CASTLE HOTELS OF EUROPE

Schlosshotel Münichau in Austria, built by the Knights of Münichau in the 1300s. See the listing in chapter on Austria. (Photograph by the author)

CASTLE HOTELS OF EUROPE

Ancient Castles
Abbeys
Baronial Mansions
Ancestral Homes
Chateaux and Palaces
in Western Europe
which offer
hotel accommodations

SIXTH EDITION
(First two editions were
published in 1964 and 1966 under the title
Castles of the Old World)

International Standard Book Number 0-9600064-5-1
Library of Congress Catalog Card Number 81-84608

Published by
Robert P. Long, Publisher
445 Glen Court
Cutchogue, N.Y. 11935, U.S.A.

Printed in U.S.A.

Trade Distributor:
Hastings House, Publishers, Inc.
10 East 40 St.,
New York, N. Y. 10016

Contents

THE COVER

Château du Gué Péan, located in the Loire Valley of France. Today travelers can sojourn here where several kings of France, including Louis XII and François I, once stayed. See listing in chapter on France. (Ektachrome supplied by Le Marquis de Keguelin, owner of the castle. Electronic scanner color reproduction by HCM Graphic Systems, Great Neck, N.Y.)

1.

2.

3

Colorful Castles

A few of Europe's Most Unusual Hotels

1. Burg Hirschhorn, Germany. **2.** Bussaco Palace, Portugal. **3.** Burg Reichenstein, Germany. **4.** Schloss Itter, Austria. **5.** Burg Hornberg, Germany. **6.** Tregenna Castle, Britain. **7.** Rainha Santa Isabel, Portugal. **8.** San Filipe, Portugal. **9.** Chateau de Trigance, France. **10.** Schloss Spangenberg, Germany. **11.** Santa Catalina, Spain. **12.** Burg Schnellenberg, Germany. **13.** Guincho Fortress, Portugal. **14.** Melville Castle, Scotland. **15.** Great Fosters, Britain. **16.** Enrique II and town wall, Spain.

4.

5

6.

7.

8.

9.

10.

11.

12.

13.

14.

5.

16.

Introduction

To the Sixth Edition

When our first edition of only 52 pages was published in 1964, it was a rather tentative project, as we didn't know how many people shared our own "castle romanticism". The idea of actually staying in a historical castle in Europe appealed to my wife and me, and in the intervening years we have found that there are hosts of castle romantics who find great pleasure in staying in ancient castles, palaces, monasteries, and similar places when possible, instead of in ordinary hotels.

So, here we are with our Sixth Edition, nearly 20 years later. Our basic purpose in the book is to provide accurate information on the many hotels and guest houses (now well over 500). While we have visited most of these, situations and managements change and so does the quality of accommodations, and in many cases we must depend on information supplied by our scouts, the hotel managements, or the government travel offices.

Centuries of Tradition

Although our title is "Castle Hotels", we have included a number of old palaces, convents, monasteries and baronial mansions because they are of closely related interest. Many are the castles of the Renaissance and Baroque periods where elegance and style took precedence over the Gothic defense posture.

Most of the adaptations have been done with characteristic taste and consciousness of centuries of tradition, and the result is a most charming and romantic setting. You may cross a moat (a few with drawbridges still exist), enter gates through the outer walls, pass through cobbled courtyards, and find yourself in a castle looking much as it did 700 years ago. There are ancient wood-beamed ceilings, or perhaps frescoes or mosaics, and hand-blown glass chandeliers. Floors and stairs often are of hand-hewn stone, worn with centuries of foot traffic. Probably there is generous use of hand-wrought iron, marble, silver, crystal, alabaster, gilt, weaponry, armor, stained glass, and of course huge fireplaces. Ancestral paintings often adorn the walls. In your room you may find a canopied bed, a huge hand-carved armoire, or perhaps a centuries-old porcelain stove.

Dining may be by candlelight, and often in a vaulted room, a great Knights' Hall, or on a terrace. Architecture, interiors, antiquities and art objects reflect centuries of artistry. In some you can explore old walls and towers, stone stairways hewn out of thick walls, and peer through arrow slits or over battlements once defended by archers. Some castles are in walled medieval towns.

Some are "living castles", still the active residences of titled families which have occupied them for centuries, where only a section or a wing has been adapted for guests. We have stayed in castles where the same family has owned them for nearly 40 generations!

Many are historic landmarks under government protection. Rooms are comfortable to elegant, plumbing is usually modern, and many of the hotels are rated first class. Stone walls eight to ten feet thick make plumbing difficult, sometimes limiting private baths, but providing facilities down the hall. (One castle in Scotland solved the problem by carving a bathroom within a 30-foot-thick wall!) Where heating is a problem, the rooms are closed in winter, so the guest ordinarily need have no fears of the cold.

Interspersed among the hotel listings you will find a few castles which are restaurants only. This is clearly pointed out in each instance, but we thought you might like to know about them if you are nearby. Also, there are several medieval or ancient style banquets held in various castles, notably in the British Isles. Some typical ones are listed at the end of the chapters of Britain and Ireland.

Listings, Locations, Maps

In our listings, the key name of the castle is shown in CAPITALS, and listed in alphabetical order within the various chapters. This is the name that appears on the maps. In parentheses at top right of each listing is the general section of the country where the hotel is located, such as South, North Central (NC), NW, etc. Right under this, telephone numbers are given.

Generally the best way to reach these places is by car, and a detailed road map is almost indispensible. Michelin maps, where applicable, are good, as are others. You may have to get these in a book or stationery store in Europe rather than at gas stations. Some castles can be reached by taxi from nearby RR stations, or by hotel car arrangements.

My wife and I have been lost so many times, and frustrated by inadequate language capabilities, that we have included in our listings as far as possible, specific names and numbers of roads, and other directions.

Further Tips

As with any European hotel, **reservations should be made well in advance.** Ask for literature which often includes a small detailed road map. Your travel agent usually can help. A deposit will assure that the hotel will hold your room after the usual cut-off time of 5 or 6 p.m. We advise you to telephone if you expect a later arrival.

Occasionally you may enter a castle courtyard and be confused by several entrances. Even when you find the entrance you might think the place deserted. But don't despair. Look around, call "Hello" and someone will appear to take care of you. Many castles are run quite informally, without a front desk or reception area such as are found in more ordinary hotels.

Rates

Even within one castle hotel there is often a broad range of rates, depending on location and size of rooms (whether in dungeon or tower), single or double, bath facilities, and season of the year. With the dollar value fluctuating over a wide range, our rate categories tend to be a general guide only. They are shown in parentheses at the end of each listing, I, II, III and DL. Translated to U.S. Dollars they are:

(I) Up to $25 per person per day, incl. breakfast
(II) $26 to $45 per person per day, incl. breakfast
(III) $46 and up per person per day, incl. breakfast
(DL) Deluxe, the upper limits of category III.

These are single room rates. Persons sharing a double room would pay somewhat less. With inflation, rates tend to increase with time, and are always subject to change, various service charges and taxes, and U.S. dollar fluctuations.

Thanks for Your Help

We extend special thanks to many readers and "scouts" who send us comments on various hotels and guest houses. We welcome these, pro and con, and if you know of other hotels which fit our categories, please let us know.

A special acknowledgement is due to my wife, Ovella, who has helped compile this information from the beginning, both at home and in Europe, and organizes the vast amount of information accumulated. Also to our son Ron for his consultation on covers and other art work. -- RPL.

Austria

Dial prefix 0 -- within Austria only.

Schloss AMBERG (W)
A6800 Feldkirch **Tel. (05522) 22419**
(Voralberg)

This castle-like medieval stone mansion has been standing on the shoulder of a mountain overlooking the ancient town of Feldkirch since 1493. It was built for Countess Helfenstein by Emperor Maximilian. Central heat, outdoor pool, 30 beds. Feldkirch is in the western tip of Austria near the borders of Switzerland and Liechtenstein. (I)

Burg BERNSTEIN (SE)
7434 Bernstein **(03354) 220**
(Burgenland)

Originating in the time of Charlemagne (circa 800 A.D.), the present structure survives mostly from the 13th century. It is typical of the hilltop castle-fortresses of Austria and Germany, with thick stone walls and towers, and tiny windows on the defensive facades. The kitchen area from the Middle Ages may be seen in a rough-hewn stone vault, and the old castle well, 120 meters (396 ft.) deep, is under one of the towers. Many relics and archeological artifacts are on display. Throughout Bernstein's rich history it has been owned by Kings and Dukes of Austria, and a legend of a "white lady" ghost has come down from the 16th century. The present owner of the castle is Countess Maria Kuefstein. A hotel since 1953, the elegantly furnished castle reflects its royal history. Beautiful gardens, pool, roebuck and wild boar hunting, fishing, and a sauna are available. All rooms have running water, some with private baths. Full meals included with rooms. Closed Nov. to Spring. The village is on Rt. 50 about 60 km S of Wiener Neustadt. (I)

Schloss Amberg

Burg Bernstein

austria

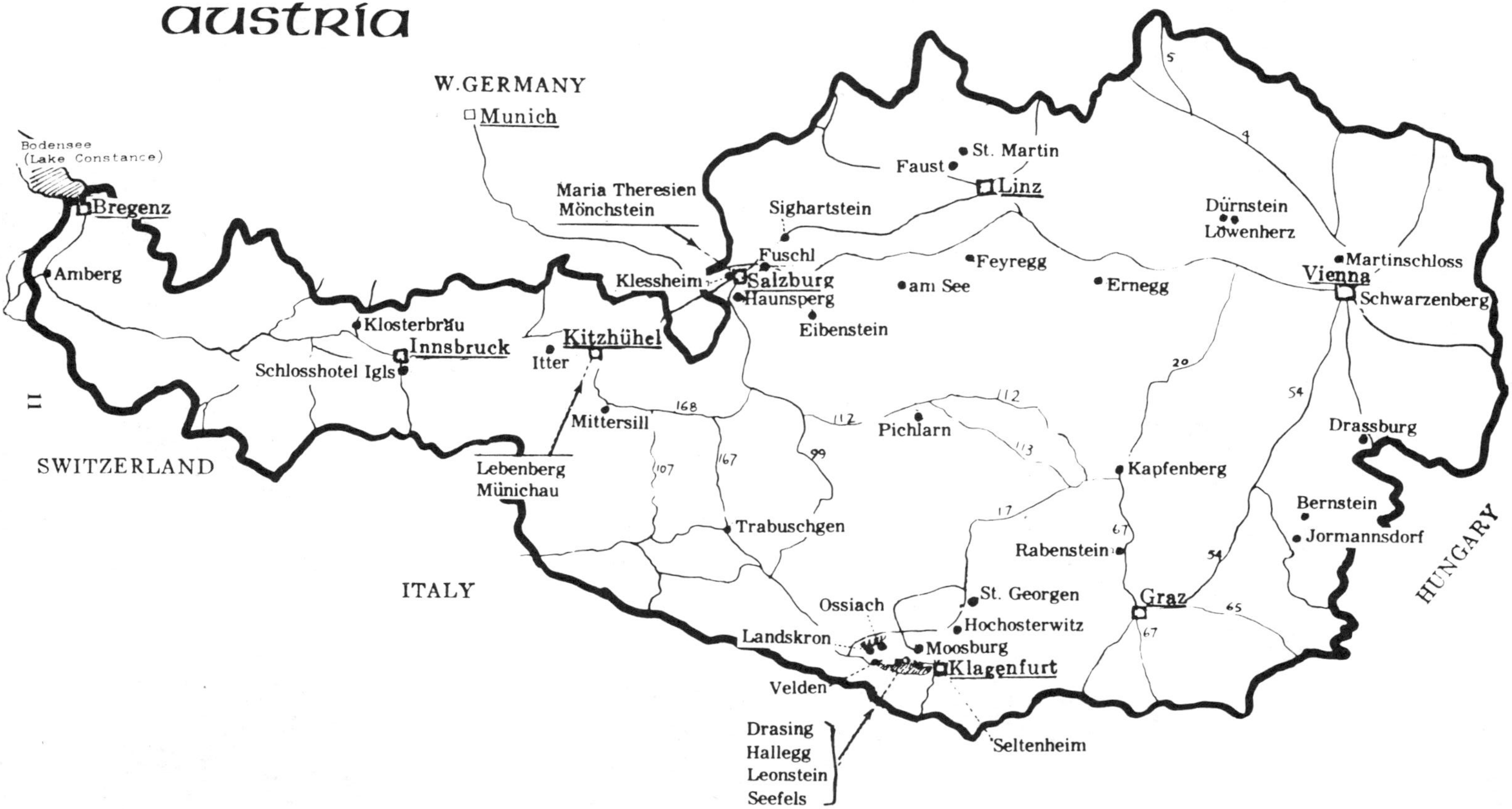

W. GERMANY
Munich
Bodensee
(Lake Constance)
Bregenz
Amberg
Klosterbräu
Innsbruck
Schlosshotel Igls
Itter
Kitzhühel
Mittersill
Lebenberg
Münichau
Maria Theresien
Mönchstein
Klessheim
Salzburg
Fuschl
Haunsperg
Sighartstein
Eibenstein
am See
Feyregg
Faust
St. Martin
Linz
Ernegg
Dürnstein
Löwenherz
Martinschloss
Vienna
Schwarzenberg
Drassburg
Bernstein
Jormannsdorf
HUNGARY
Kapfenberg
Rabenstein
Graz
Pichlarn
Trabuschgen
St. Georgen
Hochosterwitz
Moosburg
Klagenfurt
Ossiach
Landskron
Velden
Drasing
Hallegg
Leonstein
Seefels
Seltenheim
SWITZERLAND
ITALY
5
4
20
54
65
67
112
113
17
99
168
167
107

Schloss Drasing

Schloss-Pension DRASING (S)
A9201 Krumpendorf/Wörthersee
(Carinthia) (04229) 366

This 800-year-old castle in the mountains near the Wörthersee (lake) still has its knights hall and chapel, and stands guard over now-peaceful woods and grassy fields. It has been a residence for noble families for centuries and now offers accommodations for about 25 guests. Riding and fishing available. Krumpendorf is on the north shore of the Wörthersee. (I, higher in July-Aug.)

Schloss Drassburg

Schloss DRASSBURG (SE)
A7021 Drassburg
(Burgenland) (02686) 220

Although dating from the 14th century, the exterior aspect of Drassburg Castle reflects the less defensive elegance of later centuries. It stands in 25 acres of French landscaped park and garden area. Each room is designed individually and furnished in Baroque, Empire, Louis XVI or rustic style. There are also suites and apartments. Public rooms reflect the early centuries with massive pillars and vaulted ceilings, and the indoor and outdoor pools also share this setting. There is a sauna, ice skating rink, stables for riding and special hunting parties, tennis, and international cuisine. The castle is owned by Baroness Maria Patzenhofer. 30 rooms. About 65 km S of Vienna, 15 km S of Eisenstadt, near the Hungarian border. (II)

Schloss Dürnstein

Schloss Hotel DURNSTEIN (NE)
A3601 Dürnstein/Donau
(Lower Austria) (02711) 212

Built in 1632 by the Dukes of Zeltking, the palace-castle also was once the summer residence of the Princes of Starhemberg. It is now owned by the Johann Thiery family. On high ground on the bank of the Danube, it offers fine views of the river and the surrounding beautiful Wachau Valley. Above the hotel are the ruins of the ancient Dürnstein fortress where Richard the Lion-Hearted of England was imprisoned during the Crusades. The village is also the home of Katzensprung wine. Boat cruises available on the Danube. Central heat, elevator, swimming pool, 70 beds, all rooms with baths. Closed Nov 15-Mar 15. About an hour NW of Vienna. (II)

Schloss EIBENSTEIN (NC)
5360 St. Wolfgang am Wolfgangsee
(Upper Austria) 346

Surrounded by towering mountains, and situated near the Wolfgangsee (lake), Eibenstein Castle is a delightful sight with its towers and spires. The Class A hotel has central heat, elevator, sauna, indoor and outdoor pool and restaurant. 95 rooms with bath. About 40 km SE of Salzburg and 30 km NW of Bad Ischl. (I)

Schloss Eibenstein

Schloss ERNEGG (NE)
A3261 Steinakirchen am Forst
(Lower Austria) (07488) 214

Built in 1330, reconstructed and restored between 1530 and 1836, with a second story added, the castle now is an irregular square with a cone-roofed tower and an unusual arched and arcaded court. It has been owned by the titled Auersperg family for more than 300 years. There is a ghost legend of a stable boy who wanted to marry a princess of the castle, and lost his head. Recently some hitherto unknown Renaissance frescos were found under the plaster of a courtyard wall, and these have been restored to their original state. In the castle grounds is a linden tree, over 1,000 years old, 35 feet in diameter, said to be the oldest tree in Austria. Ernegg has its own 9-hole golf course, and offers tennis, swimming, shooting and fishing. Open May-Oct. 22 rooms, 2 baths. Full pension (all meals) only. Hotel car meets trains at Amstetten. Steinakirchen is on a secondary road about 20 km SE of Amstetten. (II)

↓ Schloss Ernegg →

Faust Schlössl

Schloss Feyregg

FAUST Schlossl (N)
A4082 Aschach-Landshaag
(Upper Austria) (07273) 244

15th century castle on the Danube which, legend says, was built in a single night for Dr. Faust by the Devil. Owned in the past by several noble families and a hotel since 1966, it now offers golf, tennis, water sports and fishing. 60 beds, all rooms with bath. Reached by Danube steamer direct to Aschach; bus, train, airport at Linz-Horsching (20 km). (II)

Schloss FEYREGG (N)
A4540 Bad Hall
(Upper Austria) (07258) 2591

The former summer residence of the abbots of the ancient monastery of Spital am Phyrn, the hotel now offers excellent accommodations, with riding, swimming, tennis, hiking and fishing nearby. It is also the point of departure for art excursions. 13 rooms and baths. Open all year. Express train station Linz, Horsching, or Salzburg Airport, then by hotel car. Autobahn between Salzburg and Vienna, exit Sattledt or Traun. (II)

Schloss FUSCHL (NC)
A5322 Hof bei Salzburg (06229) 253

Built in 1450 as a hunting castle for the Archbishops of Salzburg, Fuschl Castle, in more recent times has been host to such dignataries as Eleanor Roosevelt, Pandit Nehru and Nikita Khrushchev. In WWII it was the residence of von Ribbentrop of Germany and site of meetings with Mussolini. Since 1958 it's been a top resort, with its lakeside location, and offerings of tennis, golf, indoor-outdoor pool, hunting, sailing, riding, sauna and fishing. 63 rooms with baths or showers. Open Easter to Oct. 15 km E of Salzburg, off Rt 158. (III)

Schloss Fuschl

Gastehaus Schloss HALLEGG (S)
A9201 Krumpendorf/Wörthersee
(Carinthia) 49311

Hallegg Castle dates back to 1213, and an old print of 1688 shows that the castle has not changed much in the past 300 years. The austere towers, walls and battlements on the hilltop are softened somewhat by vines, foliage and woods. An open inner courtyard is surrounded by two tiers of stone columns and arches, and some of the public rooms are of ancient vaulted construction. Besides the large nearby Wörthersee (lake), there is a small lake on the castle grounds. Activities include boating, swimming, riding, tennis, hunting and fishing. Krumpendorf is on the north shore of the Wörthersee just W of Klagenfurt. 14 rooms with baths or showers. (I)

Schloss Hallegg

Schloss HAUNSPERG (NC)
A5411 Oberalm/Hallein
(Salzburg) (06245) 2662

A 14th century castle, just S of Salzburg. The towers and architecture of Haunsperg have been altered at an unknown time to give it the appearance of a later period, although its lovely interior reflects the earlier centuries. It is run as a family country mansion on a personal guest basis by the von Gernerth family which has owned it for over a century. Special holy day services are held in the 16th century chapel adjoining the castle. Most guests use the castle as a base for visiting Salzburg events, and therefore no meals are served at the castle except breakfast, plus snacks or teas on request. Spacious rooms, antique furnishings. Tennis on the grounds, other recreation nearby. Open all year. The castle is in the village of Oberalm, near the autobahn which runs S from Salzburg past the airport. Exit Hallein, follow signs to Oberalm and to the schloss. (I)

HOCHOSTERWITZ (S)
A9314 Launsdorf-
Hochosterwitz (04213) 2010
(Restaurant Only)

Balancing precariously atop a massive rock mountain, this rambling old castle-restaurant is a spectacular sight. Walls and towers cling to the cliffs, with battlements facing the surrounding territory. First mentioned in documents in 860 A.D., most of the present structures date from later centuries. The approach road encircles the mountain and passes through a remarkable series of fortified gates and drawbridges, mostly inscribed

Schloss Haunsperg

Hochosterwitz

Schlosshotel Igls

with dates of the 1500s, when the fortress was strengthened against a Turkish invasion. At one time King Ferdinand I pawned Osterwitz to the governor, Christof Khevenhuller, and in 1570 Baron George Khevenhuller purchased it. This family stills owns it. Today there is a historic collection and an armoury, waiters and performers are dressed in period costumes, and the castle is worth visiting. It is 6 km E of Donat, about 20 km NE of Klagenfurt. Average price of lunch, $8. (1981)

Schlosshotel IGLS **(W)**
A6080 Igls/Innsbruck
(Tyrol) **(05222) 7217**

An elegant old baronial mansion in a little village S of Innsbruck, located in spacious grounds. Alpine scenery. Lovely furnishings in both guest rooms and public rooms. Log fires in season, breakfast served in the lounge or by the fire in winter. Health spa facilities, indoor-outdoor pool. Views of Innsbruck 4 or 5 km away in the valley below. Elevator, dancing, summer and winter sports, riding, sauna. 18 rooms, all with baths. Bus or streetcar transportation from Innsbruck to Igls. (III)

Schloss ITTER **(W)**
A6300 Itter/Tyrol **(05335) 31113**

Snow-capped Alps surround this 1,000-year-old fortress, which has parts dating from 902 A.D. Much of the construction was added after 1520 when it was plundered and burned. Its history has been turbulent. Ownership varied between Heinrich of Bavaria and the Bishops of Regensburg. In the 1700s it was owned by Ferdinand II of Toscana, and a treaty with Napoleon in 1809 gave it to King Maximilian Josef of Bavaria. In 1877 it became the residence of Sophie Menter, whose guests often included Liszt and Tchaikovsky who played in the music room. This room still has the

Schloss Itter

mosaic ceiling from an earlier period when it was the chapel. Nazis used the castle for a political prison, and it was shelled by U.S. tanks near the end of WWII. It was remodeled as a luxury hotel in 1972. It has been open year-round, with skiing, sleighing and other winter sports available. Itter is a small village on Rt. 170 between Wörgl and Kitzbühel. (III)

(NOTE: Schloss Itter closed in early 1981 for renovation. Make inquiry before counting on it being open)

Schlosshotel JORMANNSDORF (SE)
A7431 Bad Tatzmannsdorf
(Burgenland) (03353) 223

Originally built in 1624-26, the baronial residence came into the possession of the Counts of Batthyany as a hunting lodge in 1644. Later it was a convalescent home for Austrian officers, and in 1800 was a school. In 1962 it was rennovated and modernized with the amenities needed to transform Jormannsdorf into a hotel and restaurant. Many of the antique furnishings remain, but many of the guest rooms are modern. There is also a Schloss Stube, often with musical entertainment. Rooms for 55 guests, 15 with bath; central heat. Location is about 7 km N of Oberwart, not far from the Hungarian border. (I)

Burg Hotel KAPFENBERG (SE)
A8605 Kapfenberg (Styria) 22531

A brooding stone fortress of the 12th century, this castle has overlooked a beautiful valley between mountain ranges for more than 800 years. Owned by the Stubenberg family since 1146. Fine restaurant and park. Central heat, rooms with baths or showers, 48 beds. 45 km N of Graz. (I)

Schlosshotel KLESSHEIM (NC)
A5071 Wals/Seizenheim
(Salzburg) 31177

Built in 1732 as a royal residence for Archduke Ludwig Viktor, brother of

Schlosshotel Jormannsdorf

Burg Kapfenberg

Schlosshotel Klessheim

Emperor Franz Joseph, the palace was renovated in 1938 by Hitler. His plans didn't work out, and it later became a VIP guest house of American forces. It then became a luxury hotel with elegantly furnished rooms, central heat, terraces, restaurants, swimming, tennis and a 9-hole golf course, in a setting of beautiful mountains. It played host to President Nixon on his 1972 trip to Russia and has hosted many other celebrities. Class A-1. Open June-Sept. 25 rooms,

Hotel Klosterbräu

most with bath. Pension only. 4 km NW from center of Salzburg, near main autobahn. (III)

Hotel KLOSTERBRÄU (W)
A6100 Olympiadorf, Seefeld
(Tyrol) (05212) 2621

The old monastery, built by Emperor Maximillian I in the 1500s, forms the core of this large hostelry in the center of the bustling resort town of Seefeld, up in the Alps. The ancient pillars, arches and vaults of the old structure form the main reception, lounge and dining areas and many of the guest rooms reflect the ancient character. New sections have been added, with modern facilities. Klosterbräu (Cloister Brewery) has been an inn and hotel since 1803 and is operated by the Seyrling family which has owned it for five generations. Elevator, heated pool, water sports, ski slopes within sight of the hotel. 18-hole championship golf nearby. Meetinghalls. Rooms, all with bath, accommodate 240 guests. Closed Oct-Nov and April-May. (II)

Burgruine LANDSKRON (S)
9523 Landskron bei Villach
(Carinthia)
(Restaurant only)

This is a most spectacular castle ruin on a mountain top with a magnificent view of the Julian Alps, providing restaurant accommodations only. This fortress site dates to the Dark Ages, being first mentioned in documents in 878 A.D. A castle occupied the site in the 11th century, and the present name of Landskron was first mentioned in 1351. It belonged at various times to the ruling Habsburgs, and the Emperor Maximilian I gave it to the St. George's Order of Knighthood in 1511. Soon after, the castle burned, and was rebuilt, and by 1600 was one of the most splendid of Renaissance

Burgruine Landskron

baronial manors. It was surrounded by double walls with seven towers surrounding great towers within. Lightning in 1812 reduced it to a ruin but restoration work was carefully handled. A good road and ample parking, large terraces, and excellent food served in charming stone-vaulted rooms. About 5 km N of Villach on the Ossiacher See.

Schloss LEBENBERG (W)
Lebenbergstrasse 17
A6370 Kitzbühel (Tyrol) (05356) 4301

Standing on the shoulder of a hill overlooking an Alpine valley and mountains, Lebenberg Castle was built in 1540 by the Dukes of Lebenberg, and the 11 guest rooms in the original castle are charmingly furnished in character. Operated as a pension for many years, the building was refurbished in 1965 and a new chalet-type wing was added, bringing the total number of beds to 200, most with private baths, and many on two levels. Complete health facilities, heated pool, sauna, tennis, child care, dancing, ice skating, skiing all around. It is located just outside Kitzbühel on the road toward Reith, and only 2 or 3 km from Schloss Münichau, also a castle hotel. Reservations can be made through Schloss Lebenberg for any of the other members of the Schloss Hotels of Austria. Closed mid-Oct to Dec 1. (II)

Schloss LEONSTEIN (S)
A9210 Pörtschach/Wörthersee
(Carinthia) (04272) 2816

This 15th century castle, recently transformed into a guest house, has maintained the medieval and historic tradition of the castle while adding modern amenities. Ruins of a still older Leonstein Castle may be seen on a nearby hill. Located on Europe's warmest Alpine lake, the Wörthersee, this resort offers a private beach, swimming, yachting, motor boating, water skiing, tennis, shooting and other recreations. There are weekly chamber music concerts in the courtyard in memory of the sojourn

Schloss Lebenberg

at Leonstein of Johannes Brahms. Nightclub entertainment, fine restaurant, central heat. Class A. 35 rooms with bath or shower. Open May-Oct. Pörtschach is on N side of the Wörthersee. (II)

Hotel Richard LÖWENHERZ (NE)
A3601 Dürnstein a.d. Donau
(Lower Austria) 222

Ancient monastery and inn, associated with Richard the Lion-Hearted in the time of the Crusades. Stone vaulted wine cellers and dining areas, also terrace dining, central heating, outdoor pool. Class A 50 rooms, 46 with bath or shower.

Schloss Leonstein

Richard Löwenherz

Martinschloss

Location is near the center of town along the Danube. (II)

MARIA THERESIEN Schlössl (NC)
Morzgerstrasse 87
A5020 Salzburg 41244

This baronial mansion, originally part of the Hellbrunn Castle estate which it adjoins, was built in 1612 by Archbishop Sittikus. The hotel is surrounded by a large park, with pleasant paths, ponds and gardens. The fine restaurant offers Viennese and French menus. The hotel has 38 beds, spacious rooms, 12 with baths. It has been a hotel since 1935, and owned by the Schneider family since the 1950s. Maria Theresien Schlössl is in the southern environs of Salzburg. Take Nontaler Hauptstrasse S out of the city, and branch off L on Morzgerstrasse to the castle. (I)

Schlosshotel MARTINSCHLOSS (E)
Martinstrasse 34-36
A3400 Klosterneuburg bei Vienna
(Lower Austria) (02243) 7426

The Baroque castle, situated on an ancient estate on the Danube, was built in 1766, and has had a rather remarkable history during its two-plus centuries. The castle was part of the estates of Count Hoyosh of a titled Austro-Hungarian family. Sir John Whitehead of Britain, who married Countess Breuner of the family, was credited with the invention of the submarine torpedo with which he experimented in the castle's private swimming pool. After WWI, the Trapp Family Singers lived in the castle (1920-24), and became well-known in the US some 40 years later through the show "The Sound of Music". In WW II, Martinschloss became the property of Dr. Emmer-Reissig. The Russians occupied it for years, after which it was renovated, at enormous cost, by the wife of the owner, Dipl. Ing. Eva Emmer-Reissig, who is an architect. Antiques and objects of art, including an arms collection, which now decorate the castle have been handed down from the original owners. Many of the artifacts were hidden in the depths of a 130-foot deep cistern during the German occupation. The grounds, in the outskirts of Vienna, provide park areas, and also ranges for hunting wild boar and red deer with gun

Maria Theresien Schlössl

or camera. There are castle kennels where world prize-winning dachshunds and rare Japanchin dogs are bred and trained. Class B. 54 rooms, 23 baths. Tennis, pool, sauna, water sports, good transportation to center of city. Open all year. (II)

Schloss Mittersill

Schloss MITTERSILL **(W)**
A5730 Mittersill/Land Salzburg **4523**

Built in the 12th century as a fortress-residence by the Archbishops of Salzburg, Mittersill Castle is now owned by a worldwide Christian youth fellowship, which holds conferences there. At other times it is operated as a guest hotel. It is situated on the shoulder of a mountain overlooking the town of Mittersill in the valley below. You enter through an ancient gateway and up a narrow ramp into the castle courtyard. The castle, Austrian-German style, without towers, has had a violent history. On request you can explore one or two of the unlighted dungeons, one of which originally had access only by rope through a trapdoor. The dungeons were once the scene of witch executions. A good base for summer and winter activities, including skiing in the Alps. Central heat, gothic dining room and chapel. 115 beds, 15 private baths. Approx. 100 km SE of Salzburg. (I)

Gasteschloss Mönchstein

Gastschloss MÖNCHSTEIN **(NC)**
Mönchsberg 26
A5020 Salzburg **(06222) 41363**

The castle, with parts dating from 1358, is situated in a beautiful wooded park area on top of a mountain in Salzburg. Originally a guesthouse for Archbishops, in 1654 it became a retreat for scholars of the University of Salzburg. Baron Leitner, a later owner, built the first elevator in the 1800s along the rocks of the mountainside. Later a road was added, and today a modern elevator provides nearby access from the streets below as does also a road. The castle was adapted for guests in 1949, and today it provides a lovely setting with spectacular views of the city below. Elevator, central heat. 23 beds, 11 private baths. Open Mar-Oct. (II)

Schloss MOOSBURG **(S)**
A9062 Moosburg bei Pörtschach
(Carinthia) **8206**

A 15th century castle built on the legendary site of a 9th century imperial palace. After serving as the feudal seat of

Schloss Moosburg

the manor, the castle later served as a painting gallery. Today it offers fishing and water sports on the nearby Wörthersee, also a sauna and indoor pool. 16 rooms with bath. (I)

Schlosshotel Münichau

Schlosshotel MUNICHAU **(W)**
A6370 Reith bei Kitzbühel
(Tyrol) **(05356) 2962**

This picturesque hunting castle of the Knights of Münichau dates back at least to 1314. It is situated in a flat valley among high Alps, with several skiing runs within sight. Rooms are charmingly fitted out with carved wood furniture, handsome studded doors, and the names of Knights of the Middle Ages who once occupied them. The shorter stature of those medieval warriors is reflected in the gothic arch entrances to some rooms which require the 20th century guest to bend a little to enter. Reception area, a Knights Hall and dining rooms are in thick-walled vaulted areas. Dining is in the old stable across the courtyard, reached in inclement weather by a tunnel. Elevator, central heat, 35 rooms with baths. Closed Apr and Nov. Schloss Münichau and Schloss Lebenberg, along with Schloss Kaps, in Kitzbühel, were owned centuries ago by the same nobility. It is believed the three castles were connected by tunnels spacious enough for horsemen. They are only about 2 km apart. Today Münichau is owned by the Harisch family and is about 3 or 4 km from the center of Kitzbühel on the road to Reith. The hotel provides van service to the town. (I)

Schloss Ossiach

Schloss OSSIACH **(S)**
A9570 Ossiach am Ossiacher See
(Carinthia) **04243**

An early Benedictine monastery which was secularized by Emperor Franz Josef II in 1786. Large grounds, central heating, fishing, boating, private hacks, open-air dancing and swimming pool. 90 beds. (II)

Hotel Schloss PICHLARN (C)
A8952 Irdning
(Styria) (03682) 2841

Sections of the castle are 800 years old, and other parts have been added in later years, the whole establishment having been renovated as a class A-1 hotel in 1971. Its setting is in a valley with mountains on its perimeter. Year-round activities include tennis, golf, swimming, riding, hunting, skiing, sleighing and curling. Nearby is a small airport for light planes and gliders. Central heat, elevator, indoor-outdoor pool, sauna. Full pension only. 74 rooms with bath or shower. Open all year. Irdning is on a secondary road S of Rt 112, about 80 km S of Steyr. (II)

Schloss Pichlarn

Schloss RABENSTEIN (SE)
A8130 Frohnleiten
(Styria) (03126) 2303

Perched on a high bluff overlooking the Mur River, and on a Roman road dating from 200 A.D., Rabenstein Castle makes a beautiful setting of medieval architecture and heirloom furnishings. Empress Maria Theresa (1717-1780) once stayed in the castle, and her room still holds historic portraits and other antique furnishings. The great hall is lined with armor and other medieval artifacts. Nearby are the interesting caves of Lugrotte, the old monastery of Stift Rein, and a chairlift to a mountaintop offering a view of Hungary. An 18-hole golf course is nearby. 10 beds, all rooms with baths. Breakfast only is served; a restaurant is 3 km away in Frohnleiten. Open May-Oct. About 30 km N of Graz. (II)

Schloss Rabenstein

Schlosspension St. Georgen

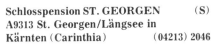

Schlosspension ST. GEORGEN (S)
A9313 St. Georgen/Längsee in
Kärnten (Carinthia) (04213) 2046

The castle, situated about a quarter mile from the southwest shore of the Längsee (Lake) is in an area of sunshine and mild climate. Its origins go back to the 11th century, and it was once a Benedictine

Monastery. Rebuilt and renovated over the years, it was remodled in 1960 and adapted as a guesthouse. Summer and winter sports abound nearby, including rowing, sailing, swimming, fishing, riding, tennis, minigolf and ice skating. The spectacular castle restaurant, Burg Hochosterwitz (see separate listing) is nearby. St. Georgen is just N of Rt 80, about 23 km N of Klagenfurt. (II)

Schloss-Pension ST. MARTIN (N)
A4973 St. Martin im Innkreis
(Oberösterreich) (07751) 6102

Dating from the 11th century, the castle is located near the Bavarian (West German) border in the Innviertel region. Not far from the spa health centers of Bad Schallerbach and Scharding, St. Martin provides a quiet place to stay. Sports are offered including swimming, tennis and riding (private stables), hunting and fishing. Public rooms retain the ancient wood-beamed construction and are decorated with antique artifacts. 28 rooms with private baths. (II)

Hotel im Palais (NE)
SCHWARZENBERG
Schwarzenbergplatz 9
A1030 Vienna (222) 725125

A former Hapsburg palace, its construction was begun in 1697 by the baroque architect Lucas von Hildebrandt. After WW II it served as Russian HQ. The proprietor now is Prince Karl Schwarzenberg. Furnished in antique style, it has fine facilities, central heat, elevator, terrace and extensive grounds. 88 beds, all rooms with bath. Open all year and Class A-1. Located just off the Ringstrasse in center of Old City. (III)

Schlosshotel am SEE (N)
A4810 Gmunden/Traunsee 4230

This beautifully situated castle stands on the shores of the lake with sweeping views of the town and the water. Spacious rooms and facilities, central heat, elevator, swimming pool. 100 beds. Location is about 2 km from the center of town. Gmunden is about 75 km E of Salzburg. (II)

Palais Schwarzenberg

Schloss-Pension St. Martin

Schloss SEEFELS (S)
Toschling 1
A9210 Pörtschach am Wörthersee
(Carinthia) (4272) 2377

Located in extensive grounds directly on the lake, this castle offers 1,000 ft. of private beach. Restaurant, tavern, sailing school, water skiing, tennis, nightclub, and nearby golf. Open May-Oct. 71 rooms with bath. Half pension, 3 days min. Class A-1. W of Klagenfurt on N side of lake. (II)

Schlosshotel am See

Schlosspension SELTENHEIM (S)
A9061 Wolfnitz/Klagenfurt
(Carinthia) 49218

The castle dates back to 1222, but was rebuilt after being partially destroyed in the 15th century during the Turkish invasions. It offers excellent views of the Karawanken Alpine range. The castle has been owned by the present family for nearly 120 years. Riding available, swimming, golf, tennis in Krumpendorf/Wörthersee, and a private beach nearby. All rooms with private bath or shower. Class B. (I)

Schloss Seefels

Schloss SIGHARTSTEIN (NC)
A5202 Neumarkt am Wallersee
(Salzburg) (06216) 251

Schlosspension Seltenheim

Situated in the lake district of Austria, this castle provides spacious views of the Alps. Founded as a fortress in the 11th century, it has for the last 600 years been in the possession of the present owning family, the Counts of Uiberacker. The original medieval castle was converted to a country manor by Count Maximilian Uiberacker in 1714. In 1950 it was adapted to accommodate guests, and drawing rooms were arranged. All guests dine together in a large hall at one table with the family of the owner. Priceless historical furniture, paintings and objects of art adorn the castle. Elevator, central heat. 13 beds, all rooms with

Schloss Sighartstein

Schloss Trabuschgen

baths. Class A-1. Open Apr 15-Oct 15. About 30 km NE of Salzburg. (II)

Schloss TRABUSCHGEN (S)
A9821 Obervellach bei Mallnitz
(Carinthia) (04782) 2042

With a history going back to the 1300s, the character of the present baronial mansion derives more from the 1700s. Art, paintings and frescoes in the public rooms reflect the elegance of past centuries, and weaponry from the Middle Ages is skillfully used in the decor. 40 beds. At intersection of 106 and 167, 65 km NW of Villach. (II)

Hotel Schloss VELDEN (S)
24 am Korso
A9220 Velden am Wörthersee
(Carinthia) (04274) 2655

Built in 1580-1603, this large castle was once the residence of the royal Khevenhueller family. Beautiful gardens and private beach on the Worthersee, Baroque style towers with cupolas, finest foods and complete services, sauna, central heat, swimming pool, water sports, tennis and dancing. 230 beds. Class A. Open May-Oct 15. Location at W end of lake. (II)

Schloss Velden

Belgium

Kasteel van BRASSCHAAT **(N)**
40 Miksebaan
B2130 Brasschaat
(Antwerp) **Tel. 031/51 83 37**

This castle-style hostelry is located in a lovely setting of parkland with a lake. Large, well-furnished rooms, good restaurant, elevator, handicap facilities, central heat. 20 rooms, 12 with baths. 9 km N of city of Antwerp. (I)

Château des BRIDES **(NW)**
1 Briedels
B8020 Oostkamp
(W. Flanders) **050/82 20 01**

The Louis XV French style château is situated in a 240 acre private estate with formal gardens and a lake. Luxuriously furnished period rooms, elevator, central heat. Only breakfast is served. 10 rooms, all with baths. Open Apr to mid-Oct. 8 km S of Bruges on the Bruges-Kortrijk road. (II)

La COMMANDERIE **(E)**
Rue Joseph Pierco 28
B4155 Villers-le-Temple
(Liège) **085/51 17 01**

This complex of ancient buildings was once the headquarters of the Knights Templar, an order established in the 12th century Crusade to protect pilgrims traveling to the Holy Land. Some towers and walls remain, as well as several buildings of the original castle enclosure. In 1312 the Pope turned the property over to the order of the Knights Hospitaler (Knights of St. John of Jerusalem), and in 1503 the complex passed to the house of Villers. The place was a major stronghold during the Middle Ages, but much of it was destroyed during the French

← Kasteel van Brasschaat

Château des Brides

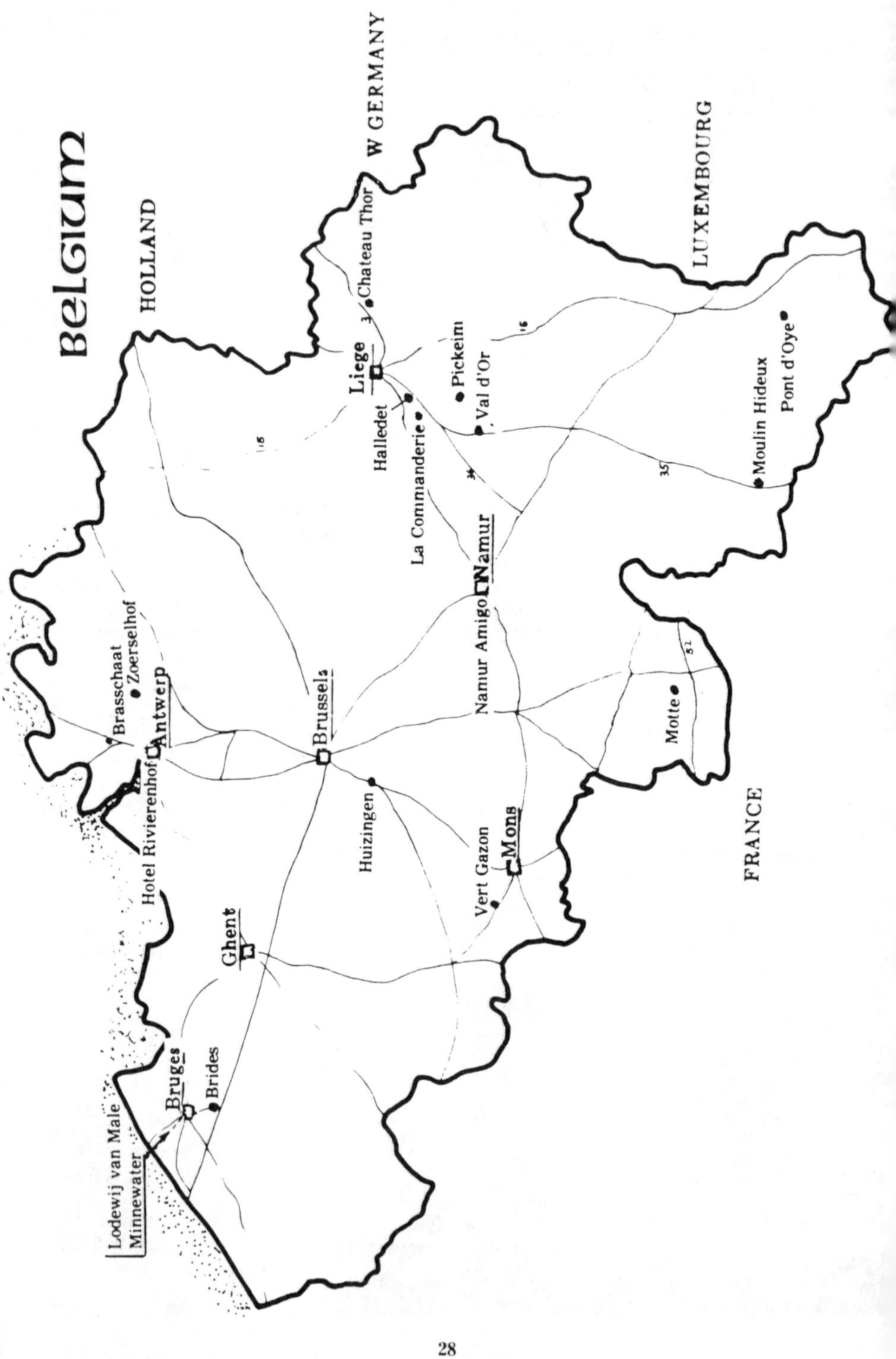
Belgium
HOLLAND
W GERMANY
LUXEMBOURG
FRANCE
Chateau Thor
Liege
Halledet
La Commanderie
Pickeim
Val d'Or
Namur
Namur Amigo
Moulin Hideux
Pont d'Oye
Motte
Mons
Vert Gazon
Huizingen
Brussels
Antwerp
Brasschaat
Zoerselhof
Hotel Rivierenhof
Ghent
Bruges
Brides
Lodewij van Male
Minnewater
35
52

revolution. Today many of the guest rooms have the old beamed ceilings some fireplaces, and the narrow stairways of the past. The dining room is especially attractive with its overhead network of massive wood beams. Excellent foods and wines. Central heat, air conditioning, bar, baby sitting service. Closed late Jan and Feb.15 rooms. SW of Liège on the Liège-Dimand Rd. near Huy and Nandrin, just off N36. (II)

La Commanderie

Hostellerie du Château (E)
de HALLEDET
B4133 Clermont-sous-Huy
(Liège) 041/75 30 04

The moated castle has twin towers of an early time, with the classic cone roofs, while the other sections are of a somewhat later vintage. It stands in a quiet park area. French cuisine and dietary meals available. Personal service. Bar, elevator, central heat. 9 rooms. On a secondary road, 20 km SW of Liège, about 3 km N of St. Severin. (II)

Château de Halledet

Du Domaine Provincial (C)
de HUIZINGEN
B1511 Huizingen
(Brabant) 02/3566177

First mentioned in history in 1191, the château was burned, rebuilt in 1545, and again remodeled to its present form in 1602. It has been the seat of several titled families over the years. Adapted for guests in recent years, it has 23 rooms and a popular cuisine. 10 km S of center of Brussels on main road to Mons. (II)

Du Domaine Prov. de Huizingen

LODEWIJK VAN MALE (NW)
488 Maalseweg
B8310 Sint-Kruis, Bruges
(W. Flanders) 050/33 57 63

Old château-style mansion with several towers, in an estate setting, with a lake, the hotel has central heat, bar and other facilities. 6 km E of Bruges on the road

Lodewij van Male

Minnewater

toward Ghent, W of Maldegem (not on the autobahn). (I)

MINNEWATER Hotel (NW)
Minnewater, 2C
B8000 Bruges (W. Flanders) 050/33 82 26

This picturesque old palace, directly on the lake in a quiet, pleasant setting is only a five minute walk from the center of the old city. The name is said to mean "Lake of Love". Modern conveniences have been added such as central heat, and the menu features seafoods and selected wines, special dietary meals and garden dining. 10 rooms. (I)

Manoir de la Motte

Manoir de la MOTTE (S)
Rue de la Motte
B6374 Boussu-en-Fagne
(Namur) 060/34 40 34

The castle, with its square tower and leaded windows, dates from the 14th century, and retains much of the character of that period. But modern facilities and central heating have been added. It was prominent in Belgium's history and heraldry, a historical saga which continued into the 1940s when Hitler built his headquarters nearby, the remains of which can be visited. Fine foods and wines are a specialty of La Motte. 10 rooms. There are at least three towns named Boussu in Belgium. Boussu-en-Fagne is near the French border, about 5 km N of Couvin, on a secondary road W of Rt. 5. (I)

Auberge du MOULIN HIDEUX (SE)
6831 Noirefontaine 061/46 70 15

This old mill is situated in a parklike area of woods, garden and a small lake. It has been beautifully converted for guests, offering 10 rooms and 3 apts, a restaurant, and tennis nearby. Noirefontaine is 150 km SE of Brussels, nót far from the borders of France and Luxembourg. (II)

Moulin Hideux

Château de Namur Amigo

Château de NAMUR AMIGO (C)
1 Ave. Milieu du Monde
B5000 Namur (Namur) **081/22 26 30**

Situated on a hilltop, this castle-style hotel offers an attractive setting with fine views. It specializes in its cuisine, and also offers dietary menus. Bar, pool, tennis, handicapped facilities, central heat, 31 rooms. (II)

Château de Pickeim

Château de PICKEIM (E)
Route de Liège, 31
B5360 Hamois-en-Condroz
(Namur) **083/61 12 74**

The château-style baronial mansion has two castle towers, broad grounds, and tastefully furnished rooms. Dietary meals available, wheelchair facilities, baby sitting, bar, central heat. Closed most of January. Hamois is on a secondary road E of N35, about 45 km SW of Liege on N36. (I)

Château du Pont d'Oye

Château du PONT d'OYE (SE)
Rue de Pont d'Oye, 1
B6720 Habay-la-Neuve
(Luxembourg) **063/42 21 48**

In the 1700s the iron works of Pont d'Oye were very prosperous, and the iron master built the romantic château for his

Hotel Rivierenhof

wife, La Marquise du Pont d'Oye. It became a center of society, counting among its guests Voltaire, King Stanislas of Lorraine, Queen Elisabeth and King Leopold I. The quiet setting is in a forest area with streams on the grounds. Period furnishings, restaurant, bar, central heat. 22 rooms. Habay-le-Neuve is on Rt. 48, about 15 km W of Arlon, in the SE corner of Belgium. (II)

Hotel RIVIERENHOF **(N)**
244 Turnhoutsebaan
B2100 Deurne (Antwerp) **031/24 25 64**

Originating in the year 1382, Rivierenhof has stood for centuries as a noble mansion, and was remodeled to its present form in 1858. In 1921 it was acquired by the Province along with its large wooded estate and was adapted as a hotel-restaurant and public park. Boating, tennis, other recreation, facilities for children, baby sitting, dietary meals, central heat. 15 rooms. Deurne is located in the NE environs of the city of Antwerp. (I)

Chateau Thor

Château THOR **(E)**
Astenet 86
B4711 Walhorn-Astenet **087/65 90 37**

Built in the 1600s, this small, walled castle has been a hotel since 1947. Facilities include a restaurant, lounge, library, terrace and gardens. It is in a park area and also offers fishing. 8 rooms, 2 with baths. Closed Dec 15 to Feb 15. S of Aachen between E5 and N28, N of Eupen. (II)

Castel de Val d'Or

Castel de VAL d'OR **(E)**
62 Grand Rue
B5292 Ocquier (Liège) **086/34 41 03**

Originally a fortified farmstead and stage coach inn dating from the 11th century, the hostelry was burned along with the village in the 17th century wars. Rebuilt to its present form in 1653, it now offers a popular restaurant with outdoor

Château le Vert Gazon

dining in the courtyard, bar, wheelchair facilities. 14 rooms. Closed part of Aug-Sept and part of Jan-Feb. About 30 km SW of Liege. (I)

Château le VERT GAZON **(SW)**
1 Route de Mons
B7980 Stambruges-Grandglise
(Hainaut) **069/57 59 84**

A towered baronial mansion in a setting of broad grounds and formal gardens, this hotel offers a range of facilities, including, tennis, golf, swimming, boating and riding. It is noted for the cuisine in its recommended restaurant. 8 rooms with baths. Closed certain periods in Jan

Zoerselhof

and June. It is 7 km from a well-known castle, Château de Beloeil. Location is S of Ghent and W of Mons. (II)

ZOERSELHOF **(N)**
98 Zoerselhofdreef
B2153 Zoersel (Antwerp) **031/12 03 19**

Built in 1667 as a monastery, the structure served this function until its monks were driven out in 1780 during the French revolution. Since then it has been owned by various barons and noblemen. In 1952 it was adapted as a guest house and now offers promenades, woods, spacious grounds, and a historic chapel. 18 rooms. On N579 about 20 km E of Antwerp. (I)

Britain

(Scotland is listed separately)

Armathwaite Hall

ARMATHWAITE HALL Hotel (NW)
Bassenthwaite
Keswick, Cumberland Tel. 551

Located on its own estate of 130 acres of deer park, woodland and lake front, this magnificent baronial mansion offers accommodations in a beautiful setting in the lake country of the west of England. Boating, tennis, fishing, golf, hunting, swimming and climbing are offered. Log fires in season, conference rooms, handicap facilities, special Christmas rates. 37 rooms with baths, central heat, elevator. 16 km NW of Keswick. (II)

Ballygally Castle

BALLYGALLY Castle, (NE)
Candelight Inn
Ballygally, Co. Antrim,
NORTHERN IRELAND 212

The small Scottish-style castle was built in 1625. Overlooking the sea, it offers bathing, boating, tennis, golf, and a trout fishing stream on the grounds. There is a dungeon bar in a tower. Conference rooms, special Christmas deals. Ballygally is about 35 km N of Belfast and 7 km N of Larne. Limousine service arranged from Belfast airport. (II)

BODYSGALLEN HALL (W)
Llandudno, Gwynedd,
WALES Deganwy (0492) 83130

Standing on a high prominence among acres of beautiful gardens, this 17th century Welsh manor house has been built around a surviving 13th century tower which may have been a lookout tower for nearby Conway Castle. The name, Bodysgallen, goes back to the 5th century when a king built an abode (bod) for his eldest son, Cadsaalen. The manor has many historic aspects, and in the garden is a small maze dating from the 1600s. There are several fireplaces and fine wood paneling, and many of the rooms have panoramic views. Restaurant, bar, TV room, riding nearby. 16 double rooms, most with baths. Llandudno is on the north Wales coast, N of Conway, near Great Ormes Head. Open Easter-Oct. (II)

Bodysgallen Hall

BOVEY HOUSE (SW)
Beer (nr Seaton)
Devon **Branscombe 241**

Thought to have been built in the 1100s by the Abbots of Sherborne, Bovey House has a rich share of English history. There is a monk's hiding place, tower room, a King Charles room, mellow stone and mullioned windows. The property was a wedding gift to Catherine Parr, one of Henry VIII's queens. Private gardens provide much of the produce, and the atmosphere is that of a private country house. Bar, game room, putting green, central heat, 13 rooms, 1 private bath. Beer is just W of Seaton, and about 10 km W of Lyme Regis. Near sea and resort of Sidmouth. Open Jan-Nov. (I)

Castle of BRECON Hotel (W)
Brecon, Breconshire,
WALES **Brecon (2942) 2551**

Built in and around the original 11th century castle, the hotel offers broad views of the Brecon Beacons (mountains) and the Usk Valley. The Norman castle was built in 1081 by Bernard Newmarch, half brother of William the Conqueror. Richard III imprisoned Cardinal Morton, Chancellor of England in the castle. The hotel front faces the old palace, and the town is interesting. Activities today offer salmon and trout fishing, riding, fox-hound hunting, boating, tennis and nearby golf. Restaurant, conference rooms; 32 rooms, most with baths, one with canopy bed. Brecon is about 65 km N of Cardiff. (II)

BROCKHAMPTON COURT Hotel (W)
Brockhampton, Hereford,
Herefordshire **Howcaple (098 986) 239**

Situated in the lovely Wye Valley, this noble, towered baronial mansion, rebuilt in the 1800s, affords fine views, and walks, horseback riding and drives in the woods and hills. Spacious lounges, halls,

Castle of Brecon

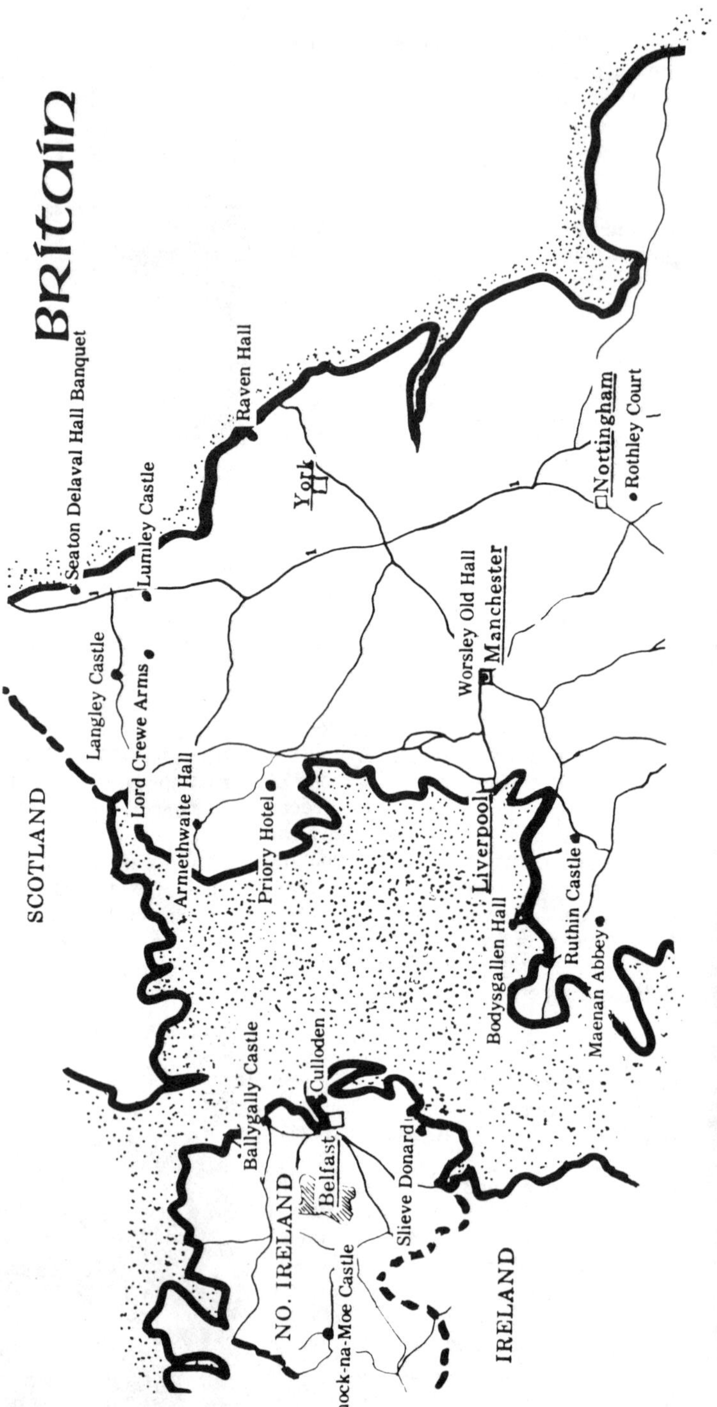
Britain
SCOTLAND
Seaton Delaval Hall Banquet
Lumley Castle
Langley Castle
Lord Crewe Arms
Armethwaite Hall
Priory Hotel
Raven Hall
York
Worsley Old Hall
Manchester
Nottingham
Rothley Court
Liverpool
Bodysgallen Hall
Ruthin Castle
Maenan Abbey
Ballygally Castle
Culloden
Belfast
Slieve Donard
NO. IRELAND
Knock-na-Moe Castle
IRELAND

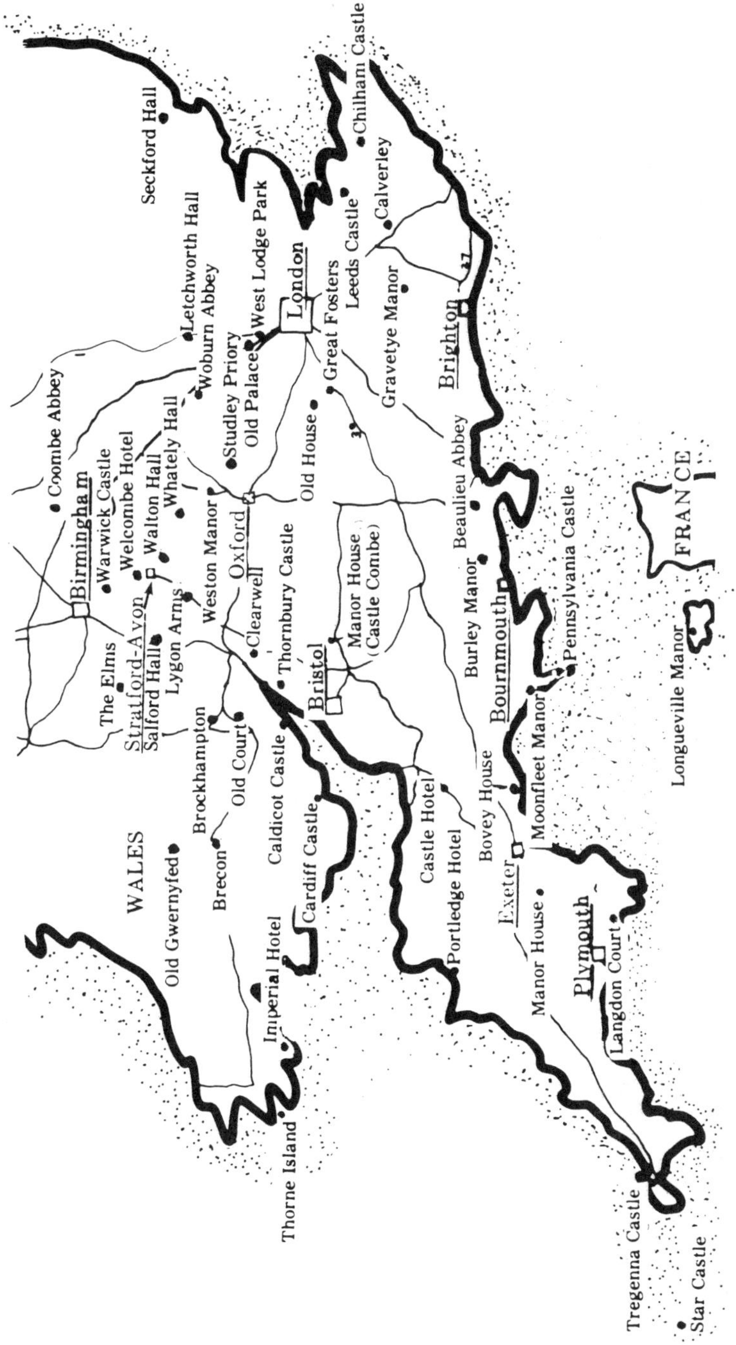
Seckford Hall
Chilham Castle
Calverley
Leeds Castle
West Lodge Park
London
Great Fosters
Gravetye Manor
Brighton
Letchworth Hall
Woburn Abbey
Studley Priory
Old Palace
Old House
Beaulieu Abbey
Coombe Abbey
Birmingham
Warwick Castle
Welcombe Hotel
Walton Hall
Whately Hall
Weston Manor
Oxford
Clearwell
Thornbury Castle
Manor House
(Castle Combe)
Burley Manor
Bournemouth
Pennsylvania Castle
FRANCE
Longueville Manor
The Elms
Stratford-Avon
Salford Hall
Lygon Arms
Bristol
Brockhampton
Old Court
Caldicot Castle
Cardiff Castle
Castle Hotel
Portledge Hotel
Bovey House
Moonfleet Manor
Exeter
Manor House
Plymouth
Langdon Court
WALES
Old Gwernyfed
Brecon
Imperial Hotel
Thorne Island
Tregenna Castle
Star Castle

Brockhampton Court

Burley Manor

Calverley

and a banquet room are lavishly decorated with ornamental wood carving. Fresh produce is served from its own gardens. Tennis, golf putting course, conference rooms, special Christmas deals. 28 rooms, open all year. 11 km N of Ross-on-Wye, watch for sign on entrance road running W from B4224. Transportation from Ross, Fawley, Hereford and Gloucester stations. (II)

BURLEY MANOR Hotel (S)
Burley, New Forest,
Hampshire (042 53) 3314

This Tudor style manor house was built about a century-and-a-half ago and derives from earlier manor houses on the site since 1251. The Crown took over much of the estate in 1801 but the present grounds comprise a 54-acre park. The manor was converted into a hotel in 1932. Riding, walks, often dancing and folk singing. Two-day stay minimum. 29 rooms, most with baths. 8 km E of Ringwood. (II)

CALVERLEY Hotel (SE)
Crescent Road
Tunbridge Wells,
Kent TN1 2LY 26455

Built before 1738 as a residence for titled families in this ancient resort town, Calverley has a 250-year history closely identified with royalty. In 1762 it was enlarged by Lord Egmont, and for 20 years was occupied by the 4th Duke of Leeds. It was the residence of the Duke of Chandos, and later of the Princess Sophia. The Duke and Duchess of Kent resided there in 1797, and in the early 1800's the Princess Victoria and Duchess of Kent occupied it every summer. In 1840 it became a hotel, and when Queen Adelaide was staying there she hosted Queen Victoria, Albert and the Prince of Wales. Le Comte de Paris and the Duc d'Orleans in exile stayed there in 1866. Today Calverley offers a spacious park area only 5 minutes from the center of town. Beautifully furnished public and private rooms, terraces, lounges, elevators, central heat, 39 rooms. About halfway between London and Hastings. (II)

CASTLE Hotel (SW)
Castle Green, Taunton (08 23) 2671

A record of the original Taunton Castle in 710 A.D. is found in the Anglo-Saxon Chronicle, the earliest history in any modern language. Conquests and burnings dispatched earlier strongholds on the site, and a third castle was built before the Norman conquest in 1066. By 1127 a Norman castle had been built, and King John often stayed there. It was rebuilt in 1495, and in the wars of the mid-1600s, underwent siege. About 300 years ago much of it was dismantled, but a section remained as a hostelry, with towers and part of a moat. Some of the interior is still medieval, and some rooms are in the towers. Guests of the Castle hotel have included Queen Victoria, Edward VII and Edward VIII, and sovereigns of other lands. Excellent facilities, dining and amenities. Located in center of town. Remaining ruins of earlier castles can be seen in the garden. Central heating, elevator. Location is near Stonehenge. (III)

Castle Hotel

Culloden

CULLODEN Hotel (E)
Holywood, Co. Down,
NORTHERN IRELAND
Holywood (02317) 5223

The former palace of the Bishops of Down stands amid lawns and gardens sloping down to the shore of Belfast Lough. Built in the latter half of the 19th century, the towered and turreted palace offers luxurious accommodations, a gothic cocktail lounge and attractive rooms. Available are golf, sailing, tennis, deer stalking, handicap facilities, central heat, elevator. 25 rooms, most with baths, some canopy beds. Open all year. 11 km NE of Belfast. Open all year. (II)

The ELMS (C)
Abberley, nr Worcester
Great Witley (029 921) 666

A Queen Anne country house of the early 1700s, The Elms is in a setting of small villages. Over the years it has built a reputation for first class food, comfort and a congenial atmosphere. Lounges are warmed by great fireplaces, even though central heating is adequate. Clock golf, tennis, boating and fishing on nearby Severn River, hunting with three packs. Handicap facilities. 18 rooms,

The Elms

Gravetye Manor

some canopy beds. 19 km NW of Worcester on Worcester-Tenbury-Ludlow Road, A443. (II)

GRAVETYE MANOR (SE)
East Grinstead,
West Sussex RH19 4LJ
Sharpethorne (0342) 810567

Built as a nobleman's home in 1598, Gravetye had periods of prosperity and neglect. By the 19th century it was a derelict and a hiding place for smugglers. It was restored by William Robinson who added fine oak paneling in the original building and the newer wing. He added extensive gardens until his death at 98, in 1935. The 30 acres of gardens and trees on the estate are still widely known and visited. The establishment was recently honored as Britain's "Hotel of the Year". Fishing available, other activities. 15 rooms with baths, central heat. Open all year. 56 km S of London, near Gatwick airport where Laker planes land. (III)

GREAT FOSTERS (SE)
Stroude Road
Egham TW20 9UR, Surrey 3822

The hunting lodge, built in the mid-1500s, was a favorite country place of Queen Elizabeth I. Originally fortified, the old moat still is there around two sides of the building. Remarkable for its masonry and its carved woodwork, this great country house is a charming monument to the concepts of Tudor England. Its massive oak beamed halls, carved ceiling, canopy beds, huge fireplaces and priceless Elizabethan furnishings make it a charming place to stay. Entrance is through a low wicket doorway (a door within a door), and the reception area is pure Elizabethan. Formal gardens and grounds have been tended by experts for centuries. There is an attached tithe barn with intricate beam and timber work

Great Fosters, moat in foreground

where banquets and other events are held. Some rooms are in a modern wing. Golf and tennis available. Egham is a picturesque town in the SW environs of London about 2 km W of Staines. Nearby is the field of Runnymede where English barons assembled in 1215 for King John's sealing of the Magna Carta, and the Kennedy memorial also is near. Great Fosters is W of Heathrow airport and about 2 km S of B388. (III)

Imperial Hotel

IMPERIAL Hotel (W)
Tenby, WALES **Tenby (0834) 3737**

Perched atop the 15th century town walls directly above the rocks and beach, the Imperial Hotel, though not a castle, has an ideal location within the ancient fortifications. Its dining rooms, terraces and guest rooms provide thrilling views of the sea in this place on the western reaches of the Bristol Channel. Its Cliffhanger Grill is appropriately named. An elevator takes guests from the terrace level to the upper floors. Located in the Pembrokeshire Coast National Park. Partial central heating, 30 rooms, most with baths. On A478. (II)

Knock-na-Moe Castle

KNOCK-NA-MOE Castle (NW)
Mullaghmore, Omagh
Co. Tyrone,
NORTHERN IRELAND (0662) 3131

The castle is situated in 12 acres of wooded grounds. Public rooms and some guest rooms are ornamented in elegant Canadian pine woodwork. Activities include riding, fishing, shooting, golf, dancing. Handicap facilities. 21 rooms, 11 baths. Open year-round. On the Omagh-Cookstown Rd, about 56 km S of Londonderry. (II)

Langdon Court

LANGDON COURT (SW)
Wembury, Down Thomas, Devon
Plymouth (0752) 862 358

Situated in 35 acres of grounds, gardens and woodlands, the Elizabethan manor house was built in 1577. It has some

Letchworth Hall

cellars remaining of earlier structures dating from Saxon times in the 11th century. In modern times, Edward VIII sometimes stayed at Langdon as a guest of the Cory family. Central heat, 20 rooms, all with baths. Wembury is on the channel coast about 10 km SE of Plymouth. (II)

LETCHWORTH HALL **(SE)**
Letchworth Lane
Letchworth, Hertfordshire **3747**

The towered and castellated structure was built in 1625 around a 12th century castle. It stands in extensive grounds, and offers, among other activities, golf, tennis and squash. 21 rooms. 48 km N of London. About 1-2 km S of A505 on Willian Road. (II)

Longueville Manor

LONGUEVILLE MANOR Hotel **(S)**
St. Savious, Jersey,
CHANNEL ISLANDS
Central (0534) 25501

This ancient manor house, with surviving strong towers, was built sometime prior to 1367 when it was first referred to in official documents. The arched gateway and other elements are still part of the building, but much of it is "modern", dating from the 1600s. Having fallen into ruins in the 1800s, it was restored, and in World War II it was occupied by German officers. It was acquired by the present owners, the Lewis family, in 1948. Today it is one of the oldest and most attractive manor houses on the island of Jersey, not far from the French coast. Heated pool, tennis, golf, riding, handicap facilities. Open all year. 2 km E of St. Helier. (III)

Lord Crewe Arms

LORD CREWE ARMS **(N)**
Blanchland, Northumberland **251**

This 12th century hewn stone monastery inn is situated in a region rich in legends of King Arthur and his Knights of the Round Table. Many remains of Saxon England are to be seen in ruins of abbeys and monasteries. The well-preserved

Lumley Castle as it looked in a 1788 print, and today.

Roman Hadrian's Wall, dating from 121 A.D., is nearby. The historic inn has a massive stone chimneyplace in which a secret hiding place is concealed, and the bar is in an 11th century cellar. One of Britain's most authenticated ghosts, that of Dorothy Forster, is said to haunt this place, a situation dating from the early 1700s. 5 rooms in the old inn, 9 in the annex, 3 private baths. The village is interesting and quiet, off the main roads, 24 km NW of Durham. Open all year. (II)

LUMLEY CASTLE Hotel (N)
Chester-le-Street,
Co. Durham (0385) 885 326

Spanning some 700 years of history, Lumley Castle is thought to have been built during the reign of Edward I (1272-1307), by Sir Robert Lumley. It was first licensed as a castle in 1389, and the exterior, comprising four massive, battlemented, square corner towers, has been altered very little since then. It has been owned continuously by the same family, the present descendant being the 12th Earl of Scarbrough. Today the bridal suite has a canopied four-poster bed of Elizabethan times, and some other rooms also have canopied beds. The Black Knight restaurant offers a high standard of cuisine and wines. Elizabethan Banquets are held in the Baron's Hall most evenings, and there is also a ghost legend. The castle commands fine views of the countryside. Included are golf, fishing, hunting, shooting, riding, heated pool and saunas. 60 rooms, most with bath. Modern wing added. Open all year. Exit from A1(M) to A167, to Chester-le-Street, which is about 16 km S of Newcastle-Upon-Tyne. Left toward Durham, left again toward Houghton (B1284) and left on a branch road to the castle. (II)

The LYGON ARMS (SC)
High Street
Broadway,
Worcestershire (038681) 2255

Dating from the early 1500s (some sections earlier) the Lygon Arms has served as an inn for over 400 years.

Lygon Arms

History has surged around it during these centuries, and Oliver Cromwell stayed there in 1651 before the Battle of Worcester. Original Elizabethan fireplaces, beams, paneling, and ceilings, and a frieze of the 17th century enhance the inn which is furnished with fine antiques. A modern wing has been added and a cocktail bar. Located in the heart of the Cotswold area, it is a traditional center for the hunt, and is near Stratford, Oxford, Warwick and other points of interest. Central heat and tennis. Open all year with lower winter rates. 71 rooms, 52 with bath. Broadway is a most picturesque village, 43 km NW of Banbury, and 24 km SW of Stratford-upon-Avon. (III)

MAENAN ABBEY Country Hotel (W)
Maenan, Nr. Llanrwst/Wales

Set in its own 10 acre park of woods, a waterfall and footpaths to a rocky rise, this towered, castle-like house offers fine accommodations. Bar, lounges, wood fires on cool days, restaurant, and a weekly Welsh Evening with community singing in the local tradition. Fishing rights on the Conwy River. 8 rooms and baths, central heating. Open all year. Off A496 N of Betws-y-Coed in northern Wales. (II)

The MANOR HOUSE (S)
Castle Combe
Chippenham, Wiltshire (0249) 782 206

Elements of The Manor House date to the 1300s, notably an old grainary and drying kiln discovered only in the 1970s, and now part of the gift shop area. The house today is a "symphony of stone chimneys, roofs and gables bearing carved animals", standing amid broad grounds with a good fishing stream not more than 100 yards from the house. Ancient formal gardens, accented by age-crusted stone statuary, flank the house. The center of the village, one of the most picturesque in England, is a five minute walk away. Entrance hall and lounge are oak-

Manor House (Castle Combe)

paneled and have great fireplaces. The dining room has a notable frieze depicting Shakespeare's characters. Most of the present structure dates from the 16th and 17th centuries. Swimming, tennis, golf and riding nearby, fishing on the grounds. Central heat, lounge bar, facilities for handicap, special Christmas arrangements. 34 rooms, 30 with bath or shower, four-poster beds. Open all year. The picturesque village of Castle Combe is on B4039, 8 km W of Chippenham. (II)

MANOR HOUSE Hotel (SW)
Moretonhampstead, Devon (064 74) 355

Large, rambling gray stone 16th century style mansion, built about the turn of the century, with 270 acres. Situated on high ground with terraces overlooking gardens and valley. Offers golf, tennis, fishing, badminton, squash and other sports. Suitable for families. Elevators, conference rooms, handicap facilities, central heat, special Christmas arrangements. A British Transport Hotel with 69 rooms, 49 baths. 16 km SW of Exeter, through the Moor. (III)

MOONFLEET MANOR (SW)
Fleet, nr Weymouth, Dorset
Weymouth (030 57) 6948

Built about 1603, the manor house was the seat of the Mohun (or Moone) family. Moonfleet Manor has a long history related to the sea and much of it to smugglers, and figured prominently in the historical novel "Moonfleet" by Meade Faulkner. Its grounds are directly on the English Channel, facing the offshore Chesil barrier beach. Entrance to the grounds is along a narrow lane through the woods and past the historic village and churches. The bar is in "Blackbeard's Vaults" in the ancient stone cellars, where folk singing is often held on summer nights. Facilities include heated outdoor pool, walks along the shore, nearby riding, golf, tennis, swimming, conference and banquet rooms, baby care, Christmas deals. 40 rooms, 27

Manor House (Moretonhampstead)

Moonfleet Manor

with bath. Just S of B3157, 10 km W of Weymouth. (II)

OLD COURT HOTEL (C)
Symonds Yat West
Ross-on-Wye, Herefordshire
(060 081) 367

This manor house and inn dates from about the year 1272, with a Tudor Hall of

Old Court

Old Court

1680. A recent wing, built with the stones from a 15th century barn on the property, blends well with the older buildings. The name derives from the use of the house centuries ago as a local court, in which many thieves were convicted and suffered the severance of their right hands as punishment. The Old Court also has its ghost legend from the bones of a man believed to be a monk, who was bricked up into a wall and discovered just recently. There is a lounge bar with huge fireplace, a Tudor restaurant, Elizabethan room, swimming pool and gardens. It is 500 yards from the River Wye with its trout and salmon fishing. Golf is available four miles away. Elizabethan feasts are held several times a week, with a menu from ancient times, including mead wine and whole roasted pig. 15 rooms, 12 baths. Open all year, special Christmas rates. Located just E of A40, 6 km N of Monmouth, 8 km SW of Ross-on-Wye. (I)

Old Gwernyfed

OLD GWERNYFED (W)
Three Cocks, Brecon
Powys, WALES **Glasbury 376**

The Elizabethan manor house, built around 1600, is in the foothills of the Black Mountains, and hosted Charles I in 1645 while raising men and money for his campaign. The spacious grounds, minstrel gallery, the Spanish Armada mast, paneled rooms, and secret code reputedly carved by Shakespeare, which were there in Charles's time are still to be enjoyed. There is also an escape way and priest's hole cunningly concealed in the dining room and spiral staircase. Hosts Roger and Dawn Beetham will show you around the ancient house. Activities can be arranged, including canoeing, sailing, riding, pony trekking, walking, hang-gliding, cave exploring, and even skiing on artificially surfaced slopes. Excellent menus make use of the manor's own garden produce in the candlelit dining room, with its large Tudor fireplace. Guest rooms include a large 30-foot-square Tudor room. Family rooms, weekly terms. It is located on a second-

Old House

Pennsylvania Castle

ary road E of A438, about 3 km S of Felindre. (Do not confuse with Gwernyfed Park, nearby.) (I)

OLD HOUSE (SE)
Thames Street
Windsor, Berkshire 61354

While this may not be a castle, it has special historical appeal for those who would like to stay in a house not only designed by the famed architect, Sir Christopher Wren, but also was his residence. It was built in 1676, and is in a setting with terraces sloping down to the Thames River. There are nice walkways along the river, and a bridge across to Eton. It is said that there once was a tunnel connecting the house to Windsor Castle when Old House was the residence of the King's mistress. It has period furnishings and decor, and offers golf, riding, and boating. 40 rooms. About 40 km W of London center. (II)

PENNSYLVANIA CASTLE Hotel (S)
Isle of Portland,
Dorsetshire (0305) 820561

Built in 1797 in castellated style, the Georgian mansion stands high on a hill overlooking the Channel. The site was chosen by George III with John Penn, the governor of Portland, and grandson of William Penn, founder of Pennsylvania, USA. The castle for a time was the residence of Princess Elizabeth, daughter of George III. Accommodations and cuisine are excellent. There are delightful footpaths along the clifftops as well as down the steep slopes to the water. Central heat, tennis, special Christmas arrangements, open all year, 13 rooms, 10 with baths. About 2½ km S of causeway entrance to the island. (I)

PORTLEDGE Hotel (SW)
Fairy Cross, Bideford, N. Devon
Horns Cross (02375) 262

A one-time fortified Elizabethan mansion dating from the 1600s, located on 60 acres of parkland, it also has sections dating from the 13th century. It has been adapted to meet modern requirements, but maintains its Elizabethan character. Portledge has an Armada Courtyard with pillars made from timbers of a Spanish galleon. There is a private ocean beach, as well as tennis, putting green, croquet, riding, sailing and fishing. Golf at Westward Ho, 6 km away. Fascinating seaside villages nearby include Torrington, Hartland and precipitous Clovelly. 40 rooms, 30 with baths. Central heat, open Easter to Oct. 5 km W of Bideford. (I)

Portledge Hotel

PRIORY Hotel (NW)
Bowness-on-Windemere (09662) 4377

The towered neo-gothic mansion is located on an estate along the east shore of Lake Windermere, one of the attractive bodies of water in England's northern Lake Country. The first-class hotel offers 15 rooms with baths, plus cottages on the grounds. Central heating, bar, restaurant, game room, meeting rooms, TV lounge. Near 592 about 2 km S of Windermere. (II)

Raven Hall

RAVEN HALL Hotel (NE)
Ravenscar, Scarborough YO13 OET
North Yorkshire (0723) 870353

Raven Hall occupies the site of a 5th century Roman fort, and the name comes from the Raven standard hoisted later on by invading Danes. The present mansion was built in 1774 and was a retreat for George III. It was converted to a hotel early in this century, and today is owned and managed by the Gridley family. The site, 600 feet above the coast, overlooks Robin Hoods Bay and the sea. There are clifftop battlements, walkways, golf, tennis, lawn bowling, billiards, putting greens, riding, pool, children's playground, dancing and sport competitions during the high season. 60 rooms. Closed in winter. About 80 km NE of York, 16 km N of Scarborough. (II)

Rothley Court

ROTHLEY COURT (EC)
Westfield Lane, Rothley
Leicestershire LE7 7LG
(0533) 374141

The estate, originally called Rothley Temple, dates back to the 13th century when it was granted to the Knights Templar by Henry III in 1231. In 1240 they built their chapel which still stands and is open to visitors. The Babington family resided in the manor house from 1565 to 1845. Thomas Babington was a personal squire to King Henry V at the Battle of Agincourt in 1415. The manor was adapted as a hotel in 1960 and offers a historical setting with modern amenities. Golf adjacent, riding nearby, tennis, squash, restaurant open to non-guests. Meeting rooms, banquet facilities. 37 rooms, most with baths. Special weekend rates, closed Christmas. About 11 km E of Exit 22, of the M1, on B5328. (II)

Ruthin Castle

RUTHIN CASTLE (W)
Corwen Road
Ruthin, Clwyd,
N. Wales (08242) 2664

Dating from 1282, Ruthin has had a turbulent history. It withstood a siege in

Seckford Hall

1400, but two and a half centuries later, in 1646, succumbed to Cromwell's troops after a seven-month siege. It was badly damaged and remained a ruin until 1826 when it was restored. Later, the Prince of Wales was a frequent guest. In modern times it became a three-star hotel, and offers hunting, fishing, golf, tennis, croquet, and extensive grounds - 38 acres. There are dungeons and secret passages, cocktail lounge and elevators. Medieval banquets are held most evenings except Sunday, with costumes, authentic food, music, entertainment. 64 rooms and baths. 24 km N of Llangollen. (II)

SALFORD HALL Hotel **(C)**
Abbots Salford,
Hereford/Worcester
Evesham (0386) 870561

Originally a convent, built in 708 AD in Saxon times, Salford's Great Hall of today dates from the 1400s. Other sections were built in the early 1600s. The stone-floored, paneled, Abbots Bar, lounge with a log fire in season, and the old chapel restaurant, are popular. Central heating, game room, conference facilities, 12 rooms, 3 with baths. On A439 about 15 km W of Stratford-upon-Avon. (II)

SECKFORD HALL Hotel **(E)**
Woodbridge, Suffolk **(03943) 5678**

This is one of the great Elizabethan manor houses built in 1530 by Sir Thomas Seckford, in a setting of acres of gardens, lake and parkland. Splendid oak paneled rooms, beamed ceilings, carved doors, massive fireplaces, and canopy beds make no concessions to the 20th century, although private bathrooms have been added along with all amenities. A new wing also was added recently. Golf, fishing, sailing, riding, hunting. Central heat, 24 rooms. W of Woodbridge A12 by-pass. (II)

SLIEVE DONARD Hotel **(SE)**
Downs Road
Newcastle, Co. Down,
NORTHERN IRELAND **23681**

Situated at the foot of the Mountains of Mourne, and facing the irish Sea, this towered holiday hotel offers a variety of facilities. The championship Royal County Down Golf Club is next door and available to hotel guests. Besides the beach, there are forest trails into the slopes. Indoor heated pool and poolside bar, fishing, tennis, pony trekking, spacious lounges and public rooms, elevators,

Slieve Donard

conference rooms, handicap facilities, special Christmas arrangements. 112 rooms. (II)

STAR CASTLE Hotel (SW)
St. Mary's, Isles of Scilly 22317

Built during the reign of Elizabeth I (1533-1603) this star-shaped fortress-castle commands sweeping views of the sea on Britain's most southerly and western islands. Over the years it has been visited by several of England's kings and queens. It is a five-minute walk from the quays, sandy swimming beaches, and the village. Tennis, heated pool, gardens, rooms for 40 guests. Open Apr-Oct. The Isles are about 40 km SW of Lands End. Ferry service: Isles of Scilly Steamship Co., Penzance; helicopter service, British Airways, Penzance Heliport, and by Brymon Aviation, Heathrow (London), Plymouth, and other points. (II)

Star Castle

STUDLEY PRIORY Hotel (C)
Horton-cum-Studley,
Oxfordshire
Stanton St. John (086735) 203

The present Elizabethan house, completed in 1587, developed from an earlier Benedictine Nunnery founded in 1184. It became a private house when Henry VIII dissolved the religious orders. It has been in the family of descendants of John Croke for nearly 340 years, and the Croke arms, joined with those of the Cave, Blount, Bennet and Unton families, may be seen in escutcheons above the main entrance. The private chapel was consecrated in 1639 and a north wing added in 1666. Otherwise, few changes have been made except for the discreetly added bathrooms and other amenities, such as central heating and wheelchair accommodations. There are four-poster beds. 20 rooms with baths. Riding, tennis, special Christmas deals. Located in a park area 11 km NE of Oxford. From Oxford take road toward Beckley-Stanton St. John at roundabout on A40. Location is N of Stanton St. John. (II)

Studley Priory

THORNBURY Castle (W)
Castle Street
Thornbury, Bristol BS12 1HH 412647
Restaurant Only

Walls and towers in the tradition of the Middle Ages mark this castle built in the 1500s. It stands amid broad lawns, and the interior has period furnishings and objects of art. Dinners only, with an acclaimed menu of seafood, salmon, and other specialties. The town of Thornbury is about 30 km N of Bristol on a secondary road W of Rt. 38, N of the M4 and W of the M5. Closed Mondays and five days at Christmas. Expensive.

Thornbury Castle

THORNE ISLAND Hotel (W)
Thorne Island, **(Summer) Angle 225**
Angle, Pembroke, **(Winter) Angle 348**
Wales

A Victorian fort atop a precipitous two-acre island, just off the rugged Wales coast, this hotel offers the complete ambience of the sea. Built about 125 years ago, it was one of several sea forts built to defend Milford Haven. Replacing 19th century men-o-war in the bay are the hotel's fleet of sailboats from 14 to 35 feet, available to guests at nominal cost. Guests also may bring their own boats. The hotel has a partial self-catering program under which guests make their own breakfasts and lunches in individual kitchens, and the hotel serves a full four-course dinner. Single, double and three-bedded rooms accommodate 16 guests. There are two bathrooms and one shower. Spacious lounge, bar, games room, children's play area in courtyard. Motor boat ferry from Angle. (I)

Thorne Island

TREGENNA CASTLE Hotel (SW)
St. Ives, Cornwall **(073670) 5254**

Located almost as far as Lands End on England's southwesternmost peninsula, Cornwall, this 18th century castellated mansion stands on a 300-foot rise above the picturesque and ancient seaside village of St. Ives. A fine view is afforded of the village below, the harbor, and the

Tregenna Castle

Gulfstream waters beyond in the Atlantic Ocean. There are tennis, pitch-putt golf (full golf nearby), squash, badminton, heated pool, and beaches available. A good base for exploring the Cornwall coast in its wildest stretches along the seacliffs. Elevators, 88 rooms, 68 with baths, handicap facilities, central and electric heat, open all year, special Christmas deal. Hotel cars meet trains at St. Erth, 6 km, on request. (II)

WALTON HALL **(C)**
Wellesbourne, Warwickshire
Stratford/Avon (0789) 840011

This huge manor house stands on ancient estates where Saxon remains have been unearthed. Some of the cellars of the present structure probably date to Norman times, though the house was renovated mostly in the mid-1800s by the famed architect, Gilbert Scott. Walton had long been a center for society. Transformed into a luxury hotel in 1973, its setting and furnishings reflect this elegance. Especially notable are the huge stained glass windows in the reception area which show many colorful coats of arms. Broad green grounds are entered over an ancient stone bridge, and mammoth trees accent the expanse. Original stonework is restored in the public rooms and corridors, and furnishings are in period harmony. Half of the 68 rooms have baths en suite, and many have canopy beds. There are conference rooms and three dining rooms. Activities include boating on its own lake, fishing, tennis, golf, riding, gym, sauna. About 11 km SE of Stratford-upon-Avon, near Loxley, E of A422. (II)

Walton Hall

Welcombe Hotel

WELCOMBE Hotel (C)
Warwick Rd.,
Stratford-upon-Avon (0789) 3611

This is a spacious 19th century country mansion in the heart of Shakespeare country. It is surrounded by beautifully landscaped grounds and gardens with plenty of space for pitch and putt golf, tennis, croquet, walking and other activities. Recommended cuisine and wine cellars. A British Transport hotel with 90 rooms, all with baths. Central heat, handicap facilities, open all year, special Christmas deal. 3 km N of Stratford on A46 toward Warwick. (II)

WEST LODGE PARK (SE)
Barnet, Hadley Wood,
Hertfordshire 01 440 8311

In the 1500s this was a hunting lodge for Princess Elizabeth, sister of King Edward VI. Spacious grounds still surround the lodge and replacing the ancient hunting activities are tennis, putting, golf, and riding. 55 rooms, 5 with baths, many canopy beds, period furnishings. Central heat, handicap facilities. At N edge of London, 2 km from the Cockfosters Sta., Underground, Piccadilly Line. (II)

West Lodge Park

WESTON MANOR (C)
Weston-on-the-Green,
Oxfordshire **Beltchington** (08695) 621

Once a monastery, with a history from the 11th century, the present castellated structure dates from the 14th, 16th and 19th centuries. It was moated, sieged, captured, and otherwise altered by historical events. The "Ghost of Mad Maude" is one of its legends. During the Civil War of the 1600s, Prince Rupert, a royal leader, took refuge from Cromwell's troops in Weston Manor. The same night, one of Cromwell's generals and his retinue arrived for lodgings. Early next morning the Prince escaped disguised as a milkmaid. Some guest rooms are now in the well-furnished Rupert cottage on the grounds. Many antiques grace the main building, dining is in the great hall, complete with notable

← Weston Manor ↓

Whately Hall

Woburn Abbey

linen fold wood paneling and minstrel gallery, the latter with its own spiral stone stairway. 20 rooms, private baths, some four-poster beds, central heat. Tennis, squash, croquet, heated pool, nearby golf. Open all year, special Christmas arrangements. 13 km N of Oxford on A43, Oxford-Northampton Rd.; 8 km from Bicester; 56 km from Stratford. (II)

WHATELY HALL Hotel (C)
Banbury, Oxfordshire (0295) 3451

The beautiful old manor house was built as a residence for Bishop Whately in 1630. By 1750 it was adapted as a coaching inn and renamed the Three Tuns. It operated as an inn for a century, and in 1850 the old estate became a private residence again. It became a fine hotel in 1926. Much of the original elegance and furnishings remain: there is a 1687 inscription in one of the rooms, and some of the windows still have their original glass and thumb spring fixtures. There are secret staircases, and a vault which is now the cocktail bar. Although there is central heating, log fires burn in the wintertime. John Wesley stayed at Whately, as did also Jonathan Swift, who obtained the name for his Gulliver's Travels from a nearby graveyard. The famed Banbury Cross of nursery rhyme is right by the hotel. Now under Trusthouse Forte management, it has spacious public rooms, elevator, conference rooms, special Christmas arrangements. 77 rooms, all with baths. 32 km from Stratford, Warwick Castle, and Oxford, and near other points of interest. (I)

WOBURN ABBEY (SC)
Woburn, Bedfordshire MK43 OTP
Woburn (052525) 666

Not a hotel, but the beautiful palace complex, now and for three centuries the residence of the Dukes of Bedford, Woburn Abbey offers the traveler a wide variety of attractions, including a limited program of overnight accommodations by special arrangement. Such prior arrangements must be made through the Private Secretary, the cost per person being approximately $300 per night. Formal dinner also can be arranged on occasion. The palace is open to visitors for a fee, except for a few days at Christmastime. Kings and Queens of England have been guests here, and its furnishings, objects of art and other treasures have become one of the outstanding showplaces of the country. Also there are antique shops in one of the buildings, and the large estate is a vast Safari Park with roaming wild animals. The park is open every day except Christmas. The Bedford Arms offers room accommodations in the town of Woburn nearby. It is 64 km NW of London, 14 km NW of Dunstable on A50. Bedford Arms' rate is (II)

PRIVATE ARRANGEMENTS FOR CASTLES OR HOMES

Overseas visitors are invited to stay as guests of the owners in a variety of historic homes ranging from thatched cottages to castles and manor houses throughout Britain. A warm welcome is extended to the discerning traveler and great care is taken to match up the professions and interests of visitors with families on the program. Arrangements for this and other special interest tours through R&I Tours, 138a Piccadilly, London W1v 9FH.

Another organization, Landmark Trust, Shottesbrooke, Maidenhead, Berks, England, arranges for stays of a week or more in various historic places throughout Britain such as old forts, gatehouses, schools, water towers, etc. The places have been rescued, renovated and furnished with bedrooms and living rooms, adequate but not luxurious.

Festival of Castles

Wales is said to have more castles per square mile than any other country (400 sites in 11,000 square miles), and 1983 is the Festival of Castles, marking the 700th anniversary of many of them. (in Gaelic: 'Cestyll '83). Edward I founded most of the famous castles such as Caernarvon, Conway, Harlech, Caerphilly and Beaumaris in the 1200s. The British Tourist Authority plans to have a play, pageant or concert within the walls of every major Wales castle in Spring/Summer, 1983.

Medieval Banquets

On next page

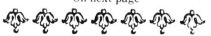

Medieval Banquets

(Scotland is listed separately)

BEAULIEU ABBEY, Beaulieu (Hampshire) Medieval banquet, entertainment. Tel: Beaulieu (0590) 612102

CALDICOT CASTLE, Caldicot (Gwent) Wales . Welsh Medieval banquet, entertainment. Tel: Caldicot (0291) 421425

CARDIFF CASTLE, Cardiff, Wales. Welsh Feast, entertainment. Tel: Cardiff (0222) 372737

CHILHAM CASTLE, Chilham, near Canterbury (Kent) Norman Keep, Medieval banquet, falconry display, informal dance in dungeon after banquet. Tel: Chilham (022 776) 561

CLEARWELL CASTLE, near Coleford (Gloucestershire) Medieval banquet, entertainment. Tel: Coleford (059 43) 2320

COOMBE ABBEY, near Coventry (West Midlands). Medieval banquet in 12th century abbey. Tel: Coventry (0203) 452406

Caldicot Castle

Cardiff Castle

Leeds Castle

LANGLEY CASTLE, Langley on Tyne, near Haydon Bridge, Hexham (Northumberland) Specialized banquets such as Dracula, Carnival Night and Henry VIII. Tel: Haydon Bridge (043 484) 481

LEEDS CASTLE, Maidstone (Kent) Kentish banquet, music from minstrels gallery. Guided tours. Tel: Maidstone (0622) 65400

LUMLEY CASTLE, Chester - le - Street (Durham). Elizabethan banquets in a 700 year-old castle. This is also a hotel. Tel: Chester-le-Street (0385) 883267

OLD COURT HOTEL, Symonds Yat West (Hereforshire). Elizabethan feast in 13th century manor house with Tudor Hall. Also a hotel.

RUTHIN CASTLE, N. Wales, 13th century castle hotel, holds medieval banquets and entertainment most evenings except Sunday. See listing on previous pages. Tel: (08242) 2664

SEATON DELAVAL HALL, near Whitley Bay, (Northumberland). Medieval banquet, entertainment, 18th century mansion. Tel: Seaton Delaval (0632) 481759

OLD PALACE, Hatfield, Herts. Medieval banquets, entertainment, year round. 15th century residence of Elizabeth I. North of London. (30)62055

Old Palace

Seaton Delaval Hall Banquet

Worsley Old Hall

WARWICK CASTLE, (Warwick, Warwickshire) Medieval banquet, entertainment in one of the great historical English castles. Usually Fri. & Sat. except July-Aug. Tel: Warwick (0926) 45421

WELCOMBE HOTEL, Warwick Rd., Stratford Upon Avon. Shakespearean banquet, food from Shakespeare's plays references, entertainment. Also a manor house hotel. Tel: Stratford Upon-Avon (0789) 295252

WORSLEY OLD HALL, Old Hall Lane, Worsley, Manchester. Jacobean banquet, entertainment. Also Duke's Cellar Restaurant in the Old Hall Cellars. A la carte. Tel: 061-799-5015

Seal of Thomas De Beauchamp,
Third Earl of Warwick, 1369

Denmark

BYGHOLM Parkhotel **(C)**
Bygholm Park
Horsens (Jutland) **Tel. 05-622333**

Bygholm Castle was originally built in the 1300s by Erik Menved. In 1775 a major building was added, and this is the section now used as a hotel. It is situated in a setting of park and beautiful gardens. Comfortable rooms, Danish and international cuisine. 38 rooms. (II)

Bygholm Castle

DRAGSHOLM SLOT **(E)**
4534 Hørve **03-453366**

First built as a bishop's palace and stronghold about 1200, and owned by the King of Denmark during the Reformation, Dragsholm Castle has been the residence of several feudal overlords, and dungeons and towers held prisoners of the Crown. Most famous was the Earl of Bothwell, husband of Mary, Queen of Scots, who was held in the tower from 1573 until his death five years later. Much of the medieval construction remains today, such as the moats, buttresses, a tower, and 8-foot-thick walls. It was badly damaged in the war with Sweden in 1694-97, and was later remodeled in the baroque style. In 1694 it was acquired by C.F. Adeler, son of a naval hero, and remained in that family for 250 years. The castle, set in a park area, is now a top tourist attraction, and during the summer months the more than 100 halls,

Dragsholm Slot

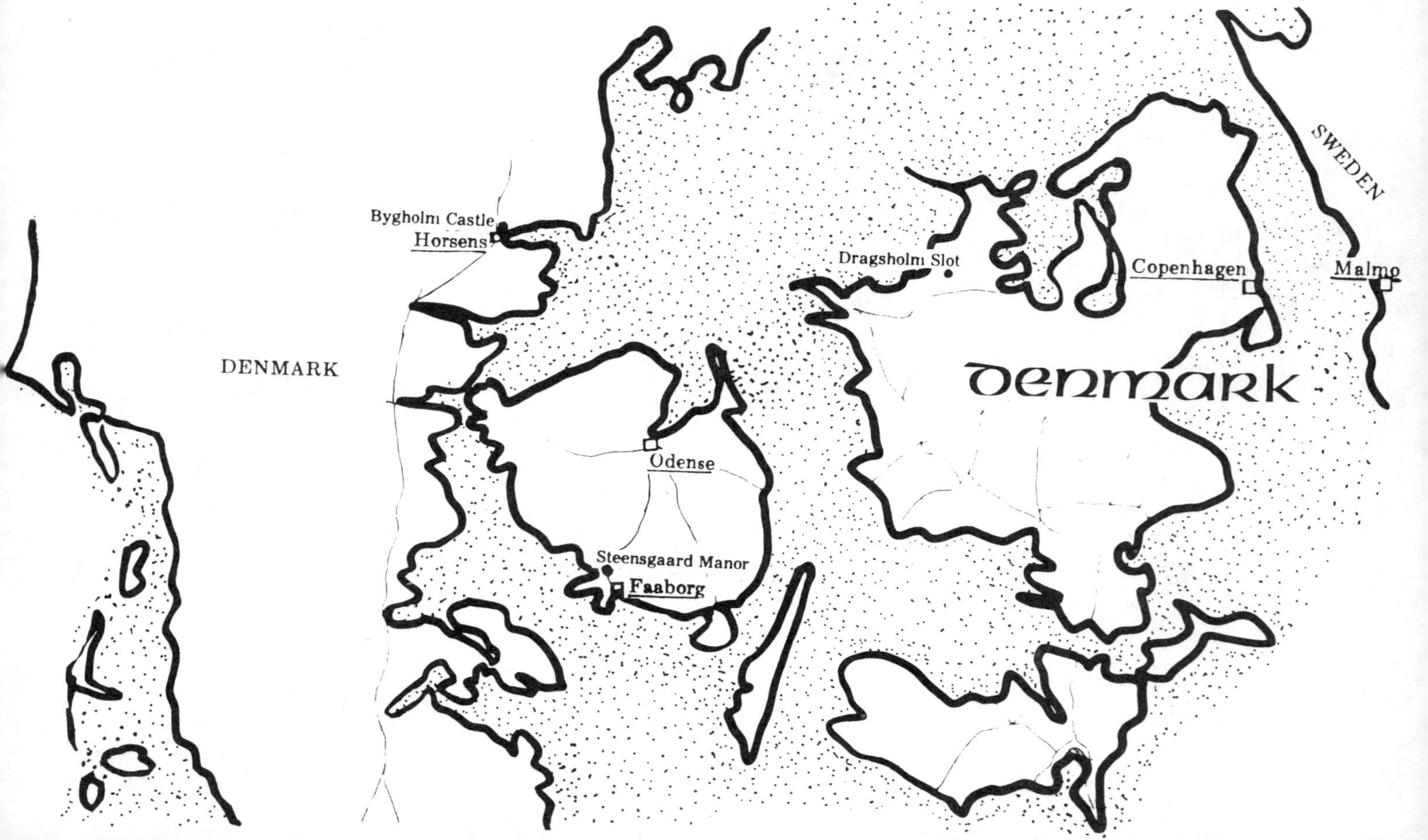
DENMARK
Bygholm Castle
Horsens
Odense
Steensgaard Manor
Faaborg
Dragsholm Slot
Copenhagen
DENMARK
SWEDEN
Malmo

Steensgaard Manor

drawing rooms and other public sections are open to visitors during the day. There is a restaurant in the old knights hall, watchrooms and kitchens, and open air dining in season on the cannon bastion with wide views of the West Zealand landscape. There is a White Drawing Room, a Golden Drawing Room, library and billiard room. You can have tea in the Count's private apartment, or a drink in front of the fire in the Knight's Room. Dragsholm has its own private chapel, established in 1731 and services are held every Sunday during the summer. At the end of a private land is a good beach stretching about 10 km along the shore, and there are picnic and strolling places. A golf course is 15 min. away at Højby, and fishing excursions also can be arranged. 25 comfortable rooms. Hørve is north of highway A4, about 87 km W of Copenhagen, and on the same island as that city. (II)

STEENSGAARD Manor (C)
Millinge, Island of Fyn **09-619490**

The manor dates from before 1310 and has had a varied history. Set in a 25-acre park which extends to the water, it includes a mile of private beach. Tennis, croquet, fishing, and other activities. Minimum stay of 3 nights requested. Recommended cuisine. 14 rooms. 4 km from Faaborg, and 41 km S of Odense, on main road to Assens. (II)

Finland

Hotelli HAIKON KARTANO (S)
(Haikko Manor)
06740 Haikko Tel. (9) 15-143033

The manor came into existence in 1632, and has had many owners, suffered war destruction and fire damage, and also has seen the splendor of empires. The present manor house, somewhat akin in appearance to the U.S. White House, was built in 1913. It is a luxury hotel and spa in 24 acres of parkland bordering on the Gulf of Finland. There is a large restaurant, summer terrace dining, indoor pool, sauna, winter sleigh rides, and complete health services. Furnishings include many antiques, and the cuisine is notable. A small excursion steamer offers cruises on the gulf and to Helsinki. Many rooms have balconies and water views. Location is just S of Porvoo, about 50 km E of Helsinki. (II)

VALTION Hotelli (SE)
Imatra (0) 54-63244

In 1903 this grand hotel was opened and attracted the rich and noble from St. Petersburg, Russia and other places to its Art Nouveau charms. Now run as a state hotel, its tall tower and massive luxury gives it the feel of a castle. Furnishings are contemporary, there is a smorgasbord, a restaurant with nightly dancing, a disco bar for those who like things louder, roulette, sauna, beach fishing, and nearby skiing in season. From the tower a visitor can see the Russian border. 65 rooms and suites. (II)

Haikon Kartano

Valtion Hotelli (Exterior and interior)

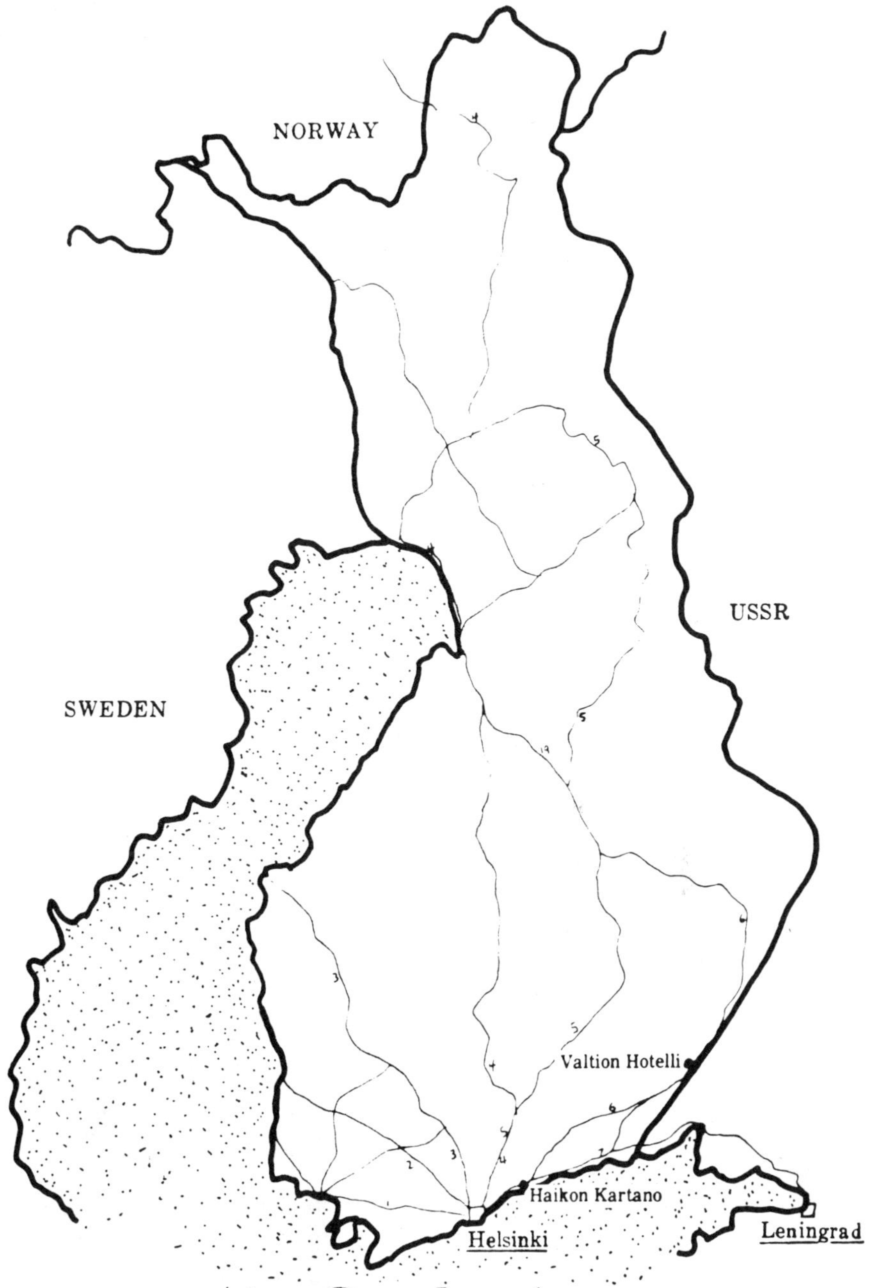
NORWAY
SWEDEN
USSR
Valtion Hotelli
Haikon Kartano
Helsinki
Leningrad

Finland

France

Hotel de l'ABBAYE (E)
74290 Talloires
(Haute-Savoie) **Tel. 44 70 81**

This large, elegant hotel, has evolved from an 11th century Benedictine Abbey in the French Alps. The Abbey, prominent in the ancient village for nearly 1,000 years, has an interesting history which has been published in a French-English booklet. The present structure reflects renovations mostly from the 17th century. From its site on Lake Annecy, about 55 km S of Geneva, the hotel provides a breathtaking view of the mountains. There's an open-air restaurant, and sports available include fishing, water skiing, boating and golf. 45 rooms, 29 with baths. Open May-Oct. Talloires is on N509a. (II)

Hotel de l'Abbaye

Château d'Artigny

Hotel d'ARLATAN (SE)
26, rue du Sauvage
(near Place du Forum)
13631 Arles **(90) 96 36 75**

Situated in the ancient walled center of the old city of Arles, near the Rhone

Hotel d'Arlatan

Château d'Ayres ↑ ←

River, d'Arlatan was built in the 12th, 15th and 17th centuries. Some of the old gates, towers and ramparts of the city are nearby, and there are also several notable Roman ruins. In the 15th (and later) centuries d'Arlatan was the seat of the powerful counts of Arlatan de Beaumont and was the most magnificent building in the city, playing host in 1516 to Queen Claude, wife of Francois I and in 1660 Princesse d'Orleans, who accompanied the young Louis XIV. Today it is elegantly furnished with antiques and objets d'art. 50 rooms, patio, garden, reading room, library, Louis XIII lounge, conference room. 3 star hotel. (III)

Château d'ARPAILLARGUES (S)
(Hotel Marie d'Argoult)
30700 Uzes (Gard) (66) 22 14 48

A residence for titled family d'Agoult in the 16th and 17th centuries, the thick-walled stone structure also was the residence of Marie de Flavigny and Countess d'Agoult. Restaurant (closed Wednesdays) with food specialties of the region, pool, tennis, nearby riding. 26 rooms, 2 apts. Rated 3-star. Closed Oct 15-Mar 15. Uzès is N of A9 between Avignon and Alès. Hotel is toward d'Anduze. (II)

Château d'ARTIGNY (WC)
37250 Montbazon
(Indre-et-Loire) 26 24 24

Today's elegant 18th century-style château is the latest of a series of castles on this site dating back to the 11th century. Francois Coty, famed perfumer, acquired the ancient estate, and in the early 1900s rebuilt it in its present form. It was only recently that the project was completed with magnificent period rooms and lounges. In the courtyard is a chapel, an exact reproduction of the one at Versailles. The 50-acre grounds can be explored with the aid of maps for various kinds of walks. Swimming, fishing, tennis, riding, boating, golf and other activities. Finest accommodations. 55 rooms. Open Jan.-Nov. Rt D17 W of Montbazon, W of D10, 12 km S of Tours, close to famous Loire Valley castles. RR stations: St. Pierre des Courps and Tours. Hotel cars available. (II)

Château d'AYRES (S)
Route d'Azay-le-Rideau
48150 Meyrueis (Lozere) 45 60 10

This 12th century castle still retains some of its old defense towers, and has been nicely adapted for modern travelers. Situated in a handsome park in the south of France, the hotel offers swimming, hunting, fishing, and excursions to the nearby Gorges du Tarn, sometimes called the Grand Canyon of France. The hotel also has its own heliport. 20 rooms. Meyrueis is near the intersection of N586 and N596, castle is about 1 km E on D57. Open Apr.-Oct. (I)

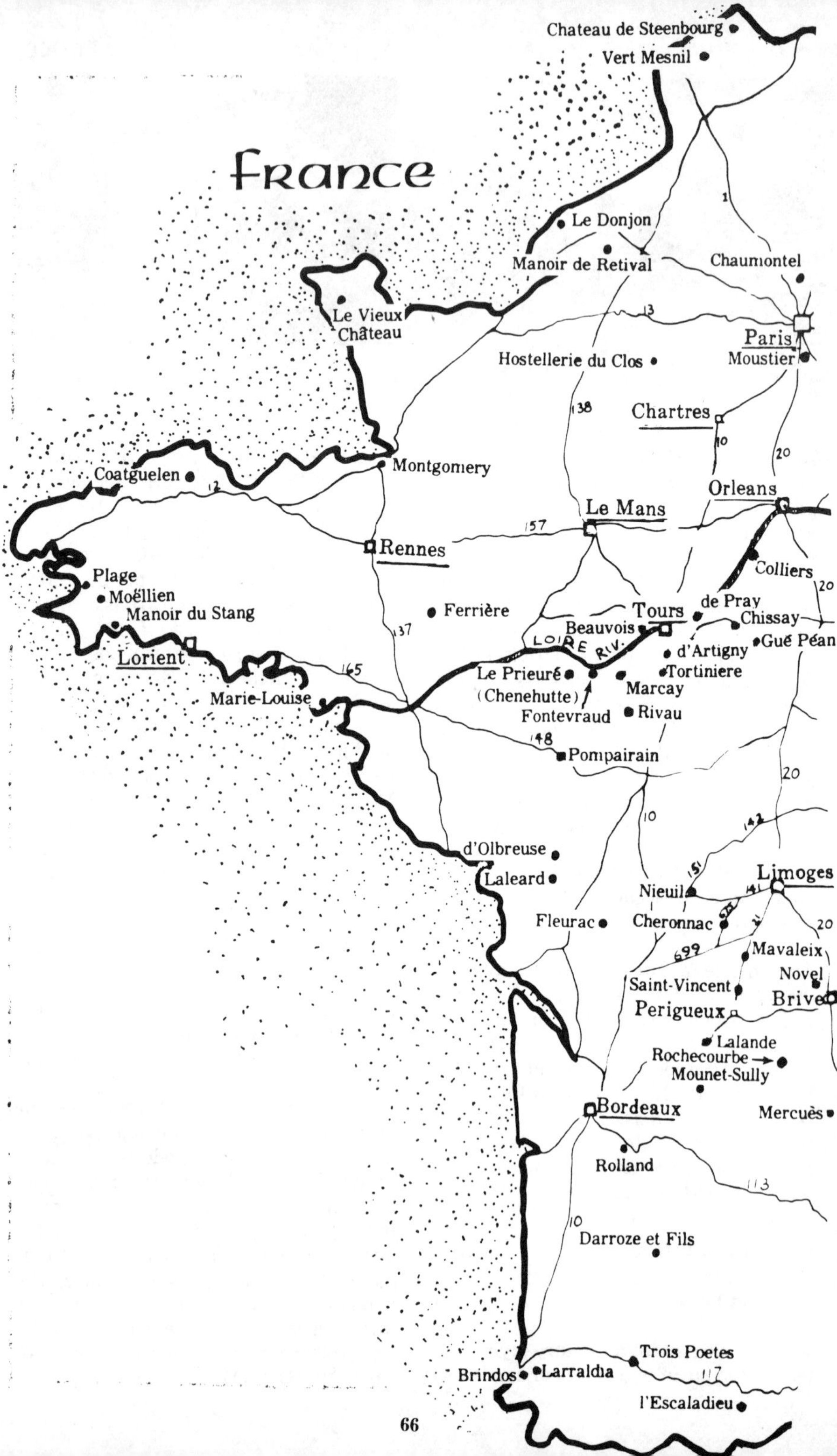
France
Chateau de Steenbourg
Vert Mesnil
Le Donjon
Manoir de Retival
Chaumontel
Le Vieux Château
Paris
Moustier
Hostellerie du Clos
Chartres
Montgomery
Coatguelen
Orleans
Le Mans
Rennes
Colliers
Plage
Moëllien
Manoir du Stang
Ferrière
Tours
de Pray
Chissay
Beauvois
Gué Péan
Lorient
Loire Riv.
d'Artigny
Le Prieuré
Tortiniere
Marcay
Marie-Louise
(Chenehutte)
Fontevraud
Rivau
Pompairain
d'Olbreuse
Laleard
Limoges
Nieuil
Fleurac
Cheronnac
Mavaleix
Novel
Saint-Vincent
Brive
Perigueux
Lalande
Rochecourbe
Mounet-Sully
Bordeaux
Mercuès
Rolland
Darroze et Fils
Trois Poetes
Brindos
Larraldia
l'Escaladieu

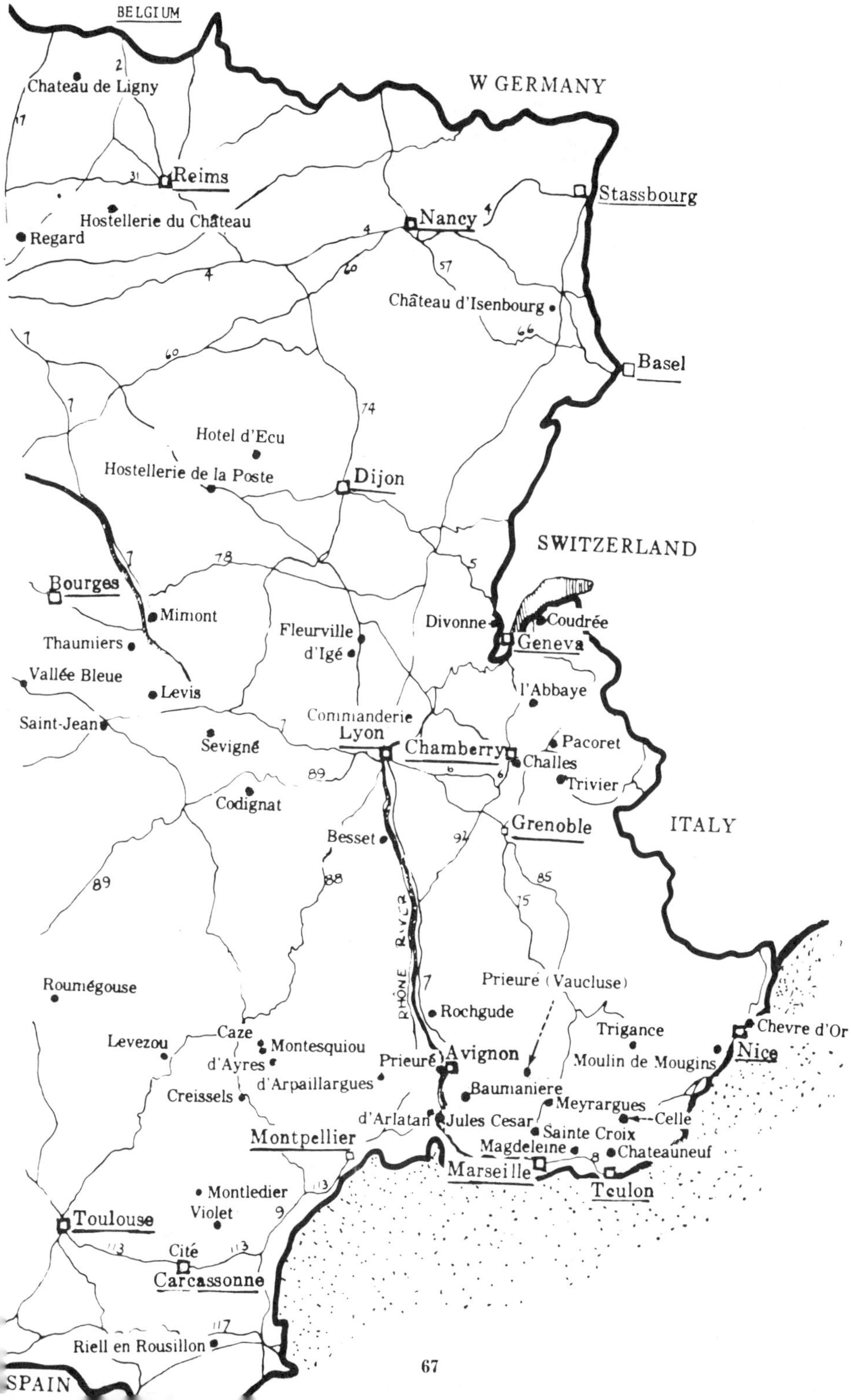
BELGIUM
W GERMANY
Chateau de Ligny
Reims
Hostellerie du Château
Regard
Nancy
Stassbourg
Château d'Isenbourg
Basel
Hotel d'Ecu
Hostellerie de la Poste
Dijon
SWITZERLAND
Bourges
Mimont
Thaumiers
Vallée Bleue
Levis
Saint-Jean
Fleurville
d'Igé
Divonne
Coudrée
Geneva
l'Abbaye
Commanderie
Lyon
Sevigné
Chamberry
Challes
Pacoret
Trivier
Codignat
Grenoble
ITALY
Besset
RHÔNE RIVER
Prieuré (Vaucluse)
Roumégouse
Rochgude
Trigance
Chevre d'Or
Levezou
Caze
Montesquiou
d'Ayres
Prieuré
Avignon
Moulin de Mougins
Nice
d'Arpaillargues
Baumaniere
Creissels
Meyrargues
d'Arlatan
Jules Cesar
Celle
Sainte Croix
Montpellier
Magdeleine
Chateauneuf
Marseille
Teulon
Montledier
Violet
Toulouse
Cité
Carcassonne
Riell en Rousillon
SPAIN

←l'Ostau de Baumanière ↑

l'Oustau de BAUMANIERE **(SE)**
13520 Les Baux en Provence
(Bouches-du-Rhone) **97 33 07**

This 16th century manor house and olive mill is in a spectacular valley setting. Charming lounges, bars, dining and other public rooms are accented with a notable collection of antique furnishings and objets d'art. It has a highly rated restaurant. Swimming, tennis and riding are offered. 26 rooms. Location is among the rocky hills of Baux, about 20 km NE of Arles, S of N99 and just E of D78f. Closed Feb. (IV DL)

Domaine de BEAUVOIS **(W)**
37230 Luynes (Indre-et-Loire) **55 50 11**

The château, situated in a large park area, in the Loire Valley, has a 15th century tower housing a dining area. Other sections date from the 1600s, with beamed ceilings, furnishings and other characteristics to match. Activities include swimming (heated pool), tennis, fishing, hunting, lake boating. Elevator. 40 rooms. Closed part of Jan. and Feb. 4 km N of town on D49. (III)

Le BESSET **(C)**
07130 Romain-de-Lerps
(Ardeche) **44 41 63**

Le Besset is a 15th century castle with two round towers and adjoining buildings, surrounded by a wall. It stands in a park of 50 acres. Rooms have beamed ceilings, four-poster beds, and luxurious appointments. Dining room and lounge have fireplaces, and there is also a dining terrace. There is a pool as well as tennis courts, and nearby fishing and hunting. 6 rooms and 4 apts. Open Apr.-Oct. The castle is on a small, winding road about 2 km W of the village of St. Romain-de-Lerps, and about 8 km N of St. Peray. This is a 4-star deluxe hotel. (IV DL)

Domaine de Beauvois

Le Besset

Château de Brindos

Château de BRINDOS (SW)
64600 Anglet (Pyr.-Atlan) 23 17 68

A towering stone fireplace and exposed stone walls provide charm and atmosphere in the spacious lounge of this old chateau located in the Basque country, near the Spanish border. It has a highly rated restaurant. Situated on a private lake, it offers fishing, riding, hunting, and nearby golf and tennis. 21 rooms. Closed Jan. 4 km SE of Biarritz. (III)

Château de la CAZE (SE)
48210 Ste. Enimie (Lozere) 48 51 01

Nestled in a deep canyon along the Gorges du Tarn road, Caze is a fine, undamanged and virtually unaltered private castle built in 1489 as a honeymoon haven. Rock Bluffs, hundreds of feet high, tower above it. The rushing river and a trout-laden tributary form the moat. Unusual cobblestone hallways on the ground and upper floor display the gleaming polish of nearly five centuries of footsteps. Hewn stone staircases, massive fireplace, vaulted dining room, and genuine antiquities, many from the Middle Ages, sustain the character of the castle. Bertrand de Mostuejouls, a valiant swordsman for the King, and known as Captain la Caze, was a famed owner of the castle. His eight granddaughters of legendary beauty, are portrayed in ceiling paintings in one of the tower rooms. Now under protection of the French government Beaux Arts, the priceless

Château de la Caze

l'Abbaye de la Celle

paintings are kept tightly closed to prevent further deterioration but may be seen on request. Terrace dining in season. Scenic river canyons are all around. La Caze is thought to be the first castle to become a hotel (1905) in France. 20 rooms, some with baths, open May-Oct. It is on the Gorges du Tarn road about 8 km S of Ste. Enimie, toward La Malene where the Manoir de Montesquiou, another castle hotel, is located. Ste. Enimie is an interesting village to explore. (I)

l'Abbaye de la CELLE (SE)
LaCelle, 83170 Brignoles (Var)

The old monastery, dating from the 11th

Château de Challes

Hostellerie du Château

century, is located in a quiet town in pleasant countryside. Furnished with antiques. Fine cuisine and local wines are featured. In pleasant weather, dining is on a terrace under giant shade trees. Some special events utilize ancient vaulted stone areas. Swimming, hunting and fishing are offered. Situated between Aix-en-Provence and St. Raphael, the abbey is 3 km S of Brignoles, off N7 toward Toulon. Open Mar.-Oct. (II)

Château de CHALLES (E)
73190 Challes-les-Eaux (Savoie) 25 11 45

The château, built in 1585, was formerly the private castle of the Marquis of Challes. It is situated in an area long attractive to travelers. Ranges of the Alps can be seen from its terraces. It was adapted as an English family style hotel. Swimming pool, tennis, handicap facilities. 72 rooms. Open May 15-Sept. 25. Located 20 km SE of Aix-les-Bains and E of Chambery, on N6. (I)

Hostellerie du CHATEAU (N)
02130 Fere-en-Tardenois
(Aisne) 82 21 13

The château dates from the 1400s and there are ruins from periods 300 years earlier. The original castle was built by Robert de Dreux, younger brother of King Louis VI of France. A later reconstruction of the castle was given by the mother of Francis I to the Constable of Montmorency (1530), and a hundred years later was confiscated by the Crown. Later, in the possession of various titled families, the castle underwent further modifications. Today it stands in attractive grounds, is nicely furnished, has a dining terrace and a recommended restaurant. Riding and tennis available nearby. 20 rooms, 7 apts, handicap facilities. 56 km W of Reims, the castle is just N of Fere-en-Tardenois and E of N367. (II)

Domaine de CHATEAUNEUF (SE)
83860 Nans-les-Pins
Le Sainte-Baume (Provence) 78 90 06

The manor house dates from the 1700s and stands in a 250-acre estate of forest and vineyards. Shade trees guard the terraces and there are tennis courts and a pool. Elegant public and private rooms, bar, banquet and conference rooms. French cuisine and Provencal specialties. 35 rooms with baths. On N560, about 45 km E of Marseille. (II)

Domaine de Chateauneuf

Château de CHAUMONTEL (N)
95270 Luzarches (Val d'Oise) 4710030

The château, built in the 1500s by the Princes of Conde, is in a lovely park setting of huge, ancient trees. Its conical towers and reflective moat add to the charm, and its dining room, and outdoor dining terraces are popular, especially on weekends. Adjacent fields produce fresh vegetables for the fine cuisine. 20 rooms, nicely furnished, some with private baths. Luzarches is on N16 about 25 km N of Paris and a little closer to DeGaulle Airport, though there is no direct public transportation from airport to castle. Frequent train service from Luzarches to Paris' Gare du Nord station. Closed August and Christmas season. (I)

Château de Chaumontel

Château de CHERONNAC (WC)
Cheronnac
87600 Rochechouart
(Haute-Vienne) 78 10 51

A classic French chateau style structure standing in a parklike area. Activities include nearby tennis, swimming, hunting and fishing. 14 rooms, open May-Oct. On D34, about 4 km W of Vayres, between Limoges and Angoulême. (I)

Château de Cheronnac

Château de la CHEVRE d'OR (SE)
Rue du Barri
06360 Eze-Village (Alpes-Mar.) 41 12 12

This small cliff-hanger, perched village is a medieval gem high on a crag on the Moyenne Corniche between Nice and Monte Carlo. The small château has an ancestry going back a thousand years to the original castle on the site which fell into ruins and was later rebuilt partially and called the "golden goat". The little hotel, with modern accommodations utilizes some sections of the ancient ruins, and offers magnificent views of the Mediterranean from its site 1200 feet up the mountainside. Visitors driving to the village must park their cars at the entrance and walk through the narrow gates and through the narrow, twisting

Château de la Chevre d'Or

Château de Chissay

streets a couple of hundred yards to the hotel. The hotel will pick up your luggage. The village is most picturesque with winding and stairway "streets" full of craft and art shops. Pack burros are used for transporting heavier goods through the village. The château has a courtyard with dining terrace overlooking the sea, as well as a charming dining room, swimming pool, terrace. Recommended restaurant. Tennis, fishing, golf nearby. 7 rooms, 4 apts, private baths. Take N7, Moyenne Corniche. 18 km from Nice airport. Closed mid-Nov.- to mid-Feb. (IV DL)

Château de CHISSAY (C)
Chissay-en-Touraine
41 (Loir-et-Cher) (16-54) 32 32 01

Chissay castle was involved in several historical events in the 1400s, having been associated with Charles VII and visited by Louis XI. In more recent times, General Charles de Gaulle stayed in the castle. Restaurant, tea room, art gallery, meeting facilities. 3 day stay requested. Open Apr-Oct. Located in the heart of the Loire castle region on RN76, N side of the Cher River, east of Montrichard. (II)

Hotel de la Cité

Hotel de la CITÉ (S)
Place d' Eglise
11000 Carcassonne (Aude) (68) 25 03 34

Carcassonne is a marvel of a walled, defensive city, perfectly preserved from the Middle Ages. It has a history going back to the an acropolis of the Gauls, a Roman castellum (from which our word "castle" derives), and a Visigoth fortress. Marked for demolition in the 19th century, the town was saved for restoration through a great effort. The hotel is in the lower city area, and utilizes an old episcopal palace built into the town walls, near the Basilica of St. Nazaire. Some rooms have canopy beds, there is a beautiful dining hall. Elevator, 60 rooms, open Apr.-Oct. About 92 km E of Toulouse on RN113 in a setting with good views of the Pyrenees. (II)

Hostellerie du CLOS (NW)
98 Rue de la Ferté-Vidame
27130 Verneuil-sur-Avre (Eure) 32 21 81

The small castle-like structure stands amid a park and garden in a quiet area about 100 km W of Paris. Unusual decorative masonry is a characteristic of the château. The cuisine includes specialties of the region. Fishing, hunting and riding are nearby. 13 rooms. Closed Dec. 15-Jan. 15. The village is at the intersection of N12 from Paris and N839 from Chartres. (II)

Hostellerie du Clos

Château de COATGUELEN (NW)
22290 Plehedel, Lanvolon
(Cotes-duNord) (96) 22 31 24

The château was built in 1750 in a spacious park of about 150 acres, and today offers relaxing greenery in a romantic setting, near the coast (6 km). Swimming, tennis, riding and fishing, and 18-hole golf 15 km. 15 rooms, 3 apts. Meeting facilities. Located near Lanvolon between St. Brieuc and Paimpol on the Brittany peninsula. (II)

Château de Codignat

Château de CODIGNAT (C)
Bort l'Etang
63190 Lezoux (Puy-de-Drome) 70 43 03

Round stone towers capped with the cone roofs of the typical French château mark this 15th century castle in the heart of the Auvergne. It stands in a 50-acre park and forest, and facilities include a heated pool, and nearby tennis, riding, hunting and fishing. A highly rated hotel with several local specialties on the menu. 12 rooms, 1 apt. Open Mar-Nov. Castle is 2 km NW of Bort l'Etang, and 18 km E of the Clermont-Ferrand airport. (II)

Château de Coatguelen

Château de COLLIERS (C)
Sur la National 751
41 Muides-sur-Loire
(Loir-et-Cher) (54) 81 50 75

The château was built near the end of the 1600s as a private residence and has served as a hotel for more then 50 years. It has been owned by the same family for over 200 years. Situated on the left bank

Château de Colliers

Château de Coudrée

Château de Creissels

of the Loire River, Colliers offers a park area, beach, boating and tennis. Nearby are the famed Loire Valley castles and palaces such as Chambord, Cheverny and Villesavin. Central heating, no restaurant, breakfast only. Open Apr-Nov. 18 km E of Blois. (II)

COMMANDERIE des Antonins (SE)
30 Quai St.-Antoine
69002 Lyon (Rhone) (16 7) 837 19 21

Restaurant Only

This restaurant is in the heart of Lyon and is a national historical monument. Dining is in a picturesque stone cavernous room by candlelight. There are also vaulted chapels and special rooms for receptions and banquets. Cuisine specialties of the region. Open all year except for major holidays: Jan 1, July 14, Aug 15, Christmas, Easter.

Hotellerie du Château (E)
de COUDRÉE
Sciez-Bonnatrait
74140 Douvaine (Haute-Savoie) 72 62 33

Since the 6th century a fortress on this site has overlooked the Swiss Alps. During the centuries it belonged to the Abbey of St. Maurice d'Agaune which ceded it to the d'Alinge family in 1245. In its elegant interior today can be seen the influence of Louix XIV and the Renaissance, in the remarkable fireplaces, woodwork, ceilings and furnishings. The character of the ancient castle has been kept even with the addition of modern accommodations. Terraces, parks, beach, water sports, riding and tennis are available. 18 rooms with bath, open Apr-Oct. About 28 km NE of city of Geneva on the SE shore of Lake Geneva. (III)

Château de CREISSELS (S)
12680 Creissels,
pres Millau (Aveyron) 60 16 69

Behind its battlements and under its towers and parapets, Creissels Castle offers lodging and fine French cuisine served family style. It is in a park setting with fine views and near a Son-et-Lumiere historical extravaganza. Open Feb-Nov, 30 rooms. (I)

Le Château de Divonne

Hotel DARROZE et FILS (SW)
40190 Villeneuve-de-Marsan
(Landes) 58 20 07

An ancient towered building houses this hotel, known for four generations for its French cuisine. Deteriorated somewhat in recent times. Its situation affords nice views of the countryside. 38 rooms. 16 km NE of Mont-de-Marsan, 120 km S of Bordeaux. (I)

Le Château de DIVONNE (E)
Route de Gex
01220 Divonne-les-Bains (Ain) 20 00 32

Situated in the Alps within sight of Mont Blanc, Divonne Castle had its beginnings sometime before 1195. It was burned, and later rebuilt in 1590. In the 1600s a wall eight feet thick was built around it, with 12 defense towers. Between 1765 and 1770, Claude Antoine de Fôret de Divonne restored the castle in the elegant style of Louis XV. Damaged again in the Revolution, it was repaired in 1850, and one early defense tower remains. Now a first class hotel, adjacent to a golf course, and nearby riding, tennis, and swimming. 40 rooms. Open May-Oct. about 30 km NW of Geneva. (II)

Le Donjon

Le DONJON (NW)
Chemin St. Clair
76790 Etretat (35) 27 08 23

Towers and old stone walls dressed in vines greet the guests at Le Donjon, which is situated near the town's seashore. It offers tennis, golf, conference rooms, park and swimming pool. Recommended restaurant (restaurant closed Wednesdays, mid-Sept to mid-June). Hotel is closed in Feb. Etretat is on the Channel Coast, 28 km N of LeHavre. (II)

Hotel de l'ECU (NE)
7 Rue August Carré
21500 Montbard (Cote-d'Or) 92 11 66

This converted convent, dating from the 1600s, is located in a medieval town of steep, winding streets and stone houses. Good food and 15 comfortable rooms. Half-pension required. Closed mid-Nov to Mar, but open Christmas holidays. 80 km NW of Dijon on N5. (I)

Abbaye de l'ESCALADIEU (S)
65130 Capvern-les-Bains
(Hautes-Pyrenees) (62) 99 55 07

The ancient Cistercian Abbey dates from 1142 and has had a turbulent history. But

l'Abbaye de l'Escaladieu

it has survived to become a medieval guest house, rich in ancient inscriptions, tombs, vaulted rooms, antiques and objets d'art. Now slightly run down but economical. It is situated on the banks of the Arros River in the Pyrenees Mountains. Gardens, terraces, conference rooms, swimming, golf, riding, fishing, hunting, are available. 15 rooms, 2 suites. About 35 km E of Lourdes, about 4 km W of Capvern. (I)

Host. Château la Ferrière

Hostellerie **(WC)**
Château La FERRIÈRE
44110 Châteaubriant
(Loire-Atlantique) **(40) 28 00 28**

The small castle style manor was built in 1750, partially destroyed in the Revolution, and restored in 1830. It stands amid broad lawns and is picturesque with its vine-covered conical towers. 15 rooms, most with baths, open all year. Food specialties of the area are featured. Châteaubriant is about 60 km S of Rennes. (I-II)

Host. du Domaine de Fleurac

Hostellerie du Domaine **(W)**
de FLEURAC
16200 Jarnac,
Fleurac (Charente) **(45) 81 78 22**

This typical French château is of Renaissance style with two neo-gothic towers, standing in spacious grounds of about 5 acres in the heart of the Cognac country. Restaurants, bar, seminar facilities. Cuisine features regional specialties. 16 rooms. Open mid-Jan to Oct 30. Located at Fleurac, 10 km NE of Jarnac via D66 and D157. (II)

Château de Fleurville

Château de FLEURVILLE **(E)**
Fleurville, 71260 Lugny
(Saone-et-Loire) **33 12 17**

The manor house dates from the 16th and 18th centuries, and there is also a much older castle tower attached. Its park area is in the Saone River valley near the vineyards of Maçon. Riding and other activities. 11 rooms, handicap facilities. Closed Feb. On N6 between Tournus and Maçon, N of Lyon. (II)

Château du Gué Péan

Château d'Igé

Abbaye de FONTEVRAUD (WC)
49590 Fontevraud-l'Abbaye
(Maine-et-Loire) (41) 51 73 52

This old abbey dating back to the Middle Ages is now run as a guest house, and also serves light lunches to the general public. From 1115 to 1793, 36 abbesses governed Fontevraud, and during those times it sheltered various daughters of Henri IV, Louis XV and the Plantagenet kings of Britain. In addition to guest rooms there are facilities for meetings, and other events. The old vaulted rooms and halls speak of past ages. Between Chinon and Saumur. (I-II)

Château du GUÉ-PÉAN (C)
Monthou-sur-Cher
41400 Montrichard
(Loir-et-Cher) (54) 71 43 01

Since Norman times the towers of this feudal castle have guarded against invaders in the beautiful Loire Valley. Ancient towers and walls surround an elegant courtyard. Two Renaissance wings are in pure Henri II style, and other sections were built in the reigns of Henri IV and Louis XIII. The historic castle was the residence of several Valois kings, and today sculpture, other works of art, and furnishings reflect this age of magnificence. It was indeed a royal residence, and over the centuries residents or guests have included Henri II, Henri III, Louis XII and François I of France, Princess Mary, daughter of Henry VII of England and sister of Henry VIII, Charles Brandon, Duke of Suffolk, Talleyrand, LaFayette, Rochambeau, Balzac, and many others. Legends of ghosts, and buried treasure beneath the Great Towers, have come down the centuries. The castle is surrounded by woodlands in which stag hunting with hounds is done, and riding for guests is a specialty. A riding school is conducted at the castle. Today's host is Le Marquis de Keguelin of the descendants of the Counts of Apremont who took up residence in the castle in 1676. It is still a private residence and accepts guests on a limited basis, usually for a stay of several days. The château also is open to visitors daily and conducted tours are offered. Montrichard is an ancient town located near many of the Châteaux of the Loire, about 30 km E of Blois, just N of N76 and Route Touristique Vallee du Cher parallel to N76. Open Easter-Nov. (III)

Château d'IGÉ (E)
71960 Igé (Saone-et-Loire) 33 33 99

This ancient castle has fortified towers and walls dating from the 12th century when it was constructed by the Counts of Maçon. Ancient exposed stonework adds authentic character to some of the hallways and the attractive dining room, and there is a spiral stairway of hewn stone. Excellent French cuisine. Nearby are swimming, golf, tennis, fishing and boating facilities. The old castle blends nicely with the ancient village. 6 rooms, 5 apts. Open Feb-Nov. Igé is about 20 km N of Macon on D134 and D85. (II)

Château d'Isenbourg

Château d'ISENBOURG (NE)
68250 Rouffach (Haut-Rhin) 49 63 53

The château, surrounded by vineyards, is of a later style than the 12th century vaulted cellars on which it stands. Overlooking Rouffach, it was the favorite residence of the Prince-Bishops of Strasbourg as early as the Middle Ages. The old cellars today form the setting for a fine restaurant where an excellent selection of wines is offered, including the special vintages of Château d'Isenbourg. Restaurant service is on the terrace when weather permits. Located in a park area, the hotel has elevators, heated pool, tennis courts and handicap facilities. 33 rooms and suites. Closed Jan-Feb. Rouffach is 12 km S of Colmar and the castle is about 4 km N of Rouffach and just W of N83. (II)

Hotel JULES CESAR (SE)
Blvd. des Lices
13631 Arles (B.-du-Rhone) 96 49 76

This 16th century convent is in a city rich in history from Roman times. The hotel has high, vaulted ceilings, spacious rooms, terraces, chapel, walkways, gardens and a restaurant. The famed artist Van Gogh used the local bridge as a subject for many of his paintings. Arles has a first century Roman amphitheatre among many sightseeing highlights. Nearby are tennis, riding, swimming, golf and fishing. 60 rooms. Closed Nov-Dec 20. Arles is on the Rhone River S of Avignon, and the hotel is on the E side of the river. (II)

Château de LALANDE (SW)
Annesse et Beaulieu
24430 Razac-sur-l'Isle
(Dordogne) (53) 54 52 30

This Renaissance style château has one tower crowned with the earlier gothic turrets, though most of the construction was in the 19th century. It is situated in a green park area of about 6 acres. Restaurant (closed Wed), receptions, meeting rooms. 12 rooms. Closed Feb. The town is on the Isle River between Bordeaux and Perigueux. (I)

Hotel Jules César

Château de Lalande

Hostellerie du Château de LALEARD (W)
17720 St. Hilaire de Villefranche (46) 94 36 48

With a great stone tower or keep, and a much more recent wing, the château mixes gothic and recent architecture. The ancient castle is associated with St. Jacques de Compostelle. Location is in a region of Roman artifacts, and several festivals. The château has its own farm for fresh produce and its regional specialties. Nearby are tennis, golf, pool and riding. 16 rooms. Open Mar 15-Nov 15. W of Angoulême and about 15 km N of Saintes. (II)

Château de Larraldia

Château de LARRALDIA (SW)
Villefranque, 64100 Bayonne (59) 25 41 04

In the land of the Basques and the Pyrenees Mountains stands this restored 17th century country château of the period French style. Surrounded by a verdant park, its setting affords lovely views of the mountains. Furnishings are antique, and some rooms have ancient slanting ceiling beam construction. Available are swimming, riding nearby, and gambling casinos in the nearby seaside resort of Biarritz, as well as beaches. 18 rooms, 3 apts. Open June-Oct. The chateau is on D137 about 5 km S of Bayonne and just N of Villefranque. (III)

Hostellerie du Lévezou

Hostellerie du LEVEZOU (S)
12410 Salles-Curan (Aveyron) 46 34 16

Built on an earlier castle site, the present structure dates from the middle 1400s. It was the summer residence of the Bishops of Rodez, and later of the Bishop of LaTour. Early in the 20th century it was acquired by the grandfather of the present owner. Some parts of the castle are designated as a Beaux Arts (fine art) landmark. Today it offers fine food, with many specialties prepared in a massive fireplace in the French tradition. Yachting and fishing available. 27 rooms. Open Apr-Nov. On RN111, 35 km NW of Millau, via N111 and N593, near Lake de Pareloup. (I)

Club Château de LEVIS (C)
03320 Lurcy-Levis (Allier) (70) 67 84 21

(Apts. only) Recently opened as an elegant timesharing resort, this castle also offers self-contained apartments with kitchenettes by day or week. Construction of the castle complex began in 1243 on the ruins of an ancient castle fortress and was completed in 1655 in a French renaissance style. Today the dozen buildings include the main château, a classic central tower flanked by two pavilions,

Château de Levis

Château de Ligny
Le Relais de la Magdeleine

East and West wings surrounding a Court of Honor, a Romanesque chapel with cloisters, stables, farm buildings and two gate cottages beside the moats. In addition to its own history through wars and peace, the castle has a notable architectural history. Jacque Hardouin Mansart, of the famed family of architects, and Lord of Levis, refinished the castle in 1752. In 1792 the de Sinety family of Levis established a porcelain manufactory at nearby Couleuvre, still operating. The castle was restored again in 1853, and in World War II its vaults hid the gold of France. Mme. Sylvia McMichael purchased the estate in 1972 for her company, Castle Holdings, Ltd. It has now been refurbished with a large collection of antiques and objets d'art. On the 33-acre estate are a 9-hole golf course, tennis, swimming, bicycle and horseback riding. There are saunas, gym equipment and game rooms in the castle. A complete library offers books in several languages, as well as an art studio. Two restaurants provide formal dining and a country kitchen as well as a snack bar. The surrounding region offers browsing, antiquing, and the Loire chateaux. Equidistant from Nevers and Moulins, the château is 18 km W of N7 and 3 km SW of the village of Lurcy-Levis. (II)

Le Château de LIGNY (N)
59191 Ligny-Haucourt (Nord) 85 25 84

The handsome round tower of the castle dates from the 12th century, although most of the structure is from the 1600s. Excavations about 60 years ago uncovered an underground bricked-up room and passages which once housed soldiers, and inscriptions on the walls from the 15th century still remain. The castle stands in a park area of about three acres not far from the Belgian border. The dining room is in the old guards hall and has a fireplace. Some bedrooms have canopy beds. Riding on the grounds, Olympic pool and tennis nearby. 9-hole golf available 30 km away. 7 rooms, 3 apts. Ligny is on D15 and D16, S of Caudry, about 60 km SE of Lille. An airport is about 7 km away. Closed Jan. (II)

Le Relais de la MAGDELEINE (SE)
13420 Genemos
(Bouches du Rhone) 82 20 05

This country mansion, built in the 1700s, was originally the seat of the Marquis d'Alberta. Legend says that Mary Magdeleine visited the area in ancient times. During WWII it was occupied by German officers and General Rommel stayed there enroute to N. Africa. Owned and managed today by M. and Mme. D. Marignane (in their family since 1935) the hostelry is furnished with family antiques and objets d'art. Public and private rooms are elegantly furnished and there is typical French price in the cuisine. Terrace dining under ancient trees, lovely grounds, and a swimming pool. Golf and tennis are nearby. Private airport (Au Castellet) 15 min. away. Genemos is 15 km E of Marseille on N96. (II)

Château de MARÇAY (W)
37500 Chinon (Indre-et-Loire) 93 03 47

This beautifully proportioned 15th century château with corner towers topped by the typical French curved conical

Château de Marçay

roofs, has been restored as an elegant hotel. Aside from its own centuries of history, it stands in the historic Loire Valley close to many points of interest and the royal castles and palaces of the area. Heated pool, elevator. 30 rooms. Open Mar-Dec. About 50 km SW of Tours, and 4 km S of Chinon, on the S side of the Loire. (II)

Castel MARIE-LOUISE (W)
Esplanade du Casino
44500 La Baule, Bretagne-Sud 60 20 60

The towered castle-like structure was built at the turn of the century in the

Castel Marie-Louise

Château de Mavaleix

seaside town of LaBaule, on the south shore of the Brittany peninsula. It is in a park area of flowers and trees, and has a heated pool as well as a beach on the Atlantic Ocean. Bar, restaurant, terraces, elevator. Golf, fishing and sailing nearby. 30 rooms. Closed early Jan to mid-Feb. Nearby towns LeCroisic and Batz-sur-Mer are attractive. About 15 km W of St. Nazaire. (III)

Château de Mercuès

Chateau de MAVALEIX (WC)
Chaleix, 24800 Thiviers
(Dordogne) (53) 52 82 01

This historic 13th century chateau in the interesting Dordogne region of southwest France, offers a variety of activities including tennis, swimming, riding, fishing and hunting. 30 rooms, 22 with baths, closed Jan. S of Limoges, and 10 km N of Thiviers on N21. (II)

Chateau de MERCUÈS (S)
Mercuès, 46000 Cahors (Lot) 57 50 32

This 11th-12th century castle stands on the site once occupied by an ancient Roman fortress. In 1360 the castle was ceded to the English who then occupied much of France, but the French soon laid siege. A relief army of English troops came, but the two armies reached a stand-off situation, and one of the most unusual settlements in history followed. They negotiated and the French bought the castle from the English for gold worth 1600 sheep and a piece of fine damask. By the 16th century most of the castle's wars were over. It was enlarged and its magnificent terrace added, an astounding feat involving transporting dirt and rock up from the plains below. The castle became the elegant residence of Bishops. It was adapted as a hotel at the end of WWII, and later renovated. Accommodations are deluxe and there is a fine restaurant. Tennis, heated pool, riding stables, elevator. 30 rooms and baths. Open Apr-Nov. Halfway between Toulouse and Limoges. N of N111, 8 km NW of Cahors. (IV DL)

Chateau de MEYRARGUES (SE)
Rte. de Chateau
13650 Meyrargues
(Bouches-du-Rhone) 57 50 32

For over 900 years this castle has stood atop its rocky hill. It was mentioned in history as early as 1024, and since that time has been the citadel of many provincial nobles and kings. Through the centuries it has been bombarded, pillag-

Château de Meyrargues

ed and partially burned. Restored and adapted as a hostelry in 1952, it provides a fine setting on the Durance River near many points of interest in the south of France. Of interest are the remains of a Roman aqueduct on the castle grounds. The dining room area is in an ancient rough stone vault, and the cuisine is pridefully served. 14 rooms, 6 with baths. Closed Dec 15-Mar 1. About 15 km NE of Aix-en-Provence on N96. (II)

Chateau de MIMONT (C)
58320 Pouges-les-Eaux (86) 68 81 44

Mists of time obscure the history of the estate. It is thought that prehistoric Druids or Celtic sects built the dolmens (large flat stones laid across upright stone supports) which have survived. An abbey was on the site in the 11th century, but it and later additions were destroyed in the French revolution. The present grand country château was built on the old foundations at the start of the 19th century. The great woods of the area have been the scene, since the 12th century, of the Chasse a Courre — hunting wild boar or stag with horses and hounds. The château is believed to have hosted Emperor Napoleon III. In modern times it came into possession of the Alasnier family. It became a hotel in 1962 (now 4-star deluxe), and has family furnishings of antiques, Charles X furniture, a pink marble staircase, ancient tapestries, oriental rugs, original paintings and other objets d'art. About 18 km N of Nevers, off N7. (III)

Manoir de MOËLLIEN (NW)
29137 Plonevez-Porzay
(Finistère Sud) (98) 92 50 40

The massive stone castle-like manor, with its high tower, had deteriorated into ruins, but was carefully restored into a 3-star hotel recently. Restaurant, walking trails, tennis, riding and beaches nearby. Open all year but the restaurant is closed Oct-Apr. 10 rooms. N of Quimper on the Brittany peninsula. (II)

Manoir de MONTESQUIOU (SC)
48210 La Malêne, Ste. Enimie
(Lozere) 48 51 12

Located in the rugged Gorges du Tarn River, this ancient fortified residence of

Manoir de Montèsquiou

Hotel Montgomery

Château de Montlédier

the Montesquiou family was built in the 1400s. Recently transformed to a comfortable 3-star hotel with central heating, baths or showers in all rooms, and authentic period French furnishings, it has the ambiance of ancient times. There are terraces and gardens, and only the highway through the village separates the castle from the river. Some rooms are in the tower, reached by the original spiral stone staircase. 12 rooms. Open Apr-Oct. The castle is in the village of La Malene which is about 14 km S of Ste. Enimie, and also about 5 km S of Château de la Caze, another castle hotel. Both Ste. Enimie and La Malêne are interesting villages, and Rt. 107 through the gorge is most scenic. (II)

Hotel MONTGOMERY (NW)
13, rue Couesnon
50170 Pontorson (Manche) 60 00 09

This old lodge was built by the Counts of Montgomery in the 1500s, and a curious highlight of French history occurred near here more than four centuries ago. King Henri II of France held a festival there on the occasion of the marriage of his sister to the Duc de Savoie, June 30, 1559. A highlight was a jousting tournament of mounted knights. As the last event, the King commanded Gabriel, Count of Montgomery, to tilt with him. An open visor and a broken lance resulted in the fatal wounding of the King, and he died there July 9, nine days later. Today the hotel's character is enhanced by fine woodwork, beamed ceilings, a 16th century staircase, and furnishings from the periods of Louis XIII and XV. The setting is in gardens and terraces. The famed offshore fortress-monastery, Mont-St. Michel, is just 9 km away. 35 rooms, open Mar-Nov. Pontorson is on N176 about 45 km N of Rennes. (I)

Château de MONTLEDIER (S)
Route d'Angles
81200 Mazamet (Tarn) 61 20 54

Dating from the 13th century, this aged castle in the Black Mountains offers an attractive setting for lake boating, swimming, riding, golf and nearby tennis, and other amenities. There is a massive square tower and a turreted round tower, which accent the adjoining buildings. Outdoor dining terrace. 8 rooms. Open all year. It is NE of the village of Pont-de-l'Arn, which is on D54 about 10 km N of Mazamet. Castle is just S of D54. (II)

MOULIN de MOUGINS (SE)
Chemin du Moulin
06250 Mougins (Alpes-Mar.) 75 78 24

This genuine oil mill, dating from the 16th century, provides a picturesque setting for its 3-star rated restaurant and guest rooms. Some of the old mechanical parts of the mill have been worked into the decor and many of the rooms have the ancient exposed beams. Mougins is located at the base of the hills of the same

Moulin de Mougins

Château de Mounet-Sully

name, 5 km from the Mediterranean beaches at Cannes. Sailing, fishing, hunting, golf, riding, and tennis are all nearby. 6 rooms. Closed Oct 25-Dec 20. On the Carnot road which runs N out of Cannes, just N of the Autoroute to Nice. (III)

Château de MOUNET-SULLY (SW)
Route de Mussidan
24100 Bergerac (Dordogne) (53) 57 04 21

The old château dates from the 1500s to the 1700s and now offers a variety of comforts and services. These include a small theatre, swimming pool, cloister, minigolf and a nightclub. 14 rooms, 12 with baths. Bergerac is about 100 km E of Bordeaux, and the castle is on N709 about 1 km NW of Bergerac. (II)

Restaurant le MOUSTIER (N)
41 bis, rue Langlois
(near des Halles, Route A6)
91490 Milly-la-Forêt
(Essonne) (6) 498 92 52

Restaurant Only

Candlelight dining is in the ancient vaulted rooms of the chapel of St. Vulfranc, in a château of the 12th and 15th centuries. Specialties of the area, including lobster bourguignon. S of Paris near Fontainbleau and Barbizon. 4-star, expensive.

Château de NIEUIL (SW)
16270 Nieuil (Charente) 71 36 38

Built in the early 1500s, this beautiful country château was once a hunting castle of King Francois I. Today, with its perfectly balanced towers, green lawns and formal gardens, it is a charming place. A hotel since 1937, it is among the earlier castles to be so utilized. Activities include swimming and tennis, and there is a recommended restaurant. 12 rooms with baths, 2 apts. Closed mid-Nov-Jan, but open for Christmas holidays. Nieuil is E of St. Claud, and 40 km NE of Angoulême. (II)

Château de Nieuil

Château de Castel Novel

Château de Castel NOVEL **(S)**
19240 Varetz (Correze) **85 00 01**

Feudal towers of the 14th century, and other elements of later centuries, as recent as the 19th, are incorporated in the castle as it stands today. It has documents tracing its origins back to 1289, and Roman coins have been found in excavations on the site, indicating an active Roman presence there centuries earlier. Complete French cuisine, elevator, heated pool, tennis, excursions arranged. Location is in a large park area. Recommended restaurant. 27 rooms. Closed Jan. 10 km NW of Brive by RN20 and 701. (II)

Château d'OLBREUSE **(W)**
79210 Usseau (Deux Sevres) **(49) 75 85 74**

This private castle has been in the Desmier family and descendants since 1350, a family connected with several of the European dynasties. Charles Desmier d'Olbreuse utilized the castle for care of the wounded in WWI, and the

La Tour de Pacoret

castle was restored in 1975 and adapted as a guest house. A round tower and other elements of the ancient castle remain, and a newer wing is attached. It is now a historic monument. Walled court, promenades, quiet area. Tavern and wine-cellar. 11 rooms, and other rooms in Le Village d'Olbreuse. Meeting rooms. Between LaRochelle and Niort, 40 km from the Atlantic coast. (I-II)

La Tour de PACORET **(E)**
73740 Gresy-sur-Isere
(Savoie) **(79) 32 44 12**

The hotel offers fine views of mountains and valley, with quiet surroundings, gardens, central heating. 12 rooms. Closed Oct 15-Mar. 2 km NE of Gresy-sur-Isere, near N90, about 37 km E of Chambery. (I)

Hotel de la Plage

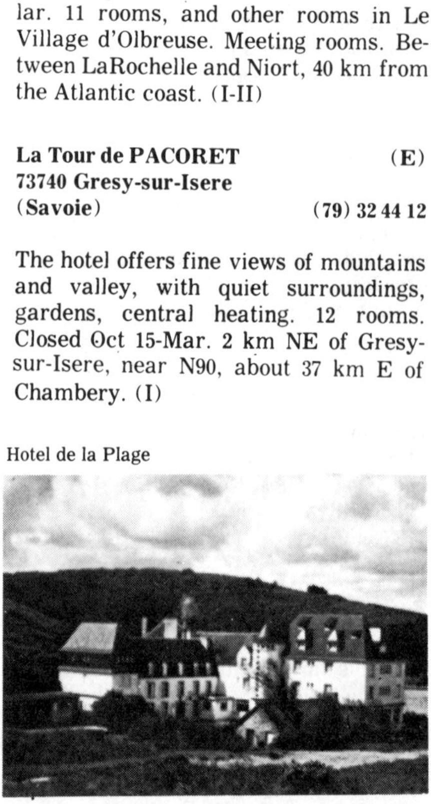

Hostellerie de la Poste

Château de Pray

Hotel de la PLAGE (W)
29137 Ste. Anne-la-Palud
(Finistere-Sud) 92 50 12

Located among the green hills at the western end of Brittany, this beautiful seashore resort offers quiet, isolated surroundings. The large, rambling mansion has one tower linking it to feudal architecture. Heated pool, tennis, riding, hunting, fishing nearby. 30 rooms, 2 apts. Open Mar-Sept. On Bay of Douarnenez (Atlantic Ocean), 25 km N of Quimper airport, on D107, a secondary road. (II)

Château de POMPAIRAIN (WC)
79200 Parthenay
(Deux-Sèvres) (49) 64 26 09

With its symphony of towers, spires and gables, this baronial mansion, built in the 18th and 19th centuries is a captivating sight. It is in a park area of some 30 acres, 1 km from the towns of Parthenay and Chatillon-sur-Thouet, where there are two pools, tennis, and meeting facilities. It offers only 6 rooms. Breakfast only. About 50 km W of Poitiers. (II)

Hostellerie de la POSTE (EC)
13 Pl. Vauban
89200 Avallon
(Yonne-Bourgogne) (86) 34 06 12

From 1707 onward this hostellerie served coach passengers traveling through, and its tradition continues as it is rated as one of France's great restaurants. Napoleon stopped here on his return from the Island of Elba to drink a bottle of Chambertin wine, his preferred vintage. Dining is in the old converted stables, and on a cobblestone terrace. Swimming, hunting, fishing, riding and tennis. 30 rooms, most with baths. Closed Dec-Jan. On N6. (II)

Château de PRAY (C)
13 Ave. Barn
37400 Amboise (Indre-et-Loire) 57 23 67

Situated in the midst of the Loire Valley, this 14th century castle makes a suitable headquarters for touring the many famed châteaux of the Loire, probably the most notable array of surviving castles in the world. Château de Pray was built in 1382 and was the home of members of the French royal court. It was adapted as a fine hotel about 1951. 16 rooms, 12 baths. Closed Jan-Feb 10. 2 km E of town on RN751. (II)

Le Prieuré
(Chenehutte les Truffeaux)

Hostellerie le Prieuré
(Villeneuve-les-Avignon)

Le PRIEURÉ (W)
49350 Chenehutte les Tuffeaux
(Maine-et-Loire) 50 15 31

Located in the heart of the Loire Valley near Saumur on that river, this castle, dating from the 12th to 15th centuries, offers magnificent views and excellent accommodations. Parks, gardens, promenades, boating, heated pool, miniature golf, fishing, tennis and beautifully furnished rooms. Ultra modern rooms also are available in modern bungalows on the grounds. 40 rooms. Closed Jan-Feb. 7 km W of Saumur on right bank of Loire River. (II)

Hostellerie le PRIEURÉ (SE)
Pl. du Chapitre 7
30400 Villeneuve-les-Avignon
(Gard) 25 18 20

The palace was built in 1322 by Cardinal Arnaud de Via, a nephew of Pope John XXII, and in 1333 he presented part of it to establish a Priory (Prieuré). They added a cloister and a strongly fortified tower to the chapel, which later was enlarged and is now the village church. The Cardinal's tomb is in a side chapel and his coat-of-arms can be seen in the keystone. During the French Revolution in 1789 the Priory was taken by the state, and over the years it was used as a school, a gentlemen's residence and a boarding house for artists. In 1943 it was transformed into a small hotel, still utilizing the old furniture and maintaining the atmosphere of past ages. Swimming, tennis, riding, elevator and air conditioning. 47 rooms. Open Feb-Nov 15. On the right bank, 2 km, across the river, from Avignon on N580. (II)

Hostellerie du PRIEURÉ (SE)
84480 Bonnieux (Vaucluse) (90) 75 80 78

Situated on a promontory in the village of Bonnieux this ancient convent of the 1600s offers guests the calm and quiet atmosphere of the old cloister. The restaurant features specialties of the Provence region. 10 rooms. Open Mar 15-Nov 15. Bonnieux is E of Avignon and N of Aix. (II)

Château du REGARD (N)
Rte. Orry-la-Ville
60580 Coye-la-Forêt (Oise) (4) 458 60 16

The château, built in the early 19th century, was given by Napoleon I to Marechal Berthier. Located in the Forest of Chantilly north of Paris, the château offers a restaurant, bar, swimming and tennis. 18 rooms with baths. Closed Aug. and Christmas Holidays. Some 30 km N of Paris. Coye is just E of N16, S of Lamorlaye. (I)

Château du Regard

Château de Riell en Rousillon

Manoir de RETIVAL (N)
76490 Caudebec-en-Caux
(Seine-Maritime) 95 11 22

The old towered baronial mansion stands in a wooded park area, with lawns and gardens. Fishing and yachting are offered. Handicap facilities, wheelchairs. 12 rooms, open Mar- mid-Dec. No restaurant. Location is in the Seine Valley on N182, about 40 km W of Rouen toward LeHavre. This road runs N of the Seine River. (I)

Château de RIELL (S)
en ROUSSILLON
66500 Molitg-les-Bains
(Pyrenees Orientales) 05 12 29

Moltig-les-Bains is a health spa in the Pyrenees near the Spanish border. The castle-like hotel overlooks the village and mountains. Dungeon lounge and bar, fireplaces, gothic style vaulted rooms, and a swimming pool on the roof overlooked by a stone tower. Hunting, fishing, riding, tennis nearby. The Pablo Casals music festival is held in the village. 20 rooms. Open Apr-Oct. 7 km N of Prades, 50 km W of Perpignan. (III)

Château du RIVAU (WC)
37120 Lemere
(Indre-et-Loire) (47) 58 14 03

This beautiful feudal castle, with its round and square strong towers, was associated with Joan of Arc before her victory at Orleans in 1429. In 1438 the castle was acquired by marriage by the House of Beauvau, and in 1441 Pierre de Beauvau obtained permission from King Charles VII to fortify the castle. Now adapted as a guest house, it also has facilities for receptions and meetings. It is S of Chinon in the Loire Valley. (I-II)

Manoir de Retival

Manoir de ROCHECOURBE (SW)
24220 Vezac (Dordogne) (53) 29 50 79

The ancient fortified manor has a cone-topped strong tower, and is small as

Château de Rochgude

Château de Rolland

castles go. It stands in a park area, and is convenient for excursions to nearby caves, castles and other points of interest. Fishing, tennis, swimming, and nearby riding. S of Sarlat. 7 rooms. Open Apr-Nov. (I-II)

Château de ROCHGUDE **(SE)**
26130 Rochgude (Drome) **04 81 88**

Situated in the beautiful Rhone valley of the Provence region, Rochgude Castle sits astride the ancient boundary between the realms of the King of France and the Papacy between 1274 and 1797. It sustained a siege by Baron des Andrets in the 1500s and suffered great damage. Partly restored in the 17th and 18th centuries, the château offers today's guests elegant vaulted rooms, huge fireplaces, a lovely 18th century staircase, beautiful antique furnishings. Cobbled courtyard, heated pool, tennis, terraces and walkways in the grounds and village. There are extensive underground cellars and dungeons. Fishing, riding nearby. Open April to Nov. 12 km N of Orange, 9 km SE from Rollene on D117 and D8. (II)

Château de ROLLAND **(SW)**
Barsac, 33720 Podensac
(Gironde) **27 15 75**

The château is the former monastery of Chartreux, partially restored by Louis XV (1715-1774). Furnishings are in keeping with that period, and interiors have wood beamed ceilings and fireplaces. It is in an area of vineyards, and there are walking paths roundabout, as well as fishing, hunting, tennis, and swimming. 7 rooms, 2 suites. Closed Jan. Barsac is 39 km SE of Bordeaux on N113. (II)

Château de ROUMÉGOUSE **(SC)**
46500 Rignac (Lot) **33 63 81**

In the 10th century and later, this towered castle was a stopping place for pilgrims to and from Rome. Located near a celebrated pilgrimage place, Rocamadour, it is also in an area of canyons, grottoes and prehistoric caves. The castle played its role as a feudal center through the Middle Ages, declined, and was restored in the late 19th century. Converted to a hotel after WWII, it now offers swimming, riding, hunting and fishing. 12 rooms, 2 apts. Open Apr-Oct 15. On N681, 4 km E of Rocamadour and N of Gramat. (II)

Château de Roumégouse

Abbaye de SAINTE CROIX (SE)
Val de Cuech
13300 Salon (Provence) 56 24 55

With elements dating from the 9th to 12th centuries, this ancient abbey was abandoned for 200 years and then restored. Today the 4-star hotel offers guests a lovely site overlooking a broad valley and rocky crags, extensive grounds and pool. Lounges and public rooms abound in vaults and archways, and antique furnishings and objets d'art. The dining room is Middle Ages — 2-story-high stone vaulted with arch windows and a minstrel gallery. Rooms are antique-furnished with modern amenities. Facilities for meetings and receptions. Riding, tennis, archeological sites, artisans' shops nearby. Just S of D16 E of Autoroute A7 about 50 km N of Marseille. (II)

l'Abbaye de Sainte Croix

Château SAINT-JEAN (C)
Parc St-Jean
03100 Montlucon (Allier) 05 04 65

This towered castle has sections surviving from the Middle Ages when it was a rest stop for the hard-riding Knights Templar and Knights of Malta, during the Crusades. Recommended restaurant, park, terrace, pool, sailing, fishing, riding and tennis. 8 rooms. Closed Dec 20-Jan 16. It is in the southern environs of the city on N689. (II)

Château SAINT-VINCENT (SW)
Route d'Angoulême
24460 Château l'Eveque
Perigueux (Dordogne) (53) 54 30 50

The massive 14th century medieval fortress dominates the town of Château l'Eveque, which also was formerly the name of the castle. The name was changed to Saint Vincent in honor of a kindly priest who was ordained in the castle in 1600. He later founded the Order of St. Vincent de Paul. The castle dates from the 14th and 15th centuries and was once the residence of the Bishops of Perigueux. Several round and square towers give the tall stone château the feudal look of the Middle Ages, and the style of the Perigord region. It has been restored as a 3-star hotel with all facilities, including swimming, tennis and riding nearby. Sitting rooms and drawing rooms, with massive wood beam structure, are charmingly furnished, and some of the guest rooms have canopy beds and elegant furnishings. The castle stands in a 40-acre park area with

Château Saint-Jean

Château Saint-Vincent

Pavillon Sevigné

gardens and ponds. Good restaurant with French cuisine of the region. 14 rooms, 3 apts. Closed Feb. 10 km N of Perigueux on N139. (III)

Pavillon SEVIGNÉ (C)
10 Pl. Sevigné
03200 Vichy (Allier) 32 16 22

Built in the 1600s, this mansion was once the residence of the writer Marquise de Sevigne. Vichy, world-renowned spa of Roman times, offers all facilities for sports and amusements. Sevigné, a 4-star hotel, is furnished impressively. 55 rooms. Open May-Oct. Vichy is about 60 km N of Clermont-Ferrand. (II)

Le Manoir du STANG (NW)
29133 La Foret-Fouesnant
(Finistere) 56 97 37

Renaissance woodwork, furnishings and objets d'art have been retained in the adaption of this centuries-old château as a modern guest house. Some gothic stone construction and hand-hewn stone spiral staircases add charm to the setting. Dining room waitresses wear traditional Breton costumes. It is in Brittany, near the Atlantic Ocean, close to beaches, golf, fishing, tennis, and sea excursions can be arranged with Breton fishermen. 28 rooms. Open May-Sept. On D783 between Quimper and the old walled port town of Concarneau. (III)

Château de STEENEBOURG (N)
Steene par Dunkerque
59380 Bergues (Nord) (20) 68 66 36

Situated close to the Belgian border, this 16th century castle has a Spanish-Flemish style, with stepped gables and towers. Pleasant grounds and lawns, and menus typical of the area, are features. 7 rooms with baths. Closed Aug. SE of Calais on D352, and 15 km from the sea. (II)

Le Manoir du Stang

Château de Steenbourg

A typical hand-hewn stone staircase.
Manoir du Stang, France, 1500s

Château de Thaumiers

Château de THAUMIERS **(C)**
18210 Thaumiers,
Charenton-du-Cher (Cher) **(48) 60 87 62**

Viscount and Viscountess de Bonneval have opened their ancestral castle to accept a limited number of guests. The present castle was constructed in the 1700s and offers quiet and elegance in spacious grounds and a reflecting lake. Location is W of Bourges a medieval city with an outstanding cathedral and other highlights, as well as associations of Chopin and George Sand. Open Easter-Oct 31. About 50 km SE of Bourges on Rt. 153. Rates on request.

Le Domaine de la TORTINIÈRE **(WC)**
37250 Montbazon
(Indre-et-Loire) **26 00 19**

This Renaissance-style castle was built about a century ago by the Count of Rigny, in an area rich in French history going back to the 11th century when a castle keep was erected. The chateau became a fine hotel in 1954 with beautiful grounds and surrounding trees, golf, riding, swimming, fishing and tennis. 14 rooms and 7 apts. Closed Dec-Jan. In the midst of the château country, the castle is about 12 km S of Tours, just N of Montbazon and slightly W of N10. (II)

Le Domaine de la Tortinière

Château de TRIGANCE **(SE)**
83840 Trigance (Var) **76 91 18**

The 12th century castle sits high above the little village of Trigance offering sweeping views of the valley and mountains. One of the castle towers dates from 1108, others from the 15th and 16th centuries. Dining room and lounge are in two ancient stone-vaulted rooms, one above the other, with connecting hand-hewn stone stairs. There are also subterranean passages and stairs into the lower towers which lend credence to the castle's ghost legend. Good restaurant with careful attention to the French cuisine. Terraces provide excellent view-

Château de Trigance

points for the scene below, and excursions to the nearby spectacular Gorges du Verdon can be arranged, as can also hunting and fishing. There is a pool and tennis. The approach to the castle is up a winding mountain road to a parking area below the castle. Guests walk up 90 stone steps to reach the castle, but baggage is taken up on a hoist. Open Easter to mid-Nov. It is about 20 km S of Castellane, just W of D955. (II)

Château de TRIVIER (EC)
73190 Challes-les-Eaux
(Savoie) (79) 85 07 27

In an area of high mountains the castle is situated in spacious grounds of about 10 acres, with a lake. There are also health springs nearby. Facilities for meetings, restaurant, wine cellar. 26 rooms. Open year-round. SE of Chambery. (I)

Château des TROIS POETES (SW)
64300 Castetis par Orthez (59) 69 16 20

The castle's origins go back to the Middle Ages, and the present structure reflects the reconstruction of about 1600. For years it was known as Château de Candau from the family which owned the estate for several centuries. In later years three French poets resided there or were associated with the castle, which provided its present name. Busts of the poets may be seen in the entrance court. Today it is a 3-star hotel and restaurant, with 10 rooms, some with shower or bath. Additional lodgings are in l'Orme de Sully, an old mansion about 150 meters away. Orthez is on RN117, near the Spanish border, about 60 km from the Atlantic coast. (I)

Château de la VALLEE BLEUE (C)
Rte. Verneuil
36460 St. Chartier (Indre) 31 01 91

The old towered château stands in spacious grounds. 12 rooms with baths or

Château des Trois Poetes

Château de la Vallee Bleue

Hostellerie du Vert Mesnil

Le Vieux Château

showers. Closed mid-Dec through Jan. Near N718 and N143, 9 km N of LaChatre, and about 29 km S of Chateauroux. (I)

Hostellerie du VERT MESNIL (NW)
Tilques, 62500 St. Omer
(Pas-de-Calais) (21) 98 28 99

The symmetrical château reflects the architecture of the 18th and 19th centuries when it was built. For many years it was the residence of a titled family. In the 1930s it was used as a seminary, and during WWII was occupied by a German general and his staff. The château was adapted as a hotel and restaurant in 1971. The dining rooms and other public areas dating from the 18th century, are spacious and attractive. There is a lounge and bar. Guest rooms are nicely furnished. 40 rooms, all with baths. Table tennis, outdoor tennis, volley ball and walks through nearby marshes available. It is situated off RN43, a 10 min. drive from St. Omer, and 40 min. from Calais-Boulogne, or Dunkirk. (II)

Le VIEUX CHATEAU (NW)
50260 Bricquebec (Manche) (33) 52 24 49

Some of these structures date from the 10th century, and were the seat of Robert Bertrand an officer with William the Conqueror at the Battle of Hastings opening the conquest of Britain in 1066. There is a tower dungeon dating from the

1300s which now contains a museum. Restaurant, regional specialties. It is located 22 km S of Cherbourg and 140 km from the famed Mont-St-Michel. 21 rooms. Closed January. (I)

Château de VIOLET (S)
11160 Peyriac-Minervois
(Aude) (68) 78 10 42

Located at the foot of the Black Mountains, Château de Violet is an old towered manor house with furnishings in character with the ancient house. It is in a park setting, and excursions may be made to nearby points of interest, including the walled city of Carcassonne, and the sea. 20 rooms and apts. Open Jan-Oct. Peyriac-Minervois is on D11, about 25 km NE of Carcassonne. The château is about 1 km N on D35. (II)

Château de Violet

CHATEAU ACCUEIL
(Castle Welcome)

Chateau Accueil is an association of private castle-owners in France who offer a warm personal reception and experience in their castles. They offer traditional French hospitality, and information about the architecture, history and cultural events, as well as emphasizing the gastronomy of their regions. They offer guest rooms and private apartments or houses. Facilities also provide for dinner parties, business luncheons and meetings.

For information: Mme. la Vicomtesse de Bonneval, La Presidente, Chateau de Thaumiers, 18210 Charenton-du-Cher, Tel. (48) 60 87 62; or Mme. Illich, la Secretaire Generale, Chateau de Memillon, Saint-Maur-sur-le-Loir, 28800 Bonneval, Tel. (37) 47 28 57; or Voyages Saulnier, 11 rue du 29-Juillet, 75001 Paris, Tel. 260 37 51, Telex 220 864.

French Print, Paris-Lyon, 1485-'99

Germany

Burg-Hotel ABENBERG (SE)
8541 Abenberg uber Schwabach

The castle, partly dating from 1071, is above a quiet village. Walls, ancient buildings and watch-towers surround an open court, with a pool, grassy areas, sunbathing and outdoor restaurant. Historic furnishings, swimming, and rooms for about 20 guests. Seven days stay suggested. Munich-Berlin autobahn exit toward Ansbach. Nearest RR station is Roth near Nürnberg. (II)

Burg Abenberg
Alte Klostermühle

Der ACHTERMANN (NE)
20 Rosentorstr.
Goslar/Harz 338

Constructed around an old tower built in the 1400s, this hostelry has an elevator, large comfortable rooms and a dining room in the tower. 96 rooms, 49 baths. About 70 km SE of Hannover. (II)

Hotel-Restaurant (C)
ALTE KLOSTERMUHLE
6301 Arnsburg uber Lich (06404) 2029

The name "Cloistermill" derives from the history of the establishment which began as the Zisterzienser Monastery in 1174. In 1803 the abbey was secularized and became the property of the Counts of Solms-Laubach. The hotel is in the former students quarters, with antique furnishings. The former mill and baking house have been transformed into a specialty restaurant, and the old brewing house of the monks imparts a rustic atmosphere to receptions and other festivities. There is a monastic chapel where weddings are often held. Available are mini-golf, horse carriage rides through the surrounding country, riding, fishing, hunting, bowling, and a children's playground. 40 beds, some rooms with bath. Arnsburg is NE of Frankfurt, near Autobahn toward Kassel, exit Butzbach toward Lich. About 10 km S of Lich, and 15 km SE of the university town of Giessen. (II)

ALTE THORSCHENKE (W)
3 Brückenstrasse
5590 Cochem/Mosel 70 59

This guest house, built in 1332 and

preserved as a landmark by the state, is furnished with many antiques. A carved wood hanging staircase and a spacious beamed ceiling dining room enhance the interior. Some rooms have four-poster beds. Elevators, handicap facilities, conference rooms, terrace. 53 rooms, 25 with baths. Closed Jan 6 to mid-Mar. Cochem is a picturesque resort town spread along the shore of the Mosel River, dominated by an impressive mountaintop 12th century castle. (I)

Alte Thorschenke

Parkhotel Wasserburg ANHOLT (NW)
Kleverstrasse
4294 Anholt (Westfalia) 20 44

Located in the flat landscape near the Holland border, Wasserburg (Water Castle) Anholt lives up to its name. It is surrounded by a wide moat and lake, and is entered across a narrow stone causeway and drawbridge. The latter is typical of Dutch drawbridges, and the castle architecture reflects the NW German and Dutch style. Some foundations of the castle are said to date from Roman times, and some of it was built in the 1100s. Throughout its history it has lain in the paths of conquering and defending armies, its latest episode being the heavy bombing of WWII. Owners since the 1600s, the Princes zu Salm, restored it at great expense after the war, using ancient tile and bricks. The huge complex now contains a museum as well as 29 guest rooms. Dining on a lake terrace, nice public rooms, elevator, conference rooms, handicap facilities. Swimming, fishing, golf nearby. Situated in a large park area, about 3 km from Isselburg-Anholt RR station. N of Dusseldorf-Köln Autobahn, exit Rocholt-Rees. Closed Feb. (II)

Wasserburg Anhol t

Schloss Arensburg

Hotel Schloss ARENSBURG (NC)
3262 Steinbergen
Rinteln on Weser (05751) 50 78

This Renaissance-style castle is among the low mountains and valleys of the Weser River. The main building dates

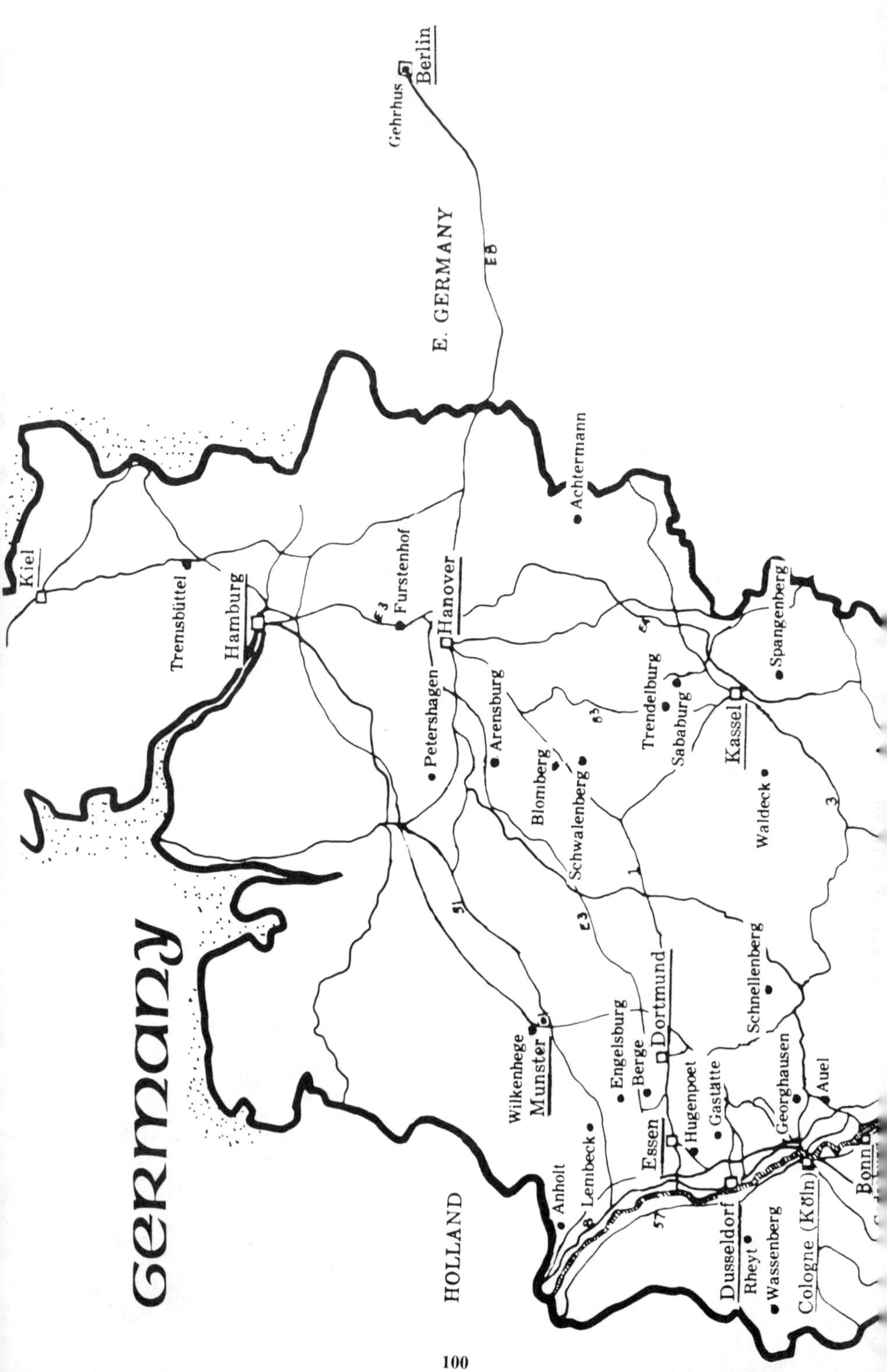

GERMANY
HOLLAND
E. GERMANY
Kiel
Tremsbüttel
Hamburg
Fürstenhof
Hanover
Achtermann
Petershagen
Arensburg
Blomberg
Schwalenberg
Trendelburg
Sababurg
Kassel
Spangenberg
Waldeck
Schnellenberg
Gehrhus
Berlin
Wilkenhege
Munster
Engelsburg
Berge
Dortmund
Hugenpoet
Gastätte
Georghausen
Auel
Anholt
Lembeck
Essen
Dusseldorf
Rheyt
Wassenberg
Cologne (Köln)
Bonn
E3
E8
E4
51
57
83
3
1

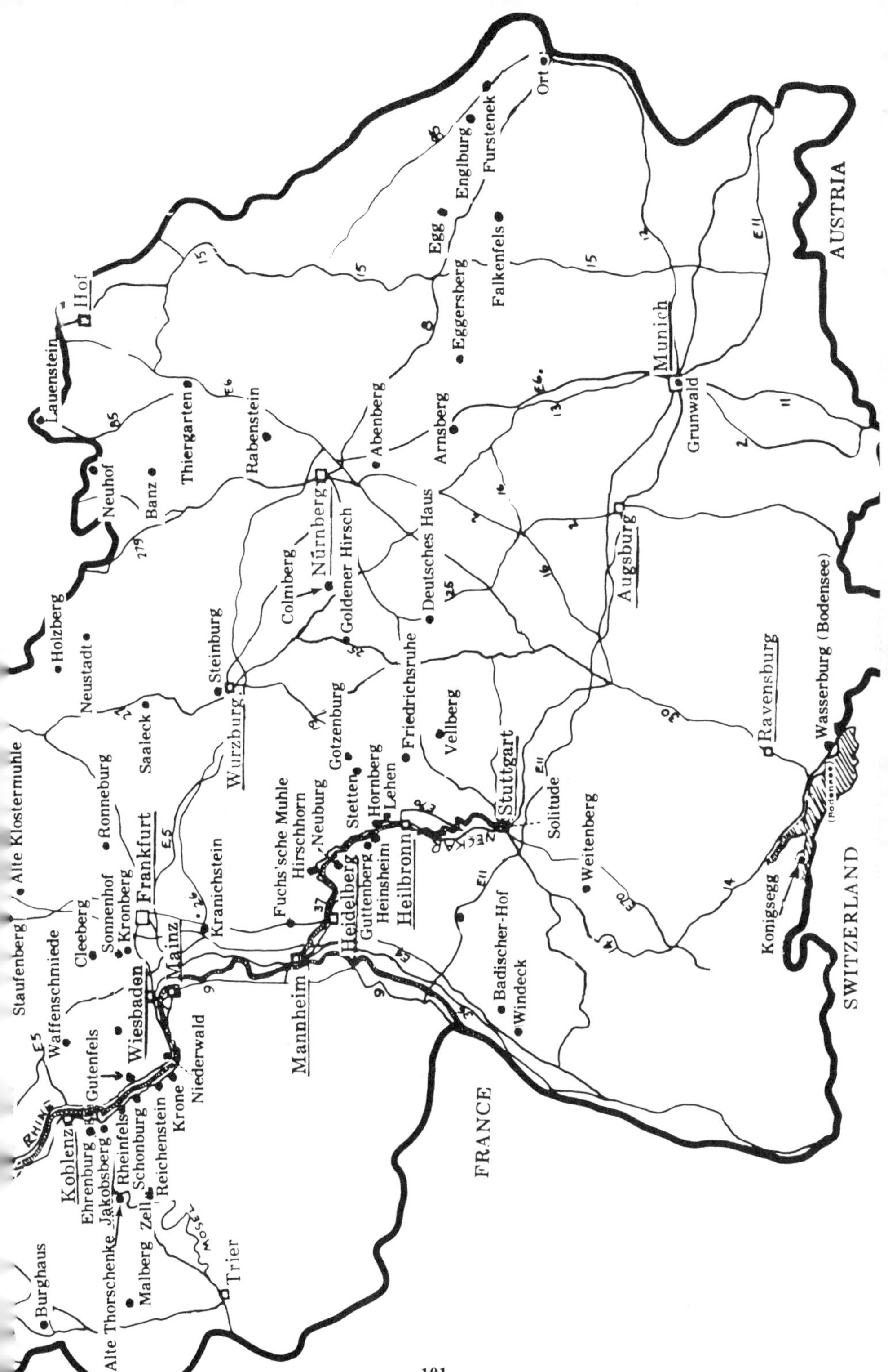

AUSTRIA
SWITZERLAND
FRANCE
Hof
Lauenstein
Neuhof
Banz
Thiergarten
Rabenstein
Holzberg
Neustadt
Alte Klostermuhle
Ronneburg
Saaleck
Steinburg
Wurzburg
Nürnberg
Colmberg
Goldener Hirsch
Abenberg
Arnsberg
Deutsches Haus
Friedrichsruhe
Gotzenburg
Vellberg
Stuttgart
Solitude
Weitenberg
Ravensburg
Wasserburg (Bodensee)
Konigsegg
Augsburg
Munich
Grunwald
Eggersberg
Falkenfels
Egg
Englburg
Furstenek
Ort
Staufenberg
Waffenschmiede
Cleeberg
Sonnenhof
Kronberg
Frankfurt
Kranichstein
Mainz
Wiesbaden
Gutenfels
Niederwald
Krone
Reichenstein
Schonburg
Rheinfels
Jakobsberg
Ehrenburg
Koblenz
Zell
Malberg
Alte Thorschenke
Burghaus
Trier
Mannheim
Heidelberg
Fuchs'sche Muhle
Hirschhorn
Neuburg
Stetten
Hornberg
Lehen
Guttenberg
Heinsheim
Heilbronn
Badischer-Hof
Windeck

Schloss Arnsberg

Schloss Auel

from 1300. Situated on a hilltop, the castle grounds have footpaths in the surrounding woods. Accommodations offer a refined and quiet atmosphere and modern amenities, among ancient buildings, walls and courtyards. 23 rooms and apts. Near the Autobahn between Hannover and Cologne (Köln), exit Bad Eilsen. In Steinbergen, 5 km from Rinteln on 238 near 83. (II)

Schloss ARNSBERG (SE)
D8079 Kipfenberg-Arnsberg (08465) 3 54

With origins going back to 1235, this old castle complex of walls and buildings stands on the edge of a precipitous rock cliff with panoramic views across the valley. There are visible remains of Roman and Celtic civilization nearby, and hiking trails round about. Ancient fossils also can be found. Vaulted public rooms, wood beam ceilings, conference rooms, chapel, wine cellars, restaurant, sun and TV rooms. New Year package arrangements. 50 beds. Location about 60 km S of Nürnberg, E6, Exit toward Eichstatt-Kipfenberg. (I)

Schloss AUEL (WC)
5204 Lohmar 21, Wahlsheid (02206) 20 41

This 1766 moated baronial residence replaced an earlier 14th century castle which was the ancestral home of the

Schloss Banz

Marquis de la Valette. Among many notables who have been guests in the present mansion over the years are Napoleon and Czar Alexander. Today the interior is exquisite, decorated with priceless furnishings, matched by finest foods and wines. Auel is situated in the Rhine Valley and offers a heated pool, Heliport, golf and riding. 25 rooms. Closed Nov. Rt 484, about 35 km SE of Cologne. (II)

Steigenberger-Hotel **(SW)**
BADISCHER HOF
47 Langestrasse, Baden Baden **2 28 27**

This old cloister, now a preserved government monument, and rated as a distinguished hotel, is in a resort city in the Black Forest region. International restaurant, conference rooms, elevator, handicap facilities, thermal baths, park and garden grounds. 75 rooms. (II)

Schloss Gasthof BANZ **(EC)**
8621 Lichtenfels/
Oberfranken **(09573) 59 77**

Hotel facilities are in an 18th century palace complex on a hilltop 1575 ft above sea level. A former monastery and duke's palace in 1803, the hotel and ballroom facilities have made it a center of many activities. Finest wines and German beers are featured. Organ and cembalo concerts in summer. Train service and other transportation nearby. 40 beds. Open Apr-Oct. Between Coburg and Bamberg on 289. In Staffelstein E of Lichtenfels. (II)

Schloss BERGE **(W)**
Adenaueralle 103
4660 Gelsenkirken-Buer **(0209) 5 99 58**

Schloss Berge is a 17th century water castle of the Counts of Westerholt-Gysenberg situated in a large park area. It is still surrounded by a moat, and approached across a stone bridge. Terraces and gardens, as well as the surrounding park, offer pleasant walking areas. Public rooms as well as private are

Schloss Berge

elegantly furnished, and there are three fine restaurants. 13 rooms. It is just N of the E3 Autobahn about 10 km N of Essen. Adenauerallee is found connecting with Kurt Schumacher Strasse. (II-III)

Burghotel BLOMBERG **(N)**
4933 Blomberg **3 71**

Situated near the market square and town hall (Rathaus), this ancient wall-enclosed fortified castle has buildings dating from the 13th, 14th and 16th centuries. Formerly the seat of the titled Lippe family, the castle now is owned by

Burg Blomberg

Das Burghaus

the state of Lippe, a first class hotel since 1974. Walls and battlements face out over the valley, and upon entering the cobbled courtyard through a gothic gate, the visitor sees a surround of half-timbered buildings. A fine restaurant and public rooms maintain the medieval charm. Footpaths lead around the hill below the walls, and shopping is just a few hundred yards away, in the center of town. The village of Blomberg is on Rt. 1, about 70 km SW of Hannover. 22 rooms, open all year. (III)

Das BURGHAUS **(W)**
Burgbergring 4
5377 Kronenburg/Eifel **(06557) 2 65**

A great baronial house, built 1766, on a high hill overlooking a broad valley. Authentic antique furnishings, charming 18th century kitchen. Original castle ruins still include elements of towers and walls which are incorporated in Quaint village houses. arches, gates, chapel, etc., which artists come to paint. Proprietor is Dr. (Mrs) Lucretia Lorent of the Faymonville-Lorent family, owners of the manor since the French revolution. 30 beds. Closed part of Jan-Feb. Turn W on E42 from B51 at Stadtkyll (4 km), near the Belgium border. (I)

Schloss Cleeberg

Schloss Colmberg

Schlosshotel CLEEBERG **(C)**
6309 Cleeberg **7 01**

This 12th century castle is located in a large natural game preserve surrounded by the Taunus Mts and dark forest. The landmark stone tower is enclosed by the old wall and other buildings of later periods. Luxurious guest rooms are rustic, all with bath, radio and TV. International restaurant, summer breakfast on terrace. The bar is in a deep vault. Conference rooms, riding, tennis, bowling, hunting, fishing, hiking, golf, skiing, airplane lessons. 19 rooms. N of Frankfurt, N of the E4 (Butzbach exit). (II)

Schloss COLMBERG (SC)
8801 Colmberg (09803) 2 62

Dating from the 11th and 12th centuries, Colmberg Castle has for 500 years belonged to the former ruling Hohenzollern family. With several stone towers and a large half-timbered central building, it is typical of the German castles of the Middle Ages. There is a castle and art museum, wildpark, library, terrace dining in season, chapel, conference facilities. 31 rooms, 16 with bath or shower. On the Burgenstrasse (Castle Road) between the walled medieval town of Rothenburg on Tauber and Ansbach. (II)

DEUTSCHES HAUS (S)
3 Weinmarkt, Dinkelsbuhl 8804

Dinkelsbuhl is an intact medieval town complete with walls, bastions, towers, gates and moats, located halfway between Nürnberg and Stuttgart on Rt 25. Hotel is within a town house dating from 1440 and has spacious rooms furnished with appropriate antiquities. 13 rooms, 3 with bath. Closed Nov-Mar. (I)

Schloss EGG (SE)
8351 Egg
b. Deggendorf/Bayer Wald (09905) 2 89

With roots back to 1100, this walled castle with its tall turreted tower presents a striking characterization of the Middle Ages. It is surrounded by thick woods and park area, and is only a few km N of the Danube (Donau) River. Guest rooms and apartments are attractively furnished, and antiques and art objects add ancient charm. You may enjoy zither music in the evening by a cellar fireplace. 7 apts, TV, central heating. Egg is 6 km NW of Deggendorf and 3 km N of Metten. (II)

Gästehaus Schloss (SE)
EGGERSBERG
8422 Obereggersberg
Riedenburg/Opf. (09442) 14 98

The castle was first mentioned in history in the 9th century, and was formerly

Schloss Egg

owned by the Bavarian Dukes and Chancellor Leonhard von Eck. It is on the Danube high over the Altmuhl Valley in the Jura Mts. Rebuilt through the centuries, most of the present structure dates from about 1600. Concerts frequently held. Valuable collections are among the antiques and other furnishings. Conference rooms. Riding and fishing are offered. 20 rooms. About 30 km W of Regensburg, E of Denkendorf exit, Autobahn E6. (I)

Schloss Eggersberg

← Parkhotel Die Engelsburg →

Burg-Hotel EHRENBURG (W)
5401 Brodenbach/Mosel (02605) 24 32

The well-preserved castle was built in 1100, and owned by the Counts Kanitz of Nassau. As with most castles, later additions have been made through the centuries. There are views of the Ehrenbachlamm Gorge. Recommended restaurant, central heat, most rooms with bath or shower. Open mid-Mar to Oct. B49 Koblenz-Trier via road to Brodenbach-Boppard. Castle is 3 km from Brodenbach. (I)

Schloss Englburg

Parkhotel Die ENGELSBURG (W)
Augustinestrasse 10
4350 Rechlinghausen 2 50 66

Built in 1701, and formerly the residence of the Duke of Arenberg, the old castle-like palace now offers comfortable and attractive accommodations right in the center of this small city. The restaurant maintains the character of the 18th century, and there is a cafe, terrace, car parking in the courtyard, and facilities for meetings and conferences. The castle adjoins the old town walls and the broad grounds in the rear are bounded by the walls and a few watchtowers, apparently dating from much earlier times. 29 rooms. (I)

Pension Schloss ENGLBURG (SE)
8391 Tittling (Bayer. Wald) (08504) 17 35

Englburg Castle, with its distinctive onion-shaped towers, has not changed substantially in its outer appearances from old prints picturing it several centuries ago. Location of the castle and its complex of buildings is above the Bavarian village of Englburg in a quiet park area with nice views. Rates include meals. Usually fully booked. Open mid-Dec to mid-Oct. B85 (Ostmarkstr., Regen-Passau) toward Tittling. Exit toward Furstenstein, turn R after 4 km to Englburg. About 30 km N of Passau. (I)

Burg FALKENFELS (SE)
8441 Falkenfels ü Straubing (09961) 63 85

This is a high-castle of impressive proportions, with two terraced circular walls, one above the other. The former owners were the Counts von Bogen and the Knights von Hohenfels. The main tower is from the 13th century, and some other sections were built later. Kitchen and wine cellars provide savoury Bavarian specialties. Guests find rustic comfort on all three floors, or can relax under old chestnut trees overlooking the Danube River. Conference rooms, swimming pool, lake for fishing on grounds. Bowlking, tennis, skating, water skiing, riding, nearby. Winter ski-lifts and slopes are only minutes away. 39 rooms, most with baths. Nürnberg-Passau Autobahn exit toward Ascha. Castle is W of Ascha. (I)

Burg Falkenfels

Waldhotel FRIEDRICHSRUHE (SC)
7111 Friedrichsruhe
b.Ohringen, Württemberg (07491) 70 78

This great baronial mansion was built in 1712, and stands in a region rich in old castles and medieval towns. It is away from traffic, offering quiet in a lovely landscape. Park area, heated indoor pool, sauna, tennis, golf, fishing. Elevator, handicap facilities. 50 modern rooms, baths, showers. N of E12, N of Ohringen. (II)

FUCHS'SCHE MÜHLE (SW)
Birkenauer Tal. 10
6940 Weinheim 6 10 31

This inn, restaurant and guest house is a picturesque old water mill dating from the 1500s. Room accommodations and

Waldhotel Friedrichsruhe

Fuchs'sche Mühle

restaurant are modern. Terrace dining, heated indoor pool, sauna, elevator. 28 rooms, most with baths. On B38 N of city, and about 20 km N of Heidelberg. (I)

Schloss Fürstenek

Fürstenhof

Schloss FÜRSTENECK (SE)
8391 Fürsteneck über Passau

A tall keep and other elements of the 12th century castle are surrounded by buildings built in later centuries to form a typical complex around a stronghold. Entrance is through an ancient gate tower archway over a bridge. The guesthouse and pension offers rooms in antique or modern decor, and public rooms maintain the ancient character. Heated pool nearby, fishing and other activities. Rooms have showers or baths. 20 beds. B85 (Passau-Schönberg) to Tittling, R on road to Fürsteneck, about 25 km N of Passau. (I)

FÜRSTENHOF (N)
Hannover STr. 55
31 Celle (05141) 2 70 51

A baroque palace of the 17th century combining modern elegance with ancient splendor. A modern wing (1970) is hidden behind the old palace. High class restaurant Endtenfang, interesting shops and boutiques, vaulted cellar bar, many meeting rooms, discotheque, elevator, indoor pool. A Beer Tavern occupies the rustic interior of the old coach house. All guest rooms have private baths. The city of Celle is worth a visit, with its streets of half-timbered buildings, the ancient city hall (Rathaus), the castle of the Dukes of Brunswick and Luneburg and of the Electors and Kings of Hannover, 1266-1866. Celle is at intersection of Rts. 3, 191 and 214, 40 km N of Hannover. Furstenhof is in the city on the road toward Hannover. (II-III)

Schloss GASTÄTTE **(W)**
Burg a.d. Wupper
5650 Solingen-Burg **(02122) 4 30 50**

(Restaurant only)

This great castle complex dominates the area and overlooks the Wupper River from a high prominence. It has high outer and inner walls, towers and keeps dating from the 12th century. It was the seat of the Bergian Counts. Visitors for a nominal entrance fee can roam through the grounds, knights hall, chapel, museum, exhibits of arms and armor and collections of artifacts. The restaurant in the castle serves both snacks and complete meals. E of Dusseldorf, Autobahn E73, exit Schloss Burg. Follow signs.

Schloss Gastätte

Schloss Hotel GEHRHUS **(E)**
Brahmstrasse 4-10
1000 Berlin **8 26 20 81**

Formerly known as the Pannwitz Palace, it was built 1912-'14 to house the extensive art and china collections of the personal attorney of Kaiser Wilhelm II. This elegant palace is in a large park in the Grunewald, 5 min. from the Kurfurstendamm in the heart of W. Berlin. Conference rooms, elevator, nearby swimming and tennis. 34 rooms and apts. (II-III)

→ Schloss Gehrhus ↓

Schloss GEORGHAUSEN **(W)**
5253 Lindlar Hommerich Bez
Köln/Suelztal **(02207) 2561**

This old baronial mansion has been the seat of noble families as far back as 1380, and the present manor house dates from 1710. It is protected by moats and surrounded by extensive grounds. Location is in a lovely section of the Suelz Valley between the Ruhr and Sieg Rivers. Excellent kitchen and wine cel-

Schloss Georghausen

lars, and one dining room is in an ancient rock-vaulted dungeon. Fishing, 18-hole golf, terrace. 27 beds. 27 km E of Cologne (Köln). (II)

GODESBURG Hotel (W)
5320 Bad Godesburg am Rhein 36 30 08

It was in the 750th year of Goda Castle (1210-1960) that the ancient building was adapted as a first class guest hotel by an unusual blend of modern architecture with ancient towers and ramparts. The medieval fortress was built by the Bishops of Cologne, and from many of the balconied rooms the famed Cologne Cathedral can be seen. The site also affords a grand view of Eifel-Foreland and the Rhine valley. The spacious Knights' Hall of the castle seats 300 people. 14 rooms. 5 km S of Bonn. (II-III)

Hotel GOLDENER HIRSCH (SC)
16 Untere Schmiedgasse
Rothenburg ob der Tauber 20 51

Located in one of the wall towers of this popular, almost perfectly preserved, walled medieval town, this hotel offers superb views of the city and surrounding hills and valleys. A most unusual setting, with terraces, conference rooms, international restaurant, elevator. 80 rooms, 47 with baths. Closed Dec-Jan. (II)

Burghotel GOTZENBURG (SW)
7109 Jagsthausen/Württ. 22 22

Medieval atmosphere pervades the spacious, antique-furnished rooms of this 12th century hunting castle where you can sleep in four-poster canopied beds and enjoy the culture of past ages. Archeological and historical museum contains the famed iron hand of Gotz von Berlichingen, legendary 16th century knight, who was born in this village about 60 km NE of Heilbronn. 14 rooms. Recommended restaurant. Open Mar-mid-Nov. Exit Neckarsulm from Autobahn, NE of Neckarsulm. (II)

Godesburg

Schloss GRÜNWALD (S)
Zeillerstr. 1
8022 Grünwald-München 6 41 16 12

Grünwald has a history going back many centuries and was a fortified location even in Roman times. It was the residence of Ludwig the Strong in the 13th and 14th centuries, and the seat of Bavarian and Austrian imperial families for many centuries. Terraces, antique furnishings. 16 rooms. Near the Isar River. 12 km from center of Munich. (I)

Schloss Hotel Burg GUTENFELS (W)
5425 Kaub, Rheinland-Pfalz 2 20

Gutenfels Castle, crowning the heights above Kaub, was built by the Knights of Falconstein in the 12th century. In 1277 it was acquired by the Count Palatine, who later built Die Pfalz Castle on an island in the middle of the Rhine (still a major landmark), which gave him a firm hold on the area. Richard, Duke of Cornwall and brother of English King Henry III, is said to have visited Gutenfels in 1257 and was enamoured of the Countess Guta there. 12 years later, when he was a widower, he returned and married her. He later became Emperor of the Holy Roman Empire, the only English Pope. Gutenfels was mostly destroyed in the 17th century but was restored in the late 19th century. Beautiful views of the mountains and Rhine. Terraces, good restaurant (closed Tues), 10 rooms. (II)

Burghotel Götzenburg

Schloss Grünwald

Burg Guttenberg

Burg GUTTENBERG (SW)
6954 Neckarmühlbach (06266) 3 88

(Restaurant only)

Featuring a restaurant with local color and specialties of food and wines, Guttenberg Castle also has daily exhibitions of flights of falcons, eagles and vultures. (11 am and 4 pm, except Mon). The castle stands on a hilltop W of the Neckar River and is worth a visit to dine, or roam through the medieval courts and rooms.

Schloss Heinsheim

Built in the Middle Ages by the Hohenstaufen Emperors, it is one of the best-preserved castles in the area. Its massive crenelated walls and towers with their loopholes for archers, give it a story-book appearance. Knightly banquets and entertainment in 15th century style are held frequently. Closed Jan. From the main Neckar River road (27) cross to the west bank at Gundelsheim.

Schloss HEINSHEIM am Neckar (SW)
6927 Bad Rappenau-Heinsheim (07264) 10 45

This baronial mansion, more than 350 years old, has been owned by the von Racknitz family for generations. The present owner is Baron Wilhelm von Racknitz. There are spacious public rooms, chapel, swimming, and other amenities. Park area, elevator, handicap facilities. It is located along the Neckar River, a region of many castles. 38 rooms. Closed mid-Jan to mid-Feb. N of Heilbronn, N of E12 Bad Rappenau exit. (II)

Burg Hirschhorn

Burg HIRSCHHORN (SW)
6932 Hirschhorn am Neckar 13 73

For 400 years the Knights of Hirschhorn held their seat of power in this castle far above the Neckar River. Built as a strong tower in 1200, curtain walls were added, both outer and inner, and a moat 48 feet deep. It was a refuge for the walled village on the river banks below. Under a curse from the mother of one of his enemies, the last Knight of Hirschhorn died in 1932. The castle, with its modern amenities, including an elevator, makes an impressive sight on its hill above the medieval village. Magnificent view from the dining terrace in good weather. No lounge or public rooms except a dining room. 19 rooms. Closed mid-Dec to mid-Jan. About 25 km E of Heidelberg on B27. (I)

Jagdschloss Holzberg

Jagdschloss HOLZBERG (EC)
8743 Bischofsheim/Rhon (09772) 12 07

This ancient hunting castle dates from 1614 and stands in the mountains about

Burg Hornberg

2600 feet above sea level, in the Hochrhon area. Its early character is maintained in complete authenticity as its accommodations come without benefit of electricity. Light derives from candles and oil lamps, and furnishings are antiquities and objects of art. In the woods around are red deer, heath-cocks, and there is trout fishing, and riding stables. 9 rooms with bath or shower. E of Frankfurt, on B279, 6 km from Bischofsheim via Hochrhonstrasse. (I-II)

Burg HORNBERG (SW)
6951 Neckarzimmern 27 58

Since 1040 this castle has dominated a hill overlooking the Neckar River. In 1480 it was purchased by the legendary Gotz von Berlichingen. For centuries its tall tower has been a landmark through this valley, and towers and ruins are open to visitors. Original open fireplaces are still used, original decorations adorn the rooms, and there is an old-fashioned blacksmith shop, shopping center, gift shop, riding, fishing, fine restaurant and a prize-winning wine cellar. 23 rooms. Open Feb 15-Dec. Located 45 km S of Heidelberg. (I-II)

Schloss Hotel HUGENPOET (NW)
August-Thyssenstrasse 51
4307 Kettwig/Ruhr 60 54

A striking moated castle of the North German style, Hugenpoet in its present form dates from the 1500s. Documents show a castle here in 1308 from which the Barons von Nesselrode protected the area and exacted tribute from passing traders. The original castle was mostly destroyed in 1478. The present structure was adapted as a deluxe hotel in 1954 and

Schloss Hugenpoet

Klostergut Jakobsberg

Schloss Konigsegg

Jagdschloss Kranichstein

today is a favorite of industrialists from the nearby Ruhr area. There is an impressive marble staircase in the entrance hall, and a marble arch is taken from another castle, Horst. In the summer its dining terrace on the moat, and park offer great charm, as do the massive fireplaces in winter. The hotel houses a fine collection of paintings, and furnishings are tasteful antiques. Recommended international restaurant. Elevator, conference rooms, tennis. 25 rooms, 19 with baths. Closed Feb. 20 km N of Düsseldorf and 15 km S of Essen. (II)

Klostergut JAKOBSBERG (W)
5407 Boppard/Rhein (06742) 30 21

Situated on a bluff overlooking the Rhine, Klostergut Jakobsberg is an old monastery with an enclosed courtyard and two castle-like towers. Originally built in 1157 by Kaiser Friedrich I, it was a monastery of the Middle Ages, mostly destroyed in the mid-1400s. Later, rebuilt, it was owned by the archbishops of Trier and by about 1640 became the property of the Jesuits. It served as a university center before the French Revolution and later was taken over by the Prussians. In the late 19th century it came into private hands and recently was renovated and transformed with all modern amenities into a hotel maintaining the ancient cloister character. Modern rooms, meeting rooms, fine restaurant, indoor pool, chapel and more. Boppard is on the left bank of the Rhine, about 20 km S of Koblenz, near the famed Lorelei rock of the big river. (II)

Schloss KONIGSEGG (SW)
7752 Insel
Reichenau/Bodensee,
Mittelzell (07534) 4 35

A 16th century castle, once the seat of noble families, still has its towers and battlements and fine water views. Tennis, boating, dancing by candle light. 26 rooms. Reichenau is an island in the Bodensee (Lake Constance) W of Konstanz and can be reached by boat from that city. (II)

Jagdschloss KRANICHSTEIN (WC)
Kranichsteiner Strasse 261
6100 Darmstadt 86 26

Built in 1572 as a hunting lodge for the Counts and Grand Dukes of Hesse, the baroque castle now houses a hunting museum as well as a restaurant and guest rooms. Contemporary and period furnishings, park area, flower gardens and riding. Menu includes wild game. 15 rooms. About 6 km NE of the center of Darmstadt. (I)

Schlosshotel KRONBERG (C)
Hainstrasse 25
6242 Kronberg/Taunus
Bei Frankfurt/Main 70 11

Empress Friedrich, mother of Kaiser Wilhelm II, built this castle as her residence in 1888 in the architectural styles of native Hessian framework and English Tudor (she was the daughter of Queen Victoria of England). It was a gathering place for European royalty, and most of the ruling monarchs were guests there. After World War I French occupation officials occupied the castle but the family remained also. During the 1920s it became a mecca for art connoisseurs, but because of maintenance costs no one lived there up to World War II. American occupation forces used it as a club for high officers and civilians, and it was widely known as Cronberg Castle. The theft of the Hessian jewels from the castle in 1945 was widely publicized. Transformed recently into a fine hotel with 54 rooms in an authentic setting and furnishings of 19th century royalty. Recommended cuisine. Golf in the 250-acre park. 15 km NW of Frankfurt/Main. (III)

Hotel KRONE (W)
Rheinuferstr. 10
Nr. Rudesheim, Assmannshausen 20 36

This 16th century half-timbered inn stands directly on the Rhine at the foot of vineyard-covered mountains. Sweeping

Schlosshotel Kronberg ↑ ↓

Hotel Krone

Burghotel Lauenstein

Burghotel Lauenstein
(Entrance)

views of the river, its marine traffic, and surrounding castles. Dining terrace, heated pool, elevator. 90 rooms. Closed mid-Nov to mid-Mar. (I-II)

Burghotel LAUENSTEIN (E)
Burgstrasse 4
8641 Lauenstein/Oberfranken 2 56

Here the guest enters through the outer wall gates into the Middle Ages. He can roam through the ancient castle, through dim vaulted halls, and on the battlements overlooking mountains and valleys. The castle, dating from the year 915, was built by the Frankonian King Konrad I on a prominence of 1800 feet altitude. Princes of Hohenzollern owned it for many centuries. Contains collections of antique furniture, interesting iron work, and peasant rooms. The great Knights' Hall is 12th century gothic. Central heating. 24 rooms. Closed Feb. Rt 85 about 35 km N of Kronach, 4 km N of Ludwigsstadt. Minimum of 3 days. (I-II)

Hotel Schloss LEHEN (SW)
Hauptstrasse 2
7107 Bad Friedichshall,
Wurtt. (74411) 74 12

Built about 1400 as a water-castle, Schloss Lehen is on the castle-road from Heidelberg to Heilbronn. It formerly was the residence of the noble family of Greeks and later of Duke Frederic of

Schloss Lehen

Württemberg. Transformed into a modern hotel and restaurant 500 years after its construction, up-to-date accommodations have been installed, including an elevator, without affecting the medieval character. The vaults of the Knights' Hall and of the esquire room have become fine restaurants. 20 rooms. About 10 km N of Heilbronn. (II)

Schlosshotel LEMBECK (NW)
4270 Dorsten (Lembeck) (02369) 72 13

The castle dates from the 12th century, with additions, and is entered over stone bridges across two moats, through walls and gateways before reaching the main building. It is situated in a large park area, with peacocks and other semi-wildlife to be seen. Part of the castle is a museum (nominal charge) filled with antiquities, everyday artifacts from the 1600s, art, tapestries, wood carvings, chinaware, tools, household things. There is riding available as well as a Schloss Disco (insulated from other areas by 8-foot-thick stone walls). Dining is in vaulted rooms at moat-level. 7 rooms with antique furnishings and canopy beds. Location is NW of Wulfen, just N of 58. Turn N off 58 toward Wulfen onto the road toward Reken and Lembeck. (II)

Schlosshotel Lembeck

Schloss MALBERG (W)
D5524 Malberg b.
Kyllburg/Eifel (06563) 22 08

The castle was first built about 1000 A.D. on a 984 ft. mountain above the Kyll Valley, close to Kyllburg. Altered through the centuries, most of the present structure was added in the Baroque style in the 19th century. The Schmitz-Malberg family has lived there since 1615, and it has been run as a guest house since 1931, with a family atmosphere. Fresh produce from the private farm enhances the menu. Gardens, swimming, fishing. 30 guests. (II)

Schloss Malberg

Hotel Pension Schloss NEUBURG (SW)
6951 Obrigheim/Neckar 73 30

The oldest parts of the castle, the cellars, ground floor and Knights Hall, date from

Schloss Neuburg

Jagdschloss Niederwald

Schloss Neuhof

970 A.D. and represent more than a millenium of history from the site overlooking the Neckar River. Other sections date from the 14th century, and an annex building was erected in 1598. The castle is located in a forest area, and has terraces and wide views. Conference rooms, park. 14 rooms all with baths. Closed Jan-Feb. B37 Eberbach/Neckarelz. Cross bridge at Diedesheim to Obrigheim, turn left upstream. (II)

Schloss NEUHOF (E)
8631 Neu-Neershof 14 (09563) 61 51

Two castle towers flank the entrance to this hotel-restaurant, although the character is that of a baronial mansion. First records date back to 1387, but the knights' hall was rebuilt as a restaurant and for conferences and festivities. The hotel was refurbished in 1973. Park area provides for walks among ponds and wild life. 18 rooms and private baths. Neershof is 6 km NE of Coburg and the castle is N of Neershof. (II)

Schlosshotel im Bad NEUSTADT (E)
Kurhausstrasse 37
8740 Bad Neustadt/Saale 7 04

Centuries of history intertwined with a long procession of rulers and nobles mark this castle. Restaurant, tea on the terrace, tennis, golf, swimming. 49 rooms. 60 km N of Würzburg. (II)

Jagdschloss NIEDERWALD (W)
6220 Rudesheim am Rhein (06722) 10 04

Dining rooms with a view of the Rhine are a feature of this one-time royal hunting lodge set among typical Rhineland vineyards. The town has a wine museum and a wine festival is held in Sept. It is also a stopping place for excursion steamers which provides a lively nightlife of restaurants and bars. Conference rooms, park area. Open Mar 15-Oct. The schloss is 5 km E of town which is on the R bank of the Rhine. (II)

Hotel-Restaurant (W)
Burg OCKENFELS
5460 Linz am Rhein (02644) 20 71

Formerly the seat of the Bishops of Cologne, the castle is situated on a bluff 300 feet above the Rhine. Terraces, restaurant, bar, conference rooms, lounges. 25 rooms all with baths. 2 km N of Linz which is on the right bank on B42, 27 km S of Bonn. (I-II)

Schloss ORT (SE)
Am Dreiflusseck, Passau 8390 3 40 72

Located on the Danube near the Austrian border, Passau is an interesting medieval town with quaint houses and hilly streets, and a boarding point for river boats to Vienna. Schloss Ort is a 13th century building with elevator and 35 modernized rooms. Closed mid-Dec to mid-Jan. (I)

Schloss PETERSHAGEN (N)
4953 Petershagen
an der Weser (05707) 3 46

The main building dates from 1306, and

Schloss Petershagen

Burg Rabenstein

the reception and dining rooms are on the second floor at the top of a hewn stone spiral staircase. Some guest rooms are in a "newer" section across the courtyard, built in the mid-1500s. The castle nestles behind a defense wall along the Weser River and was once the seat of the Bishops of Minden and Osnabrueck. Period furnishings, lawns, heated pool, terraces, tennis. The castle is now owned by the third generation of the Hestermann family. 10 rooms. Closed Feb. About 11 km N of Minden on B61 toward Bremen in the village of Petershagen. (I-II)

Hotel Burg RABENSTEIN **(EC)**
8581 Post Kirchahorn

The old knights' fortress has roots going back to the 12th century, and was prominent in the 30-years war in the early 1600s. Converted into a fine hotel in 1970-71, Rabenstein has been decorated in a style blending with its long history, and offers modern amenities. Its round and square towers, slate roofs and striped shutters look down from its hilltop prominence, and stand guard over beautiful rococo gardens and grounds. It is about 60 km NE of Nurnberg. Autobahn E6, exit Trockau or Pegnitz. Castle is SW of Kirchahorn. Watch for road sign. (I-II)

Hotel Burg REICHENSTEIN **(W)**
6531 Trechtingshausen/Rhein
(06721) 61 17

Rhine castle with magnificent view of river and its constant traffic. Rough

Burg Reichenstein

Burg Rheinfels

stonework and gothic arches of the 13th century stronghold (and restorations) evoke the robber-knights who once headquartered in its towers and battlements. Drawbridge and iron portcullis are still functional, guarding an interior gateway into the museum section of weapons and armor. Club dining room in old stable is picturesque. 12 rooms, some newly furnished, most with shower. Left bank of Rhine between Bingen and St. Goar. (I-II)

Schlosshotel auf (W)
Burg RHEINFELS
Schlossberg 47
5401 St. Goar 74 55

Sited atop a high bluff on the Rhine, the hotel stands on one of the Middle Rhine's most extensive castle ruins built in 1245. It is near the famed Lorelei and overlooks the "Cat and Mouse" river castles. There are terraces, a cannon room, Bocksberger room, knight tavern, fireplace, chapel, museum, walking paths, heated indoor pool, sauna, elevator. Food specialties include venison. 27 rooms. Located about 35 km S of Koblenz on left (west) bank of Rhine. (II)

Schloss-Hotel Rheyt

Burg Ronneburg

Schloss Saaleck

Schloss-Hotel RHEYT (W)
4050 Mönchengladbach 2,
Rheyt (02166) 2 01 02

Surrounded by a formidable moat and approached across a stone bridge and through ancient stone gateways, this old castle-like palace offers comfortable rooms, restaurant, Black Forest Stube, terrace, gardens, central heat. There is a museum with an extensive collection of art objects and antiquities. Surrounding woods offer walking areas. 3 km E of Rheyt, which is in the SW environs of Mönchengladbach, about 25 km W of Düsseldorf. (II)

Hotel RONNEBURG (C)
6451 Altwiedermus
Krs. Büdingen (06048) 71 30

Although constructed in the Middle Ages, about 1230, the old Castle's towers, walls and battlements are mostly intact. Entrance is through a formidable gateway protected by ancient iron-studded, thick, wooden doors. The main tower, one of the tallest among German castles, is a landmark seen from miles around, and at the top it has novel enclosed lookout enclosures on four sides. There is within the castle an extremely deep well, served in ancient times by a huge winch with a human treadmill wheel, still to be seen. For a nominal charge, a tour includes this, a museum of ancient farm and household artifacts in a dungeon, exploring through old halls and rooms, and a climb up the 132 steps of the high tower, if you wish. The castle is associated with Count Zinzendorf, 1736, founder of the brotherhood which later established the Amana Colonies in Iowa. Good restaurant, 4 double rooms with baths. About 50 km NE of Frankfurt and 7 km SW of Büdingen at Altwiedermus. (I)

Schloss SAALECK (C)
8783 Hammelburg a.d.
Fränkischen Saale (09732) 24 35

This 11th century castle-palace high on a hill above the Saale valley, also was once a monastery. It is surrounded by woods in an area of vineyards. 12 nicely furnished rooms offer decor in modern or period style. Closed early Jan-early Feb. About 30 km N of Würzburg, opposite the town of Hammelburg. Autobahn exit Hammelburg then take Rt B27 which is a branch road to castle. (I)

Hotel Restaurant SABABURG (EC)
3520 Hofgeismar-
Sababurg 5 (05678) 10 52

Originally built in 1334 for the protection of pilgrims to Gottsbüren, the old stronghold was partially destroyed, and rebuilt in 1490. Much of it now dates from that

Burg Sababurg

period. Outer walls surround the main buildings which are dominated by two massive strong towers. One of the towers houses some of the guest rooms, and the other stands empty, part of the castle areas, including dungeons, which may be explored for a nominal fee. The Grimm brothers, authors of the famed fairy tales, are said to have visited the castle and made it the locale of the Sleeping Beauty story. A pleasant outdoor terrace restaurant adds summer enjoyment. 15 rooms. Closed Jan 15-Feb 15. About 25 km N of Kassel in a forest area. Autobahn Exit Hann-Munden, 10 km NE of Hofgeismar past Beberbeck. (I-II)

Burg SCHNELLENBERG (WC)
5952 Attendorn im Sauerland (02722) 40 81

The castle was once the most powerful stronghold in the Sauerland, and today it belongs to the Barons of Fürstenberg as it has since the 11th century. Most of the buildings date from later centuries, but feature massive gateways, and stone bridge approaches, tower rooms, vaulted dining rooms, fireplaces, beamed ceilings and antique furnishings. If you stay here, watch out for the castle ghost, a knight in armor carrying his helmeted head under his arm. Rooms are tastefully furnished and have modern amenities. Chapel and treasury are filled with exhibits of antiques and artifacts of the ancient past. Fine restaurant, riding, pool, tennis, fishing and hunting. 47 rooms all with baths. Closed Dec. About 50 km SE of Dortmund. (II)

Auf SCHÖNBURG (W)
6532 Oberwesel am Rhein 81 98

If you have dreamed of a castle on the Rhine, this may well be it. Built on a steep rock above the village of Oberwesel, the castle is more than 1,000 years old, standing on foundations built in 966. It belonged to Emperor Barbarossa of the Holy Roman Empire in 1166, and is one of the largest and best-preserved of the ancestral castles. The Schönburger Knights headquartered here for centuries. It was partially destroyed in 1689 but was mostly restored. Today its

Burg Schnellenberg

Auf Schönburg

medieval towers and ramparts command a striking view of the river and valley. Towers, stone stairways, halls and courts may be explored. Excellent candlelight restaurant, period furnishings, tasteful guest rooms. 9 rooms. Open Mar-Nov. On left bank about 5 km S of St. Goar on the road to Delhofen. (I-II)

Schlosshotel (N)
Burg SCHWALENBERG
3284 Schieder-Schwalenberg 51 67

The castle, dating from 1231, with later additions, is on a hilltop with views of the surrounding countryside for miles around. It dominates the picturesque village of Schwalenberg. A popular restaurant overlooks the valley below. The castle is surrounded by woods with a small park where a variety of birds, deer and other wildlife may be seen. There are footpaths all around the crown of the hilltop, with views of the tile-roofed village below. Rooms are nicely furnished. A small underground bar is open weekends. Central heat, riding, bowling. 13 rooms, some with showers. On B239, Höxter-Blomberg. 9 km from Schieder (Lippe) RR station. (I)

Burg Schwalenberg

Schlosshotel SOLITUDE (SW)
7000 Stuttgart (0711) 69 10 91

This knights hunting lodge was built in 1763-67 in the Rococo style by the Duke of Württemberg. It is situated in a forest

Schlosshotel Solitude

Hotel Sonnenhof

area with attractive views. International restaurant, garden terrace, chapel. Closed Christmas to end of Jan. 33 rooms. About 10 km W of center of Stuttgart. (I)

Hotel SONNENHOF **(C)**
Falkensteiner Str.
6240 Königstein im Taunus **30 51**

Situated on the south slope of the Taunus Mts. at an elevation of 1500 feet, this baronial mansion is surrounded by its own 20-acre park. Elegant public and private rooms, terraces, balconies, and superb views over the Main Valley. Excellent food and famed wine cellars. Conference rooms, heated indoor pool, handicap facilities. 46 rooms. In Falconstein, about a 20 minute drive NW of Frankfurt/Main. (II)

Schloss SPANGENBERG **(EC)**
3509 Spangenberg/Hessen **(05663) 8 66**

This beautiful tall, towered castle is right out of the Middle Ages, set atop the tallest hill in a most picturesque medieval town. The approach is through outer defense walls, across a wooden bridge (formerly a drawbridge) over a deep, dry moat, and into the cobbled inner court. A visitor can walk the walls above the moat all around the castle, as well as walking around the grounds. It was originally built by the Knights of Treffurt, 1214-1238, and was acquired by the Hessian Counts in 1350. It was strengthened and refortified by Count Wilhelm IV in 1631, and was the strongest of the Hessian castles. Nevertheless the French captured it in 1758. Even then it had not seen its last war as it was bombed during WWII and restored again. Many of the modern-furnished rooms offer excellent views over the moat to the old red-tiled roofs of village houses below. Spangenberg village boasts street after street of beautifully kept half-timbered buildings, some dating from the 14th century. Popular restaurant, and a breakfast room for guests. Forest walking, fishing, riding, conference rooms. 23 rooms. Closed Jan-Feb. On 487 about 25 km SE of Kassel and 11 km E of Melsungen. (I)

Schloss Spangenberg

Burg STAUFENBERG (C)
6301 Staufenberg 15 69

Though it was built in 1311, the castle now has central heating and modernized rooms. Nearest RR station is Lollar, about 2 km, car pickup on request. Buses every 15 min. 13 rooms. Closed July. Castle is less than 1 km off B3, 25 km S of Marbac and about 10 km N of Giessen. (I-II)

Schloss STEINBURG (C)
8700 Würzburg (0931) 5 04 34

The castle was first built during the reign of Bishop Iring van Reinstein (1254-1266). In that century, monks from the Ebrach Cloister planted the first Silvanerrebe, marking the beginning of Germany's biggest wine region. In 1897 the castle was rebuilt by Peter Schneider following plans by the architect Pfannes to take advantage of the views over the Main River. On July 19, 1912 King Ludwig von Bayern visited the castle and personally planted a vine. The present owner, Franz Bezold, acquired the castle in 1937 and adapted it as a hotel and winerestaurant now famous the world over. Conference rooms, bar, heated pool, sauna, gardens. 37 rooms. most with baths. (I-II)

Schloss Steinburg

Schloss STETTEN (SC)
7118 über Künzelsau/Württemburg 40 77

A well-preserved, virtually undamaged castle dating from the early Middle Ages, about 1000 A.D., the ancient fortress-residence has been the seat of the Stetten family for 37 generations. Dr. Wolfgang Frhr. von Stetten heads the family residing there at present. A document still in existence shows that a member of the family was present in 1033 when German Emperor Konrad II laid the foundation stone of a nearby monastery. The ancient fortress still has its arrow-

Schloss Stetten

Jagdschloss Thiergarten

slitted towers and walls, gate houses and courts. A most interesting chapel, dating from the 1400s utilizes part of an earlier round stone tower as its apse, and houses a still-functional 500-year-old organ. The vaulted Burgkeller has been made into a fine center of "Castle Gastronomy", and there is also a Swiss restaurant. A dining room for special functions is in a picturesque dungeon-like vault, illuminated with wall torches and table candles. Activities include table tennis, children's playground, heated outdoor pool, and Icelandic riding horses for beginners and experienced riders. Rooms for 45 guests are in two buildings, and there is a special apartment available in the ancient half-timbered gatehouse which presides over the entrance and old moat. The 900-year-old castle is 25 km N of Schwabisch-Hall, and is near the new Autobahn to Kunzelsau. Closed Jan-Feb. (I)

Jagdschloss THIERGARTEN (E)
Oberthiergärtnerstr. 36
8581 Thiergarten
bei Bayreuth/Oberfranken (09209) 7 11

Located just south of the town of Bayreuth, this old hunting castle is near many points of historical and cultural interest and has a good restaurant. The Richard Wagner opera house is in the town, and his grave and a monument to him are on the large castle grounds. The castle has been host to many famous musicians including Toscanini, and other

↖ ↓ Schlosshotel Tremsbüttel

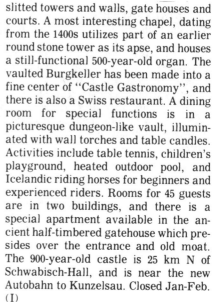

figures such as Edward VIII of England. 12 rooms. Closed part of Jan. About 75 km NE of Nurnberg. (I-II)

Schlosshotel TREMSBÜTTEL (N)
Schlossstrasse 6
Bargteheide/Holstein 65 44

This was a hunting lodge of the Dukes of Holstein-Gottrorp in the 17th century, and later a deep moat was added. Rebuilt to its present elegant style in the 19th century, it again became a duke's residence. It is in a large park area. The building is notable for its carved ceilings, fine woodwork, staircase, other decorative elements and objects of art. Excellent dining, and wine cellars. Rooms are well-appointed. Activities available include tennis. There is a vintage auto museum adjacent. 19 rooms. 36 km NE of Hamburg on Hamburg-Lubeck Autobahn, exit Bargteheide. Follow signs on B404, the castle is about 8 km away from Bargteheide. (II)

Burghotel Trendelburg

Burghotel TRENDELBURG (EC)
3526 Trendelburg 1
Kreis Hofgeismar 10 21

Just when Trendelburg was built is lost in antiquity, but it is known that it existed before 1300. In 1367 it was the seat of the Bishops of the area, in the intervening centuries imperial families have resided there, and it has been owned by the Von Stockhausen family since the 16th century. Guests today may reside in the old round towers which have been fitted out with modern conveniences. From the high towers and terraces there is an excellent view of the village and valleys below. Known as one of the Germany's best-preserved castles, it is in the center of an area framed as the origin of Grimm's Fairy Tales. Carriage riding, heated pool, international cuisine. Conference rooms, handicap facilities. 22 rooms plus 30 beds in guest house. Open Feb. 15-Dec. On Rt B83, 35 km N of Kassel. (I-II)

Burghotel Trendelburg
(Entrance beside the great tower)

Schloss Vellberg

Hotel-Restaurant **(SW)**
Schloss VELLBERG
7175 Vellberg **20 74**

A fortress has stood on this high rock prominence for over 850 years, having been first documented in 1102. The first castle was destroyed in 1523 by the Swabian Alliance, and was rebuilt in its present form soon after. From 1102 it was the seat of the lords or knights of Vellberg, a family line which ended in 1592. The castle today is in the irregular step-gable form, built upon the gothic substructure. Walls and defense outpost towers lend an atmosphere of the Middle Ages to Vellberg. There are rooms in a "honeymoon tower", dining in vaulted and wood-beamed rooms, banqueting hall, sun terrace for dining, and a castle chapel often used for weddings with a white coach and top-hatted horsemen for bridal parties. Bar, swimming, sauna, tennis. 4 rooms. On a secondary road about 10 km SE of Schwäbisch Hall, and 60 km NE of Stuttgart. (I-II)

Waffenschmiede

WAFFENSCHMIEDE **(W)**
in der Burg Hohenstein
6209 Hohenstein 2
(bei Bad Schwalbach) **(06120) 33 57**

Located atop a steep mountain, this massive 800-year-old Hohenstein Castle overlooks the Aar River. The castle was built in the second half of the 12th century and owned by the Counts von Katzenellnbogen. Johann III von Katzenellnbogen enlarged it in 1422. It had a deep moat and wealls 8 feet thick. In the 30 years war it was partially destroyed and is preserved now by the state of Hessen. There are broad sunny terraces offering panoramic views of the landscape. The restaurant is popular, and in season one can enjoy fireside dining. Regional fish, meat and game specialties are offered. The hotel section has recently been enlarged and now has 8 rooms, done in a modern style with private baths. Park area, conference rooms. About 25 km N of Wiesbaden, on B54 between Bad Shwalbach and Limburg, or by rail and bus from Wiesbaden and Limburg. (I-II)

Burghotel Schloss WALDECK (C)
3544 Waldeck am Edersee 53 24

Schloss Waldeck

Perched on a high rim of the Edersee (a large lake), this spectacular Medieval stronghold dates back to 1120, and through the centuries has been the seat of noble families. Additional wings and sections were added around 1500, and it reached its zenith as a noble castle about that time. 200 years later it served as a national prison, and in 1760 came under siege in the Seven Years War. For a nominal charge you can go down into the dungeons and see an ancient kitchen, and museum relics of the past. The Waldeck mountain castle played its role through all the turbulent history of the area and remained well-preserved, being adapted as a hotel as early as 1906. It is extremely picturesque with its towers and battlements right out of the Middle Ages. There is a steep cobblestone drive up and through very narrow archways through outer walls. If you are a hotel guest, you can drive all the way into the inner cobblestone courtyard and park. On weekends and holidays the place is thronged with local area people visiting the restaurant and enjoying the fine view from the courtyard and terraces. Festive banquets, nearby tennis, boating, riding. Some of the guest rooms are found on the upper floors after negotiating a hand-hewn spiral stone stairway. 20 rooms, breakfast room, restaurant, bar, outdoor terrace. Open Mar-Oct. About 4 km off 485, 32 km SW of Kassel. (I)

Burg WASSENBERG (NW)
Kirchstrasse 17
5143 Wassenberg 40 44

Burg Wassenberg

With a chronicle going back to Kaiser Heinrich II (1002-1024) the castle has been a guardian of history for almost a thousand years. It has many associations with royalty and titles including nobles of Flanders and the archbishops of Koln (Cologne). Antique furnishings, spacious dining rooms, extensive menu. A special cuisine features dishes "as the knights of old used to eat". 12 rooms, with bath or shower, some with balconies. Location on B221 Aachen-Venlo Road near Holland border. (I-II)

Schloss Wasserburg (Bodensee)

Schloss WASSERBURG **(S)**
Hampstrasse 5
8992 Wasserburg (Bodensee) **56 92**

The manor, directly on Lake Constance (Bodensee), dates back to the 8th century, with the present buildings dating partly from 1280. Facilities and activities include beach, boat landing, fishing and excursions. Beautiful views of lake and mountains. 14 rooms. Open Apr-Oct. (II)

Schloss WEITENBURG **(SW)**
7241 Weitenburg,
Kreis Tübingen **(07457) 80 51**

Weitenburg Castle dominates a hilltop overlooking the Neckar River, a small stream in this area. First mentioned in history in 1062, the castle was remodeled and buildings added, mostly in 1585. Since 1720 the Barons von Rassler have been proprietors. There are fine canopied beds, porcelain stoves, massive wood antique furnishings, objects of art, a gothic chapel which is the setting for many weddings, wood-beamed dining room (venison a specialty), and terrace overlooking the valley. Facilities include an indoor heated pool, sauna, riding, carriages, conference rooms. A hotel since 1954. 32 rooms, 28 with baths. Adjacent village of Borstingen, S of Rt. 14, between Stuttgart and Horb. Turn S from 14 at Ergenzingen. (I)

Schloss Weitenberg

Hotel Schloss WILKENHEGE **(NW)**
Steinfurterstr. 374
4400 Münster, Westphalia **(0251) 21 30 45**

Wilkenhege is the ancient residence of the Bishops of the area. Originally built in 1311, and mostly rebuilt in 1550, it reflects this period but still has its moat. Built mostly of brick, it reflects the typical construction of the north German plain where stone was not widely available. Adapted as a hotel in 1955, it provides modern facilities. Attractive dining room, popular cuisine, and terrace dining in season. Conference rooms, dancing, golf, handicap facilities. 38 rooms with baths. Steinfurter Strasse is Rt. 54 running NW out of Munster. The castle is on a small road, Wilkenhege, to the R as you travel NW. (II)

Schloss Wilkenhege

Burg WINDECK (SW)
Kappelwindeck Str. 104
7580 Buhl, Baden (07223) 2 36 71

Mellowed through centuries, this "Gaststatte" is in the Baden-Baden Black Forest area and offers all health and recreation facilities. It has its private vineyards, and the site provides views of the Rhine basin. Recommended restaurant. Closed Jan. 2-Feb 14. 9 rooms. Between Baden-Baden and Freudenstadt. (I)

Burg Windeck

Hotel Schloss ZELL (W)
Schloss Strasse 8
5583 Zell/Mosel 40 84

The charming wine village of Zell squeezes along the Mosel River shore between the water and the steep, vineyard-smothered bluffs. The castle, typical of the smaller fortified residences of the Middle Ages, is in the center of town on the main street. Built mostly in 1220, it was once the residence of the Archibishops of Trier. On March 12, 1512, Kaiser Maximilian I was a guest in the castle, and you can stay in the suite he occupied even today. Decorations and furnishings are genuine antique, including many oil paintings from the 1500s. A massive wooden winepress, from the 1600s, stands in the courtyard, reminding visitors that this castle in the home of the original Zellar Schwartze Katz (Zell Black Cat) wines. An old print shows an outcropping of black rock far above the castle which had the form of a crouching cat, and Jakob Bohn, castle proprietor, will tell you that this is the origin of the name. He proudly serves the delicate

Schloss Zell

white Mosel wines from the castle's own vineyards. Recommended restaurant. 9 rooms and apts., mostly reached by way of winding, circular stairway up one of the towers, lined with relics and fossils unearthed nearby. Closed Dec. 10-Jan 20. From the main road along the north side of the Mosel, cross to the south side at Alf, 3 km E of Zell. There is a foot-bridge across the river at Zell. (I)

15th century German print
(New York Public Library)

Greece

CASTELLO (NW)
Dassia, Corfu Island **Tel. 30 184**

The former summer residence of King George II, this Florentine Chateau is situated in a large park with excellent views. Refurbished in 1971, there is a restaurant, nightclub, private beach, tennis and dancing. 76 rooms. 12 km N of Corfu. (II)

Hotel CAVALIERI (NW)
4 Kapodistriou
Kerkyra, Corfu Island **39 041**

Located in a baronial mansion built in the 1600s by the Venetians, this hotel is located on the island used as a resort by the royal family. Refurbished in 1974 it has spacious rooms, a roof dining garden and beautiful views of the sea. Antique furnishings and decoration. 50 rooms and bath. (II)

KAPETANAKOS Castle (S)
Areopolis, Mani Region **0733-51233**

One of a number of castles of the region, formerly the strongholds of local "warlords", this old tower is now part of the government's program of authentically restoring buildings of historic and architectural interest for the tourist trade. The castle was built in 1856 and has 6 guest rooms for 17 guests. Breakfast only, served in a common lounge, includes pastries and other regional specialties. Rooms have wash basins but no private

Castello

Hotel Cavalieri

GREECE

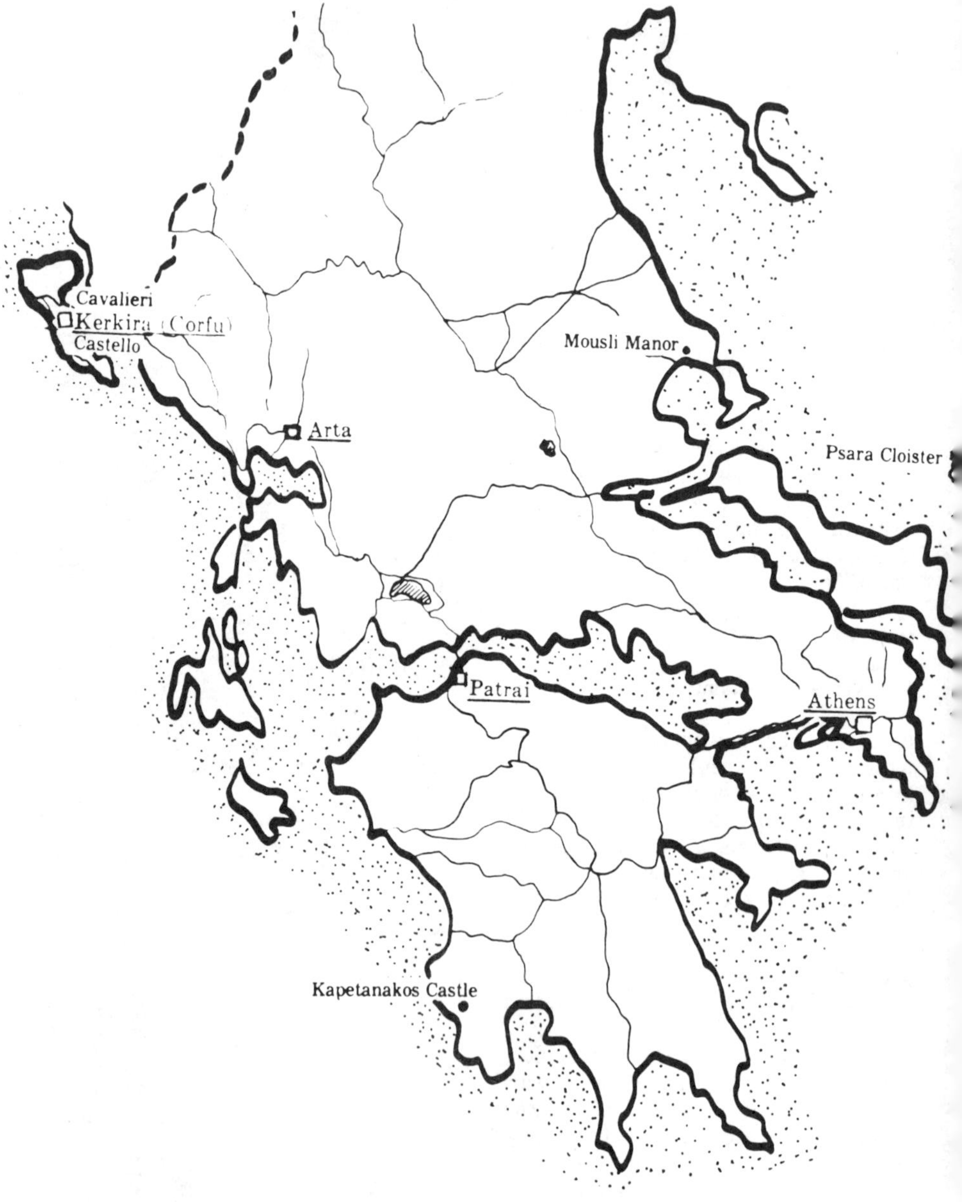

Cavalieri
Kerkira (Corfu)
Castello
Arta
Mousli Manor
Psara Cloister
Patrai
Athens
Kapetanakos Castle

baths. Furnishings are traditional and authentic. Location is near the southern tip of the Peloponnesus, about 2 km from the Mediterranean coast and 16 km (10 mi) from the Diros stalactite caves which can be visited, including underground boat excursions. The village of Areopolis, offering interesting shops and restaurants, is about a 3 hr. drive S from Athens. (I)

Kapetanakos Castle

MOUSLI Manor House (E)
Makrinitsa, near Volos (Thessaly)

This is the first of several old manor houses being restored and operated as guest houses by the Greek National Tourist Organization. Originally built about 1750, the manor belonged to the Mousli family for 200 years. It stood uninhabited after WWII until purchased by the government in 1966. Recently restored, the three-story house maintained the original character even though several bathrooms and showers were added. Original wood was used in the restoration to maintain authenticity. There are now 8 guest rooms, a breakfast room and central lounge. Volos is a port town on an east coast bay about 225 km N of Athens. Boats ply between Volos and Euboea and Sporades. Makrinitsa is about 6 km N of Volos. (I)

Mousli Manor

PSARA Cloister (E)
Island of Psara 0272-61293

This 13th century monks' cloister is one of the government-run facilities offering guest accommodations. It is located on a tiny eastern Aegean isle which has only the one steep, cobblestoned village and no roads. Dominating the village is the interesting church of St. Nicholas, of the 13th-14th century Byzantine period, and the cloister below. The ancient cells now each provide space for 1 to 3 persons, totaling 12 guests. The cloister has been restored authentically and offers good accommodation, through with no private baths. (I)

NOTE: The government tourist program also has restored several complete villages, such as those at Oia on Santorini Island, and Mesta on Chios Island, where accommodations are offered.

Holland

De Campveerse Toren
Hotel s'Gravenhof

De CAMPVEERSE TOREN (SW)
2 Kade
Veere (Zeeland) (01181) 291

Built in the 1400s as a harbor castle, this building is mentioned as an inn as early as 1558, and is considered the oldest inn of the Netherlands. Prince Willem van Oranje ate his wedding dinner here in 1575, and since then many well-known world figures have been guests, including Prince Rainier and Princess Grace of Monaco. Situated at the entrance to the port, the castle commands an excellent view of Veerse Meer (the sea). Terrace and bar. At least a five-day stay is requested. 40 beds. Closed Jan. (I)

Hotel s'GRAVENHOF (E)
Kuiperstraat 11
7201 HG Zutphen (05750) 13917

The hotel-restaurant is an old mansion dating from the 1500s. Located across the street from the St. Walburg Church, the guest enters through a gatehouse into a grassy court yard lined with cafe tables and chairs. The mansion is at the back. There is a good restaurant, terrace, nicely furnished rooms offering 19 beds. Most rooms with baths or showers. 23 km E of Apeldoorn. (I)

Hotel GROOT WARNSBORN (EC)
Bakenbergseweg 277, Arnhem 455751

This elegant palace-like country mansion was once the residence of Count Reinald de Vierde, and is now furnished in comfortable modern style. Facilities

holland
Groningen
Lauswolt
E35
N90
N91
Amsterdam
E10
Het Wapen
Hooge Vuursche
E8
Apeldoorn
s'Gravenhof
E9
Amersfoort
den Treek
Oud Wassenaar
Utrecht
t'Kerckebosch
Arnhem
Groot Warnsborn
The Hague
Rotterdam
E37
N93
W GERMANY
Tilburg
N97
Eindhoven
Campveerse Toren
Middelburg
BELGIUM
Maastricht
Wittem
Neubourg

Groot Warnsborn

Kasteel de Hooge Vuursche

include conference rooms, fireplace lounge, music at dinner, air conditioning and other amenities. The mansion stands in park and garden grounds. 29 rooms in main building and annex. Arnhem is about 100 km E of Amsterdam. (II)

Hotel-Kasteel (C)
de HOOGE VUURSCHE
Hilversumsestraatweg 14
Baarn (Utrecht) (02154) 12541

The name means 'Castle of the High Fires'. It is a first class hotel in lovely woods near the Royal Palace and in the area of bulb fields and other castles. Grounds are enhanced with illuminated pools and fountains, and meals are served in a garden terrace, on the Louis XV banqueting hall. (Full-pension guests may take meals at any of three affiliated hotels in the area.) Le Caveau (The Cave) nightclub has a nightly piano entertainer. Elevator, bar, golf, swimming, tennis and riding are available. 49 beds. 37 km SE of Amsterdam. (II)

Hotel t'KERCKEBOSCH (C)
31 Arnhemse Bovenweg
Zeist (Utrecht) (03404) 14772

This old country-seat near Utrecht has been transformed into a fine hotel and restaurant. Situated in private woods, its terraces and grounds offer fine views of the private park area, and stables have

Hotel t'Kerckebosch

Hotel-Restaurant Lauswolt

been recently added. Conference rooms, restaurant. 58 beds. About 10 km E of Utrecht.

Hotel-Restaurant LAUSWOLT (N)
10 van Harinxmaweg
Beetsterzwaag (Friesland) 1245

The palace-like country mansion dates from the mid-19th century and stands on an old manor dating to 1625. The mansion became a hotel in 1955 and is surrounded by a park and gardens of 2000 acres where grazing deer may be seen. The bar offers entertainment, and the cuisine is international. There are tennis courts, 9 hole golf nearby, riding, and yachting, swimming and water sports on the Frisian Lakes. 41 beds. Beetsterzwaag is about 7 km S of Drachten. (II)

Kasteel NEUBOURG (SE)
1 Rijksweg
Gulpen (Limburg) 1222

With a tall tower dating from 1350, 17th century wings and courts, and a moat, this fine old castle stands in the center of a lovely park. It was the home of the noble family of the Count of Marchant and d'Ansembourg, and now is a first class hotel. Elegant dining and public rooms, gardens and terrace. 49 beds. Between Aachen (Germany) and Maastricht. (Only 3 km from Kasteel Wittem, another castle-hotel.) (II)

Huize den TREEK (C)
23 Trekerweg
Leusden (Utrecht) (03498) 1425

This old mansion stands in spacious grounds with gardens and a lakeside terrace. Furnishings are 17th century and there is an elegant restaurant. Elevator, 26 beds. Closed mid-Jul to early Aug and just before Christmas to Jan 2. Leusden is about 5 km S of Amersfoort, and the hotel is SW of Leusden. (I)

Het WAPEN VAN AMSTERDAM (C)
Noordereind 221, s'Graveland 61661

The mellowed hostelry originated in 1672 and was used as a court house by French soldiers. Around 1730 it became an inn with a stable added to accommodate stagecoach horses on the Amsterdam-Utrecht route. The two buildings were

Kasteel Neubourg

Het Wapen van Amsterdam

joined by a third, built as a theatre at the end of the 19th century. Today the old stable is a party room and the theatre is a cozy restaurant with open fire and typical Dutch menu. The hotel was renovated in 1976. s'Graveland is about 40 km SE of Amsterdam and just W of Hilversum. (I)

Kasteel Oud WASSENAAR (W)
1 Park Oud Wassenaar
Wassenaar (Zuid-Holland) (01751) 79045

Restaurant only

Situated within walking distance of a beach on the North Sea, this castle has entertained many heads of state, even during its relatively short history of less than a century. It was built like a royal palace, and the Nazis occupied it during World War II. Afterwards, the Netherlands government used it to house such visitors as Montgomery of Alamein, Winston Churchill, Nehru and India, Baudouin, King of Belgium, and others. Patronized in recent years by many other world figures, it was the locale in 1967 of the festivities of the wedding of Her Royal Highness Princess Margriet. About 5 km N of The Hague.

Kasteel WITTEM (SE)
3 Wittemerallee
Wittem (Limburg) 1208

Wittem Castle, first built about 1200 by the Julemont Knights, still has an atmosphere of past centuries. Captured and destroyed, it was finally rebuilt in 1611. Its situation near the meeting of Holland, Belgium and Germany places it on well-traveled modern roads. A hotel since 1955, it is surrounded by a lovely park with old trees, moat and picturesque bridges. Recommended restaurant. 18 beds. Near Rt E39 midway between Aachen and Maastrict. (II)

Kasteel Oud Wassenaar

Kasteel Wittem

Ireland

ARD NA SIDHE Hotel (SW)
Caragh Lake (Kerry) **Tel. 5**

This ancient manor house with the Gaelic name is surrounded by extensive grounds and gardens. Modern amenities are offered in an atmosphere of open fires, tasteful antiques and the quiet of the green countryside. Dining and lounge areas are furnished in period style, with mullioned windows giving onto broad green grounds. It is near Killarney in the SW tip of Ireland where the climate is mild. Golf, fishing. 22 rooms. Open May to end of Sept. About 145 km SW of Shannon Airport and 96 km W of Cork Airport. (I)

ASHFORD Castle (NW)
HA590 Cong (Mayo) (094) 22644

A great castle with an international reputation, Ashford is situated on Lough Corrib, Ireland's second largest lake. Although most of the present structure was built about a century ago, it incorporates an original 13th century castle, and a French château added in 1715. In the 1500s troops of Queen Elizabeth battled

Ard Na Sidhe

Ashford Castle

IRELAND
NO. IRELAND
(Britain)
Sligo
Mount Falcon
Belleek Castle
Newport
Castlebar
Breaffy House
Ashford Castle
Galway
Dunguaire
Knappogue
Dromoland
Bunratty
Shannon Airport
Limerick
Matrix
Ballyseede
Ard Na Sidhe
Butler Arms
Cork
Blackrock
The Castle
Ballymaloe
Bellingham
Cabra Castle
Slane Castle
Dublin
Barberstown
Robertstown
Cliff Castle
Fitzpatrick Castle
Kilkea Castle
Carlow
Killoskehane
Longfield
Cashel
Tipperary
Cahore Castle
Wexford
Bargy Castle

through the area, finally storming the castle, and later it became an English fortress. Modern development of the estate was a vast project begun in 1852 when nearly a million trees were planted in the thousands of acres of land. Nearby are several ancient abbeys, churches and points of archaeological interest. The interior of Ashford is notable for its fine woodwork, great hall and fireplaces -- one of which is 20 feet high. Finest food and accommodations are offered. Amenities include fishing, heat, elevators. 77 rooms with baths. About 50 km N of Galway. (II-III)

BALLYMALOE House (S)
Shanagarry, Midleton (Cork) 62531

The castle was built in the late 1400s by descendants of the Norman Knights of Kerry, Fitz-Geralds. The family lived in the castle in some poverty until 1602 when the owner was Knighted after the nearby Battle of Kinsale. During a 40-year period of prosperity they expanded the castle. It was acquired in 1645 by the Earl of Orvery and was held by Anglo-Irish families. There is a record of Oliver Cromwell and William Penn visiting the castle. A 14th century keep remains in its original form and most of the present buildings are constructed around the old castle wall. Public rooms are decorated with portraits, commemorative stones, elk antlers, historical

Ballymaloe House

mementos and objects of art. The house stands in a 400 acre farm and the recommended restaurant, the Yeats Room, relies heavily on their own produce. Facilities include a bar, swimming pool, tennis court, golf course (not championship standard), riding, nearby fishing and hunting, and indoor and outdoor children's play equipment. Ivan and Myrtle Allen are present owners and managers. 23 bedrooms, most with baths, 15 in the main house and some in the old guards (gate) house. Ballymaloe is 30 km E of Cork City on the Ballycotton Road, and 3 km from the south coast. Closed short periods in winter. (I)

BALLYSEEDE Castle (SW)
Tralee (Kerry) 21585

The castle was built with beautiful stone craftsmanship in the 1400s, and a wing

Ballyseede Castle

Barberstown Castle

was added in the 1600s. The castle and its 12,000 acres were given to Sir Edward Denny by Queen Elizabeth I. Sir Edward granted the estate to the Blennerhasset family in the 17th century, providing for an annual rental of one red rose from the gardens. A member of the latter family resided in the castle until 1967. Adapted as a luxury hotel, the castle now has 300 acres of grounds. There is a Tudor bar and public and private rooms are tastefully decorated to maintain the character. Medieval banquets are held frequently in the 16th century Stone Hall. Central heat. 13 rooms. About 100 km SW of Limerick. Open all year. (II)

BARBERSTOWN Castle Hotel (E)
Straffan (Kildare) 288206

The tall keep dates from 1172 and represents the oldest of three architectural styles of the castle. There is an Elizabethan wing (1594), and an Edwardian wing (1830). A dining room is on the Norman-decorated ground floor of the keep, and the first floor (one flight up) is the lounge with views of the countryside. The second floor is a bedroom, and winding stone stairs lead to the roof of the tower. A legend says there is a man entombed in the top of the tower in keeping with an ancient lease which was to expire if ever he was buried underground. The other wings have 15 spacious guest rooms, 6 with luxury baths en suite. Some have canopied beds. There are: handsome lounge bar, TV lounge, central heat, restaurant. Dining specialties include fish and lobster dishes. In nearby Castletown House, and in 17th century Robertstown House historic banquets are held frequently in season. Straffan is about 27 km W of Dublin. (II)

BARGY Castle (SE)
Tomhaggard (Wexford) 35203

Bargy is a medieval castle most of which was built 800 years ago, on the site of previous fortresses dating back to before Christ. Known as Burgie then, the castle is still inhabited and owned by the de Burgh family. It was once taken under siege by Cromwell, who held it 48 hours only to be driven out by bees. There is a banqueting hall, minstrels' gallery, banners, coat-of-arms and armor, fine carved panelling and furniture of the Middle Ages. Open fires and central heating, and many amenities including four-poster beds. The family prides itself on the menu of fresh foods and its wine cellars. There is a drawbridge-spanned moat,

Bargy Castle

Belleek Castle

Bellingham Castle

Blackrock Castle

and the castle stands in 170 acres of park, woods and fields near the sea, with miles of deserted sandy beaches. Tennis, volley ball and croquet, with nearby fishing, boating, riding, and championship golf at Rosslare and Wexford. 18 rooms, 14 with baths. Open Easter-Oct. 16 km S of Wexford town, 10 km SW of Rosslare Harbour Continental and UK ferries. Reduced rates for longer stays. This is rated as a guest house. (Ask about charges for wine and other drinks before ordering). (II)

BELLEEK Castle (NW)
Ballina (Mayo) (096) 22061

First mentioned in documents in 1584, the castle was the seat of the Bourke family whose descendants still own it. It is thought to have been built in the 1300s. The Armada Bar, decorated as a Galleon captain's cabin, is built with actual timbers from the wreckage of the Spanish Armada in the 1500s. A Spanish ship's figurehead, washed ashore in 1588 is a special attraction. Grounds comprise 3,000 acres of park and woods. Good fishing, hunting, motorboating, sailing, beaches 3 miles away, picnics and barbecues on sandy river island beaches, are all available, also baby sitting service. Dining is on hand hewn antique tables, and you can watch the cooking in the fire of a medieval Celtic oven. Open fireplaces as well as central heat. Weekly rates given. 56 rooms, 42 with baths. Ballina is 205 km N of Shannon. (II)

BELLINGHAM Castle (NE)
Castlebellingham (Louth) (042) 72177

The ancestral castle of the Bellingham family has turreted walls and towers, and stands in broad grounds which have been prominent in Irish and English history. Entrance to the castle is through a drive and elegant gateway. The village is an old-world stopover on the main Dublin-Belfast highway, and is three miles from the attractive fishing village of Annagassan. Central heat, baby sitters. 12 rooms. Castlebellingham is 13 km S of Dundalk and 70 km N of Dublin. (I)

BLACKROCK Castle (S)
Cork (Cork) (021) 293737

Restaurant only

This time-mellowed castle on the harbor, two miles from the center of Cork, is a top restaurant for dinner only and not a hotel. Built in 1605 by the British as a harbor defense, it now offers beautiful water views from whence Drake and William Penn once sailed. Candlelight, music, roof terraces, and widely varied menu add to the historic charm. Also, frequent medieval banquets are held here.

Breaffy House

BREAFFY HOUSE Hotel (NW)
Castlebar (Mayo) (094) 22033

Located in the lake and mountain country of the West of Ireland, Breaffy House offers Grade A accommodations in its own setting of 60 acres of woodland. Fishing, shooting, riding, golf, walking trails, and bathing. Excellent foods and wines, central heating, baby sitters and elevator. 43 rooms. 3 km SE of Castlebar, it is on the main Castlebar-Claremorris-Dublin road. Closed Christmas season. (II)

BUTLER ARMS (SW)
Waterville (Kerry) 5

Square, battlemented corner towers give this great country house the aspect of a castle as it stands amid gardens and spacious grounds, facing the sea. It is on the warmer southwest coast, and provides renowned fishing for sea trout on Lough Currane, salmon fishing in season, and four other private fishing lakes. Deep sea fishing is also available. There is a championship golf course 1½ km away, riding is nearby, and on the hotel grounds are hard tennis courts. The guest house has been under the management of the Huggard family for three generations, and offers homey atmosphere. There are sun and bar lounges, TV room, and a recreation hall. Waterville, in the SW corner of Ireland is on the "Ring of Kerry", surrounded by lakes, the Atlantic coast and mountains. It is 80 km W of Killarney. (I)

CABRA Castle Hotel (E)
Kingscourt (Cavan) (042) 67160

The imposing castellated mansion, located just outside the village of Kingscourt, has sections dating from Norman times. A historical highlight was during the reign of James II who stayed in Cabra Castle during the Williamite Wars. Some of the rooms have canopied beds and gothic windows, and the various lounges and bars are elegant. Located in spacious grounds in an area of hills and glens, the castle has a nine hole golf course, riding, fishing in several lakes, and a hotel 'jaunting car' for trips. Walking trails are offered in the forest

Butler Arms

park across the road. Central heat, baby-sitters. 24 rooms and baths. About 43 km N of Dublin, and 19 km SW of Dundalk. (3 km NE of town on L14). (I)

Cabra Castle

CAHORE Castle Hotel (SE)
Cahore (Wexford) (055) 27338

This old stone baronial mansion has a central turreted tower, and stands in wooded grounds. It has 500 yards of sea frontage, and miles of sandy beaches in this warmest area of the British Isles. Fishing nearby. Impromptu singing by guests and patrons nightly in lounges. Individual electric heat in rooms. 11 rooms but no private baths. Open May-Oct. 3 km from Ballygarrett and Clonevan. (I)

Cashel Palace

CASHEL PALACE (S)
Main St., Cashel (Tipperary) 9

This Archbishop's palace was erected before 1728, and has a south face built of red brick and a north face of stone. The latter faces the famed Rock of Cashel. Rooms are spacious, and furnishings are Georgian and modern. There is a grill room and cocktail lounge, central heating and baby sitting service. Nearby are fishing, hunting and golf. The nearby Rock of Cashel is one of Ireland's greatest historical monuments -- a remarkable collection of ecclesiastical ruins. The round tower, 92 feet high, dates from the 10th century. Cormac's chapel was built in 1127, and the Cathedral of St. Patrick was built a century later. 20 rooms. 19 km E of Tipperary, about 56 km E of Limerick. (II)

The Castle

The CASTLE (S)
Castletownshend,
Skibbereen (Cork) (028) 36100

Townshend Castle has been the ancestral home of the Townshend family for many generations, and is still the residence of Mrs. R. M. Salter-Townshend who offers part of the castle for guest rooms and apartments. Situated directly on the village harbor, it offers views of the

Cliff Castle

water, and of the three tower-like islands which stab upward offshore. This was the scene of a naval battle in 1602 between English and Spanish squadrons. Rooms have hot and cold running water, and most face the sea. Nearby are the ruins of Glenbarrahane Castle and Church, and an ancient stone fort. 5 rooms, no private baths. The village is about 8 km E of Skibbereen. (I)

CLIFF CASTLE Hotel **(E)**
Coliemore Rd.,
Dalkey (Dublin) **(01) 850255**

This towered castle stands on a cliff with a commanding view of the southwestern end of Dublin Bay. It has its own private beach and boating harbor, indoor pool, putting green, and golf is available nearby. 12 rooms, 3 private baths. 13 km S of Dublin, 19 km from airport; frequent rail and bus service. Open all year. (I)

DROMOLAND Castle **(W)**
Newmarket on Fergus
(Clare) **(061) 71144**

This sprawling stone castle, with its turrets, ramparts and towers, is a well known modern hotel. It is situated among rivers and lakes on a 1500 acre estate, once the residence of Ireland's ancient kings. Originally built in 1570, the castle was rebuilt in its present form about a century and a half ago by the Fourth Baronet, Sir Edward O'Brien, and still maintains the character of ancient times with its splendid wood carvings and objects of art. Salmon and trout fishing, water sports, sailing, tennis, riding, and a championship golf course. Central heat, baby sitter service. 67 rooms and baths. Open Apr-Nov. 13 km from Shannon Airport. (III)

Dromoland Castle

Fitzpatrick Castle

FITZPATRICK Castle Hotel (E)
Killiney Hill Rd off Dalkey Ave.
Killiney (Dublin) (01) 851533

The castle (formerly called Killiney Castle) was built about 1741 and has been restored and refurnished completely, giving it an authentic baronial atmosphere. There is a Dungeon Bar, lounges and other public rooms furnished with period antiques. Besides single and double rooms, there are suites for 2 to 6 persons. There are also facilities for banquets, seminars and private parties, heated indoor pool, tennis, squash, central heat, baby sitter service. Three golf courses are nearby and the castle estate adjoins Victoria Park. 48 rooms and baths. Location is just W of Dalkey, 15 km S of the center of Dublin and 27 km from Dublin airport, from where a courtesy coach is available. (II)

KILKEA Castle (SE)
Castledermot (Kildare) (0503) 45156

Said to be the oldest inhabited castle in Ireland, Kilkea became a castle-hotel in 1968. Built in 1180 by an Anglo-Norman knight, its gray granite walls and towers portray typical Norman characteristics, with battlements, arrow-slits and gothic windows. It even has a legendary haunted room said to be visited on occasion in past ages by a ghost on a white charger, but now the room is a fully-equipped bathroom, which the ghost (thus far) has not seen fit to visit. Fishing and hunting available in over 100 acres of grounds, and a championship golf course is nearby at Carlow. 55 rooms and baths. Castledermot is 72 km SW of Dublin. Castle is about 5 km NW of Castledermot. (I)

KILLOSKEHANE Castle (SC)
Borrisoleigh
(Tipperary) **Borrisoleigh 5**

The castle was built in 1580 by Theobald Walter Butler. Today it stands in 14 acres of grounds in the foothills of the Silvermine Mts. Now privately owned by the Browne family which acquired it in 1977, the castle has undergone major restoration work, and is operated as a guest

Kilkea Castle

Longfield House

Castle Matrix

house where guests are made to feel like members of the family. It is an approved country home by the Irish Tourist Board. There are 8 rooms, two with baths. Open all year. The town is about 30 km E of Shannon Airport. (II)

LONGFIELD House (SC)
Cashel (Tipperary) (0504) 42261

The historic country mansion was built in 1770 on the remains of an earlier castle. It incorporates many of the fortress characteristics -- such as six-foot-thick walls -- and it formerly had iron-lined shutters. Built by the Long family, the estate was sold in 1846 to Charles Bianconi, after Captain Long was murdered by local political assassins. Bianconi had made a fortune by buying up many of Napoleon's horses after the Napoleonic wars and setting up an Ireland-wide stagecoach system. He brought many elegant accoutrements to the mansion from Italy, many of which remain today. Longfield now is owned by the Irish Georgian Society and operated as a guest house, with some sections open to the public as a museum. It contains valuable collections of Bianconi, Coppinger and O'Connell memorabilia as well as the collection of Hayes watercolors. Public and private rooms are elegantly furnished. Indoor and outdoor activities for children, as well as tennis, bicycling, riding, rough shooting, and golf nearby. Local produce dominates the cuisine. Fully licensed bar, central heat, baby-sitters. 10 rooms, 7 baths. (I)

Castle MATRIX (SW)
Rathkeale (Limerick) **Rathkeale 139**

More than 500 years of Irish and English history encompass this castle, whose tower was the scene of the murder in 1487 of James Fitz-Thomas (Fitz-Gerald) 9th Earl of Desmond. A century later, the Desmonds, outlawed by Queen Elizabeth I, were in rebellion, and Walter Raleigh, sent by the queen, lived in the castle in 1580. Edmund Spenser, English writer, also was staying in the castle during the occupation. The Queen gave the estate to the Southwell family, and Robert Southwell was first to cultivate Raleigh's Virginia potatoes of the Old World in the fields of Matrix Castle. The Jacobean wing was added in 1616. In the 1641 Irish rebellion the castle was seized by the Irish, and then retaken by siege by Cromwell's forces. In 1709 it was the main colony of German Protestant refugees, and in 1756 John Wesley established a Methodist community in Rathkeale. The castle fell into ruin early in the present century, and was restored in 1970 by Col. Sean O'Driscoll, Irish-American architect. It is now the scene of frequent medieval banquets which include sumptuous meals prepared in the ancient way, and entertainment. Rooms are modernized with central heating, but suites also have woodburning fireplaces, and furnishings include Elizabethan and Jacobean antiques, original prints, paintings and historic documents. Summer courses in arts and crafts are given. 10 rooms. (Reserve early) Located 30 km SW of Limerick, and about 52 km from Shannon Airport. Closed in winter. (II)

Mount Falcon Castle

MOUNT FALCON Castle **(NW)**
Ballina (Mayo) **(096) 21172**

In a setting of woods and fields, Mount Falcon Castle offers country house holidays with a variety of possibilities. This includes salmon or trout fishing on the River Moy or Lough Conn, winter pike fishing or winter shooting of small game. There is also sea fishing, tennis, pony riding, a children's playroom and nearby golf. Or you can relax in front of a log fire. Dining is family style with much of the produce coming from the castle's own farm. All 11 rooms with bath. Open all year. Grade A. Ballina is about 64 km W of Sligo. (II)

NEWPORT HOUSE **(NW)**
Newport (Mayo) **(098) 41222**

The manor house was built in the early 18th century and stands in gardens and a park area on the banks of the Derrydeevagh River. Rooms and furnishings are of the period, with many pictures and antiques. A notable feature is the grand staircase of the main hall with a gallery and dome. For 200 years the manor was the home of the O'Donels, descended from the fighting Earls of Tir Connell and cousins of "Red Hugh" of Irish history. For a time the 6th century Cathech, battle book of the O'Donnells was kept at Newport House but is now in the Royal Irish Academy. Fishing for sea trout and salmon is done in private areas on the river and lake, and boats leave the quay on the grounds for sea fishing. 18-hole championship golf at Westport, and also a 9-hole golf course, riding and game rooms. Cuisine based on the manor's own produce, with a notable wine cellar, is offered. 28 rooms and apts with baths. 18 km W of Castlebar, 10 km N of Westport and 175 km NW of Shannon. (I)

SLANE Castle **(E)**
Slane (Meath) **24207**

Restaurant only

This castle, part of which is still a private residence, devotes the lower section to a restaurant with recommended cuisine. The castle is in a nice setting and the restaurant decor is in keeping with the historical venue. The small town of Slane is about 35 km N of Dublin between Navan and Drogheda. Closed Mon, Tues and Dec 21-31. Luncheon not always available, check first.

Newport House

Medieval Banquets

These banquets first became popular when introduced at Bunratty castle some years ago, and are now held in several castles and other historic places. They can be booked through travel agents or directly. For reservations at Bunratty, Dunguaire and Knappogue, Tel. (061) 61788, or your travel agent. These are not hotels unless so noted.

BALLYSEEDE Castle (SW)
Tralee (Kerry) 21585

This is also a hotel. See listing on previous pages.

BLACKROCK Castle (S)
Cork (Cork) (021) 293737

This is a restaurant, listed on previous pages.

Bunratty Castle

BUNRATTY Castle (SW)
Bunratty (Clare)

Every evening of the year this 15th century castle of the Earl of Thomond rings to the laughter, music and entertainment of its medieval banquets. After a reception in the great hall, the banquet is held in the Main Guard. Waitresses and entertainers and famed Bunratty Castle Singers all are dressed in authentic costumes, and the hall is hung with period tapestries and portraits and furnished with antiques. Mead wine and specially prepared foods are served in the 15th century manner. The castle, with its furnishings from the collection of Lord Gort, is worth seeing, as well as its surrounding medieval park and restored buildings and cottages. Twice nightly banquets at 5:45 and 9. All-inclusive price about $26. Bunratty is about 5 km E of Shannon airport.

DUNGUAIRE Castle (W)
Kinvara (Galway)

This tall, brooding, feudal castle is the appealing and intimate setting for a sumptuous banquet, similar to that at Bunratty, followed by dramatic entertainment. Included is instrumental music, song and extracts from the works of Synge, Yeats, and others. Held twice

Dunguaire Castle

nightly at 5:45 and 9 p.m., from about May 15th to Sept 30th. Departures for the event are from Galway RR station and Salthill. Banquet is about $26.

KNAPPOGUE Castle **(SW)**
Quin (Clare)

This McNamara Castle, built in 1467, is the scene twice nightly of a medieval banquet which has as its entertainment theme the story of Ireland and its history. The pageant has been written for this event by Bryan MacMahon, and includes musical interludes. Since the 1400s the castle enjoyed continuous occupation by successive Norman and Irish families until 1923 when it was partially damaged by fire. Now beautifully restored, it is an outstanding example of medieval architecture, enriched by later renaissance refinements. As in the other castle banquets, the lavish meal is served by attractive hostesses and entertainers with pomp and pagentry, and courses are described in detail. Banquets are at 5:45 and 9 p.m., May through Oct. About $26.

Castle MATRIX **(SW)**
Rathkeale (Limerick) **Rathkeale 139**

This is also a hotel, listed on previous pages.

ROBERTSTOWN House **(E)**
Robertstown (Kildare)

This historic house in the village is the setting of banquets held each Thursday and Friday from May to September. Located on the Grand Canal from Dublin to the Shannon River, Robertstown was established in the 1700s as a port of call for packet barges. Inspired by those times, they are candlelight banquets with Georgian-style feasting, and also canal barge trips. June-Sept. About $12.

Knappogue Castle

Italy

Hotel APRILE **(C)**
Via Della Scala 6
50123 Firenze (Florence) Tel. (055) 216 237

This is the 15th century Palazzo del Borgo, once owned by the ruling Medici family. Located in the center of Florence near the RR station, its rather plain facade hides an attractive interior of decorated and vaulted ceilings, and nice furnishings. There is a bar, small garden, excellent cuisine, elevator, family accommodations. It is adjacent to the beautiful Santa Maria Novella church as well as to the nearby Arno River and other points of interest. 40 rooms including some apts, with baths. (I)

La BADIA **(C)**
05019 Orvieto **(0763) 90 359**

The abbey, dating from the 1100s, houses this first class hotel-restaurant. It comprises a church of Romanesque-Lombardesque style, and a notable tall 12-sided tower. There are frescoes of the 12th, 13th and 14th centuries, reflecting the years when the abbey was the center of the Benedictine Monks and Premontres Canons. In the 15th century it was a holiday retreat for Cardinals. In the past century it has belonged to a noble family which meticulously restored it, maintaining its medieval character. Today it has 22 rooms, all with baths, and some suites with rooms on two floors. The restaurant features produce from the abbey's own farm. Swimming pool, tennis, conference facilities. Orvieto is a medieval town 126 km N of Rome midway between Rome and Florence on the Autostrada del Sole. Closed Jan-Feb. (II)

La Badia

Castello di Balsorano

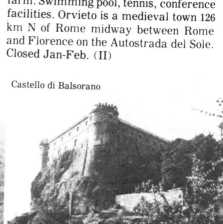

Castello di BALSORANO (S)
67052 Balsorano (l'Aquila) (0863) 95 236

This 12th century castle stands high on a hilltop with its feudal towers and battlements to be seen from miles around. Facilities include restaurant and bar in authentic medieval stone vaults or dungeons, and a great beam-ceilinged hall houses a notable arms collection. There is an inner courtyard paved with ancient stones. In furnishings and decor the atmosphere of the ancient fortress has been maintained. Mountain sports nearby. Central heat. 11 rooms. About 104 km SE of Rome, on the road toward Avezzano, some 20 km E of Frosinone. Class IV. (I)

Torre de Cala Piccola

Torre di CALA PICCOLA (W)
58019 Monte Argentario,
Porto S. Stefano
(Grosseto) (0564) 825 133

Situated atop spectacular 400-foot Mount Argentario overlooking the Mediterranean on a little coastal island north of Rome, this hotel is built around an ancient Saracen tower erected as a lookout by pirates. The hotel comprises a main building as well as vine-clad cottages, all with balconies facing the sea. The main bar is in the lower vaulted rooms of the old tower with its arrow-slit windows. An antique shop and boutique filled with Italian goods are nearby, and a restaurant on the beach. Sea bathing, skin-diving, swimming pool and air conditioning. 53 rooms and baths. Open May-Sept. Hotel is reached by private road off the Via Aurelia (N1), 142 km N of Rome. Train station: Orbetello, and 20 km taxi or hotel car ride. (II)

Grand Hotel CAPPUCCINI (C)
Via Tifernate
06024 Gubbio Umbria
(Perugia) (075) 922 241

Situated within the walls of the ancient 16th century monastery, this hostelry maintains the character and decorations of the earlier centuries. It is set on a hill just outside the town. Central heat, handicap facilities, park area, hotel car from station. 39 rooms with baths or showers. Gubbio is NE of Perugia, which is about the center of Italy. (I)

Hotel CAPPUCCINI CONVENTO (SW)
84011 Amalfi (Salerno) (089) 871 008

Foundations of this ancient convent go back to 1000 A.D., and much of the present structure dates from the 1200s when Cardinal Pietro Capuano restored the chapel and built the cloister in sumptuous style. Capuchin monks occupied it for nearly 300 years, and in 1826 it was acquired by the Vozzi family and transformed into a guest house. In the intervening years it has hosted many of

Cappuccini Convento

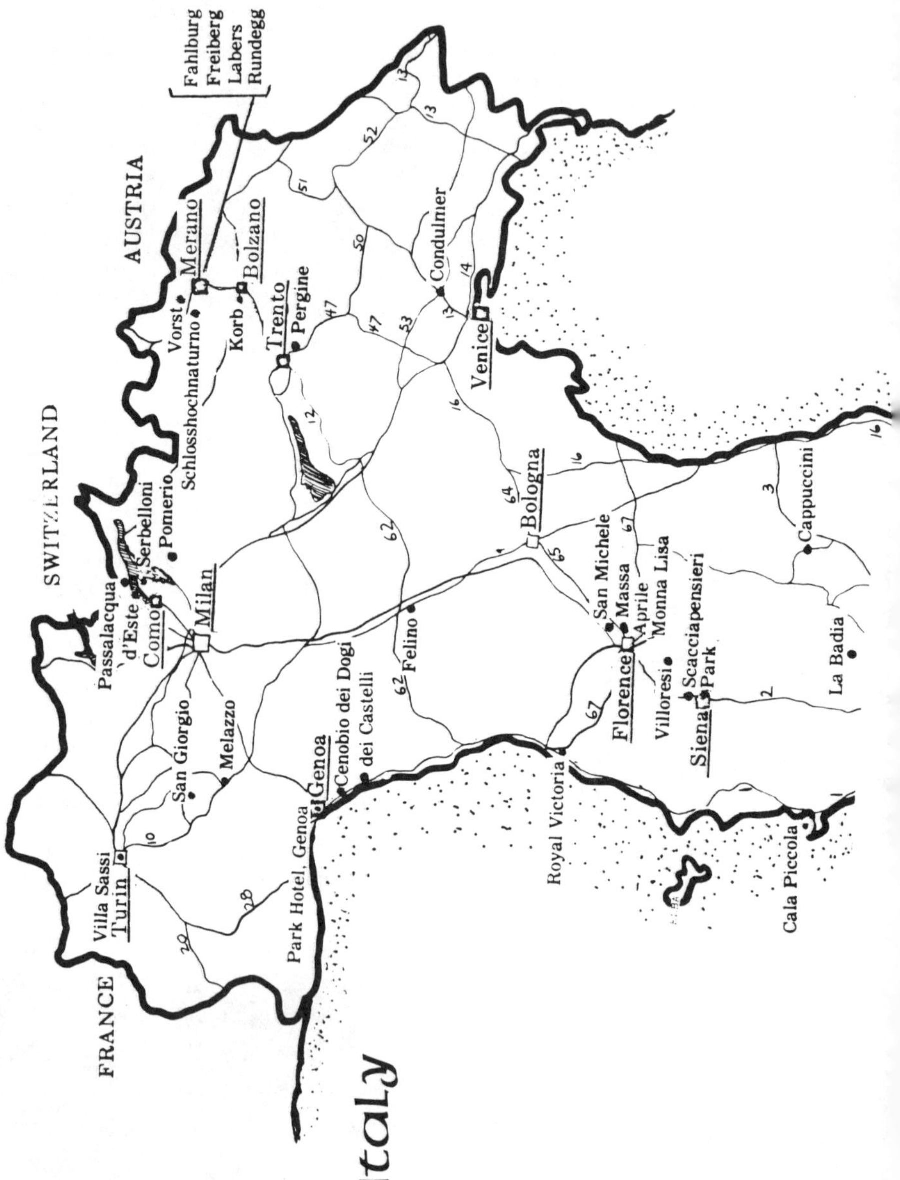
Italy
FRANCE
SWITZERLAND
AUSTRIA
Villa Sassi
Turin
San Giorgio
Melazzo
Passalacqua
d'Este
Como
Serbelloni
Pomerio
Milan
Schlosshochnaturno
Vorst
Merano
Korb
Bolzano
Fahlburg
Freiberg
Labers
Rundegg
Trento
Pergine
Condulmer
Venice
Bologna
Genoa
Park Hotel, Genoa
Cenobio dei Dogi
dei Castelli
Felino
San Michele
Massa
Aprile
Monna Lisa
Florence
Villoresi
Scacciapensieri
Park
Siena
Royal Victoria
Cappuccini
La Badia
Cala Piccola

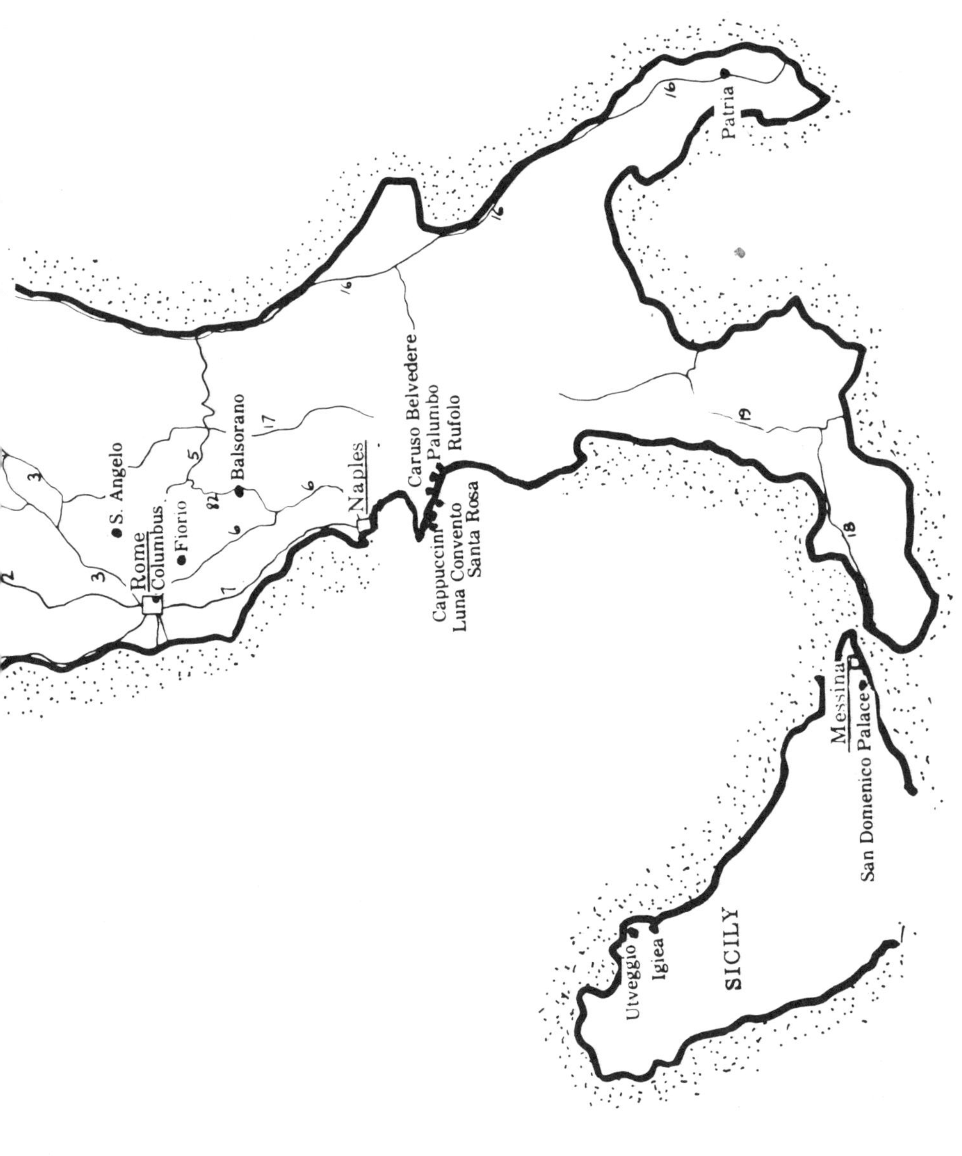
Rome
Columbus
S. Angelo
Fiorio
Balsorano
Naples
Caruso Belvedere
Palumbo
Rufolo
Cappuccini
Luna Convento
Santa Rosa
Patria
Messina
San Domenico Palace
SICILY
Utveggio
Igiea

Caruso Belvedere

the royal families and ruling monarchs of Europe as well as such personages of America as Theodore Roosevelt, Henry Wadsworth Longfellow, Samuel F. B. Morse, and many others. In the past these guests had to walk up the long stone stairways to the convent on the high cliffs overlooking the town of Amalfi. But now there is an elevator to accommodate the guests. The convent houses a fine collection of paintings and objects of art, antiques, and furnishings. Dining terrace, promenades, and many of the rooms overlook the Mediterranean Sea. 48 rooms, 36 baths, bus service to beach. Central heat, elevator, handicap facilities. Amalfi is on Rt SN12, about 70 km S of Naples. (I)

Cenobio dei Dogi

Hotel CARUSO BELVEDERE (SW)
84010 Ravello (Salerno) (089) 857 111

Built in the 11th century and known for centuries as d'Afflito Palace, this old villa has been a well-known hotel since 1903. The location is spectacular, some 900 feet above the rugged Mediterranean coast with sweeping views of the sea through its arched terrace. Menus feature house specialties and the Grand Caruso wines which originate in the surrounding vineyards, and are also sold in the U.S. Attractive accommodations and furnishings, an art collection. 26 rooms, most with baths, and many with private balconies. Central heat. Ravello is 65 km S of Naples and 29 km W of Salerno. (I)

Grand Hotel dei CASTELLI (NW)
Via Penisola
16039 Sestri Levante
(Genova) (0185) 41 044

Although much of the hotel is modern, it incorporates segments of an old castle and is in an area of several ancient castles. Located in a park area, it offers lovely sea views along the Riviera and of the ancient village. Elevators connect to the hotel's private beach and the town streets. Swimming in a protected pool and in the open sea. In season there is dancing and entertainment in the hotel. Bar, restaurant with regional and international food, banquet hall, terraces, central heat. 46 rooms with baths, luxurious furnishings. Open May-Sept. 10 km S of Rapallo. (II)

CENOBIO dei Dogi (NW)
Via Cuneo 34
16032 Camogli (Genova) (0185) 770 041

Former seat of the Bishops of Genoa, this manor house on the beach, north of Portofino is set in lovely grounds and terraces along the Riviera. Beach, swimming pool, tennis, handicap facilities, elevator, central heat. 74 rooms with baths. 10 km S of Genoa. Closed Nov-Dec. 21. (II)

Hotel COLUMBUS (C)
33 Via della Conciliazione
Rome (06) 65 64 874

The elegant hotel was built in the 1400s as a Cardinal's palace, and later served as a convent. Like many Italian renaissance palaces, its plain and austere exterior enfolds an inner court, sculptured, vaulted halls and rooms, coffered ceilings, carved stone fireplaces, period furnishings, paintings, antiques and objects of art. Elevators and air conditioning. 107 rooms, 80 baths. Central heat. Convenient to St. Peter's, about two blocks from the Piazza on the main street running straight into it. (II)

Hotel Columbus

Villa CONDULMER (NE)
31021 Mogliano Veneto Zerman
(Treviso) (041) 450 001

An 18th century villa built on the remains of an earlier monastery, and today a luxury hotel and restaurant, in a fine park with nearby lake, golf, riding, tennis and swimming. Specialty foods and wines of the area are served. 33 rooms with baths. Central heat, handicap facilities. About 22 km N of Venice toward Treviso. (I)

Villa Condulmer

Villa d'Este

Villa d'ESTE (N)
Via Regina
22012 Cernobbio (Como) (031) 511 471
(In U.S.: 800-223-6800. NY 212-838-3110)

This is one of the finest resorts in Europe. The magnificent villa was begun in the 1500s by Cardinal Gallio, and later became a palace of an Empress of Russia, a Princess of Wales, and other royalty. It was adapted as a hotel in 1873 and now offers every facility and comfort. Beautifully furnished, spacious bedrooms, dining rooms, lounges and terraces for tea concerts and dancing. Activities include tennis, golf, riding, swimming indoors and out, water sports, boating. The location, directly on Lake Como, provides lovely grounds and gardens. 180 rooms, most with baths. Air-conditioned, central heat, handicap facilities. Open April-Oct. On N side of Lake Como. (DL)

Hotel Schloss FAHLBURG (N)
Prissian I39010 Tisens
bei Meran (0473) 90930

Fahlburg Castle was built in the 12th century, and was remodled as a Renaissance castle in 1640. Today it is one of the few remaining castles which preserves its original character of the latter period. It is owned by the Earls of Brandis and operated by members of the family. The village and castle are situated on a high plateau on the south side of the Alps, in the old Austrian sector of Italy. Breakfast available in the "Old World Kitchen". Pleasant walks through the grounds, and excursions to Meran (16 km) and the Dolomite Mountains available. (I-II)

Castello di FELINO (N)
43035 Felino (Parma) (0521) 802 142

Restaurant only

This restaurant is in a massive 9th century feudal castle inside vine-covered walls. Entrance is across a stone bridge high over a dry moat. There are towers, battlements and inner courts. Whiskey gallery, Italian and French wines served in an underground area. Dining rooms

Castello di Felino

Schloss Fahlburg

with wood beam ceilings. Recommended cuisine. Closed Dec-Feb and Mon. 2 km S of Felino.

Villa FIORIO (WC)
Via Dusmet 25
00046 Grottaferrata (Roma) (06) 945 276

This old villa, not far from Rome, offers luxury accommodations as a Class I hotel. Swimming pool, central heat, conference rooms, garden area. 21 km SE of Rome, 3 km from Frascati. (I-II)

Hotel Castel FREIBERG (N)
Fragsburg Via Cavour
39012 Merano (Bolzano) (0473) 44 196

Situated high on the shoulder of a mountain, this luxury hotel incorporates much of an ancient castle dating from 1357. Many additions and alterations were made by several successive titled families who owned the manor. A Renaissance gallery and a completely wood paneled baronial hall enhanced the castle later on, and it has recently been restored to full splendor. There are beautiful dining rooms and well-furnished public lounges, a vaulted bar, indoor and outdoor pools, gymnasium, tennis, conference and banquet rooms. 38 rooms. Open Apr-Oct. Located on Via Labers, 7 km from the center of Merano. (II)

Castel Freiberg
(Exterior and interior)

Grand Hotel Villa IGIEA (SW)
90142 Palermo (Sicily) (091) 543 744

Built in a curious mixed architectural style of castle and villa, this air conditioned luxury hotel is situated in a park area directly on the sea. There are gardens with palm trees and other flora and ruins of an ancient temple. Swimming pool and sea bathing, tennis, central heat, elevator, handicap facilities. The bar is in an old stone vaulted area. 91 rooms all with baths, and private suites. Car service from station. (III)

Villa Igiea

Castel Schloss KORB (NE)
39057 San Paolo Appiano
Appiano, Missiano
(Eppan-Bolzano) (0471) 52 199

Korb (Corba) is a feudal castle in a spectacular setting among rugged mountains. The character of past centuries has

Castel Schloss Korb

been preserved in decorations and furnishings, with massive stone structures and wood beamed ceilings. Good restaurant. It is situated in a park area. Heated pool, tennis, elevator, central heat. 52 rooms. Open Apr-Nov. About 75 km S of the Austrian border in the German-speaking section of Italy near the Brenner Pass. 4 km N of Appiano. (II)

Hotel Castel LABERS (NE)
Via Labers 25
Merano (Bolzano) (0473) 26 085

Located in the South Tyrol, the southern Alpine slopes, the castle is more than 600 feet above the town of Merano with a sweeping panoramic view of the mountains and valleys. It is surrounded by woodlands and vineyards. Mountain cable car, winter sports, swimming pool, walking trails. Elegantly furnished, elevator, international cuisine, bar. It is in the old Austrian-German language area of northern Italy. 31 rooms, most with baths. Open Mar-Nov. 3 km E via Scena. (II)

Hotel LUNA CONVENTO (SW)
(Torre Saracena)
Lungomare, 84011 Amalfi
(Salerno) (089) 871 002

The 12th century cloister has a beautiful setting along the Mediterranean coast. Good restaurant, beach, pool, central heat, handicap facilities. 42 rooms with baths. Hotel car from station. (I)

Castel Labers
(Exterior and interior)

Villa la MASSA (C)
50010 Candeli, Bagno A Ripoli
(Firenze) (Florence) (055) 630 051

With sections surviving from the 1300s, this old villa now is a charming hotel in private grounds overlooking the Arno River. Patio, dining room, terraces, spacious rooms. Air conditioning, central heat, elevator, pool, handicap facilities. 28 rooms with baths. 7 km E of Florence, hotel car from station. (II-III)

Castello di MELAZZO (NW)
15010 Melazzo, Acqui Terme
(Alessandria) (0144) 41 113

This may be one castle in which you would not like to "live like a king", for it was here that Edward II, King of England (1284-1327) was held a prisoner for more than two years. The exterior of the massive fortress-castle, dating from the 1300s, has remained virtually unchanged, but the interior has been

Hotel Luna Convento

Villa La Massa

Castello di Melazzo

Monna Lisa

restored. The castle is the ancient seat of the Aleramici family which held the region of Alto Monferrato in medieval times. It has been a restaurant and hotel for some years, with vaulted room or terrace dining, period furnishings, and walkways around the grounds and walls. Open May-Sept. 8 rooms, 6 baths. About 50 km SE of Turin (Torino), Acqui is just S of Alessandria. (I)

MONNA LISA (C)
Borgo Pinti 27
Firenze (Florence) **(055) 296 213**

Behind the unprepossessing facade of this ancient building on a small street in Florence there is a surprising interior -- a palace mostly built in the 1300s. The Patriarch of Constantinople lived here during the Ecumenical Council in 1439. Later it belonged to the Neri family, and in 1515 St. Philip was born there. The splendid ceiling painting in the large hall was done by Bernardino Pocetti (1542-1612). Public and private rooms are furnished in period pieces and objects of art, and there is a notable hanging staircase. There is a lovely garden behind the old palace. Bar, restaurant, parking area. (I-II)

Hotel PALUMBO (SW)
Via S. Giovanni del Toro, 28
84010 Ravello (Salerno) **(089) 857 244**

From its perch 1200 feet above the famed Amalfi Drive stands the 12th century Palazzo Confalone, now the Hotel Palumbo. It has been owned by the Vuilleumier

Park Hotel (Siena)

family since 1875. The palace commands sweeping views of rugged mountains and the Gulf of Salerno far below. It is elegantly structured with arch and pillar vaulting, stone staircases, tile inlaid floors, paintings and objects of art. Some private rooms have vaulted and arched ceilings, and tile floors covered with rugs. The restaurant is noted for its international and regional cuisine, and especially for its own Ravello Espiscopio wines. Gardens, terraces, central heat. 32 rooms. 3-day stay requested. (Ravello is about 70 km S of Naples. (II)

PARK Hotel (NW)
Corso Italia 10, Genoa (010) 311 040

This villa in the city of Genoa dates from the 1600s, and has period furnishings, spacious rooms, some original frescoes, and interesting art and artifacts. Gardens and nearby beach. Elevator, central heat, handicap facilities, open all year. 20 rooms, most with baths. (I)

PARK Hotel (C)
Via di Marciano 16
53100 Siena (0577) 44 803

In the 15th century this was the villa of a noble family and the glory of those years is reflected within the ancient walls. Modern amenities such as air conditioning in the rooms, heated pool, and appropriate furnishings provide for today's comforts. There are terraces, gardens, surrounding vineyards, and a good restaurant. Elevator, central heat. It is situated on Marciano Hill about 2 km N of the town with superb views. 20 rooms, most with baths. Open all year. (I-II)

Palazzo PASSALACQUA (N)
22010 Moltrasio (Como) (031) 29 03 71

(Apartments only) Situated on the spectacular precipitous shores of Lake Como, this neo-classic palace comprises sections dating from 1000 A.D., and a church from approximately that era. The palace was converted to its present form in 1740 by its new owner Count A. Passalacqua, under the skill of Carlo F. Soave, architect. The Passalacqua family line ended and around 1900 an English baroness, Ruby von Nalder Sederholm, owned it. Since about 1970 it has been owned by Hungarian-born British anthropologist and writer, O.K. Maerth, who has completely restored the palace, and decorated it with a collection of art objects, many from the Orient. The palace offers 3 apartment suites only on

Palazzo
Passalacqua

ground floor, with gardens. Each one accommodates 4 to 6 persons, with bedrooms, sitting rooms, kitchens, baths. Rates (1981) approx. $275 week for 2 persons, to approx. $600 per week for 6. Chef available. Two restaurants and food stores nearby. Swimming at private beach; boat excursions. Moltrasio is 8 km N of the town of Como, and 7 km from the Swiss border town of Chiasso.

Hotel PATRIA **(SE)**
Piazzetta Riccardi 13
73100 Lecce **(0832) 29 431**

A 15th century castle is the setting for this modest historic hotel. Attractive dining room, spacious guest rooms, elevator service are offered. Central heat, 60 rooms, 29 with baths. Closed most of August. Location is in the "heel" of Italy. (I)

Castel PERGINE (Al Castello) **(N)**
38057 Pergine Valsugana
(Trento) **(0461) 531 158**

A great deal of history and legend surrounds this 13th century castle which is located about 3 km E of town. It was for centuries the seat of the Pergine family which dates back to the tenth century. The restaurant offers local cuisine including snail delicacies. Excursions may be made to nearby lakes and thermal health resorts. Park area, bar, handicap facilities. 23 rooms. Open mid-Apr to mid-Oct. 11 km E of Trento on Rt 47. (I)

Castello di POMERIO **(N)**
Via Como 5
Pomerio d'Erba (Como) **(031) 611 516**

Castello di Pomerio is a restored 12th century manor house, with an 18th century villa as an annex. Furnishings

Castel Pergine

Castello di Pomerio

are luxury antiques, and surroundings are the mountains of the Lake Como region near the Swiss border. Centuries of history surround the place, with the original castle being given in 835 A.D. by Emperor Lotario, son of Charlemagne, to the Monastery of St. Ambrose of Milan. In 1383, the present structure was acquired by Jacopo dal Verme, a military leader. Many noble families have owned it since that time. Today there are restored 14th century frescoes which are among the most important non-religious frescoes in Italy, preserved because they were covered with thick layers of plaster through the centuries. Dining is in a series of ancient rooms providing for large or small groups, with a notable menu and wine list. Tennis, pool, bocce court, sauna, gardens, and open air dining are offered. Golf at Montorfano (5 km). 30 rooms, all with baths, refrigerator/bar. Pomerio is 10 km E of Como. (III)

ROYAL VICTORIA Hotel (NW)
Lungarno Pacinotti 12
56100 Pisa (050) 23 381

Overlooking the Arno River, this old palace is built upon medieval towers, and was adapted as a comfortable hotel in 1842 by the present owner's family. It is located in the middle of the city on the street along the right river bank. Bar, restaurant, elevator, central heat, garage in the building, handicap facilities, 80 rooms, all with baths. (I)

Villa RUFOLO (SW)
84010 Ravello (Salerno) (089) 857 133

With a rich history of several centuries, this villa was once the residence of Pope Adrian IV, the only English Pope, who reigned from 1154-1159. As a hostelry, the villa has been host to many luminaries since, such as Alphonso XIII, Lord Byron, Richard Wagner, Greta Garbo, and Leopold Stokowski. Wagner made this the setting of his opera Parsifal, and Wagnerian concerts are held here each year. It is situated near the Amalfi Drive, far above the Mediterranean, among the spectacular mountains and precipices of the area. Accommodations include pool, elevator, local food and wines. 28 rooms, most with baths. Hotel car at station. 65 km S of Naples, and 29 km W of Salerno. (I)

Villa Rufolo

Schloss Rundegg

Torre S. Angelo

Schloss RUNDEGG (NE)
Schennastrasse 2 (Via Scena 2)
39012 Merano (0473) 34 364

This old castle, nestled among the high mountains of the southern Tyrol, comprises square towers and other elements from the 1100s, and the main structure dates from about 1580. The name comes from the former owner, Archduke Leopold of Rundegg. Many of the antique furnishings are from the Paravicini family, early owners of the castle. After careful restoration the castle was opened in 1978 as an elegant hotel. Public rooms have grand staircases, arches and vaulting structure, decorated walls and ceilings, and spacious private rooms are furnished with antiques. Facilities include a pool, sauna, solarium and massage center. All rooms have bars, safes, color TV, private baths. The 12th century tower room is unique with 8 windows and panoramic view in all directions. Open all year. (II)

San Domenico Palace (in distance)

Torre S. ANGELO (C)
Stada Provinciale
00019 Tivoli (0774) 23 292

This towered 15th century castle is sited on a hill providing views of the valley and town below. There are olive groves and gardens and an outdoor swimming pool. Public and guest rooms are nicely furnished. There are: conference rooms, restaurant, bar, lounges, central heat, elevator, hotel car transport and 30 rooms. Location is about 30 km E of Rome, close to points of interest in and around Tivoli. The castle is off Via Quintilio Varo, past Villa Gregoriana. First Class. (II)

SAN DOMENICO PALACE (S)
Piazza San Domenico 5
98039 Taormina (Sicily) (0942) 23 701

Formerly a 14th century monastery, this elegant hotel is said to be one of the most renowned in Europe. Situated in a lovely valley, the view one way is toward Mt. Etna, the volcanic peak, and the other is dominated by an ancient Greco-Roman theatre. There are views of the sea, and within the walls are gardens and cloisters. Among the colonnades are the enigmatic stone warriors of the ancient past, protected by a strongly-worded papal bull of Pope Clement XII in 1738. Still to be seen, the command threatens severe penalties and curses to anyone who would remove any of them from the monastery. Splendidly furnished public lounges, dining rooms, and private rooms maintain the elegance. There is outdoor terrace dining in San Domenico once called "a balcony on the eternal spring", and a Sicilian mandolin orchestra plays most evenings. Heated pool, walkways, tennis, beach, local and international cuisine. Completely air conditioned. 100 rooms and luxury apartments. Elevator, hotel car. About 50 km S of Messina. (II-III)

Castello di SAN GIORGIO (NW)
San Giorgio, Monferrato
15020 Alessandria (0142) 806 203

The high tower and other elements date from the 10th century and blend with later medieval and renassaince sections to form the massive structure. It stands atop a hill with village and vineyards creeping up the sides, and approached by a narrow, winding road. Fine restaurant, wine cellar, authentic antique furnishings, park, outdoor sculpture and fine views. In the lower parts of the castle is a hewn stone tunnel leading to the ancient deep well which supplied water in case of a siege. Central heat, 11 rooms with baths. About 20 km SW of Casale Monferrato about half way between Milan and Turin. (I-II)

San Giorgio

Villa SAN MICHELE (C)
Via Doccia 4
50014 Fiesole (Florence) (055) 59 451

This deluxe villa is a 15th century monastery whose facade and loggia are said to have been designed by Michelangelo. Its priceless art treasures may now be seen in other places in Florence, notably the triptych on the high altar of Santa Trinita and another in the Academy. The Franciscans were driven from the monastery by Napoleon in 1808, it was reestored in 1952, named a National Monument, and is now an elegant hotel with air conditioning, woods, terraces, cloister, and a view over Florence from the NE. 31 rooms, all with baths. Central heat, car at station. Closed Nov-mid-Dec. (III-DL)

Villa San Michele

Albergo Santa Rosa

Villa Sassi

Villa Scacciapensieri

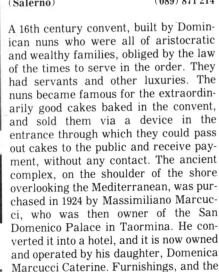

Albergo SANTA ROSA **(SW)**
84010 Conca dei Merini
(Salerno) **(089) 871 214**

A 16th century convent, built by Dominican nuns who were all of aristocratic and wealthy families, obliged by the law of the times to serve in the order. They had servants and other luxuries. The nuns became famous for the extraordinarily good cakes baked in the convent, and sold them via a device in the entrance through which they could pass out cakes to the public and receive payment, without any contact. The ancient complex, on the shoulder of the shore overlooking the Mediterranean, was purchased in 1924 by Massimiliano Marcucci, who was then owner of the San Domenico Palace in Taormina. He converted it into a hotel, and it is now owned and operated by his daughter, Domenica Marcucci Caterine. Furnishings, and the cuisine, still have a personal touch. 22 rooms. Open Apr-Oct. Handicap facilities. About 3 km W of Amalfi. (I)

Villa SASSI **(NW)**
Via Traforo del Pino 47
10132 Turin (Torino) **(011) 890 556**

This one-time private villa built in the 1600s, is now a distinguished hotel set in a spacious park at the edge of the city. Highly rated, elegant restaurant. Central heat, air conditioned, hotel car. 12 rooms with baths. Closed August. (II)

Villa SCACCIAPENSIERI **(C)**
Via di Villa Scacciapensieri
53100 Siena **(0577) 41 441**

The old villa is in a lush setting of flower gardens and tropical foliage, with nice views of its surroundings. Comfortable accommodations, food fresh from its own farm, and Chianti wines from its own vineyards. Air conditioned, central heat, tennis, swimming, handicap facilities. 31 rooms with baths. Located 3 km N of city, outside the old city walls, by way of Vialle Mazzini and Strada di Malizia. Open Mar-Nov. Car and bus service. (II)

Castello SCHLOSSHOCHNATURNO (N)
Naturno (Bolzano) 87 138

Formerly called Pensione Castello, this 13th century castle is rated as a Class III pension. It provides beautiful mountain views. 10 rooms. Naturno is 15 km W of Merano in the Alps a short distance from the Austrian border. Open Apr-Oct. (I)

Villa Serbelloni

Villa SERBELLONI (N)
22021 Bellagio (Como) (031) 950 216

A palace dating from the 1600s, this villa is situated between the forks of Lake Como, surrounded by gardens. Public rooms still show original frescoes. Golf, tennis, private beach, heated pool, water sports, elevator, handicap facilities, central heat. 93 rooms, all with baths. Open Apr-Oct 10. (III)

Castel UTVEGGIO (S)
Monte Pellegrino
90100 Palermo (Sicily)

This landmark castle, abandoned for a half century, is perched atop Monte Pellegrino, 2000 feet above the sea on the north coast of Sicily. The Sicily regional government in 1981 was investing about $2.29 million in restoring the castle as a hotel, restaurant and convention center. The restaurant accommodates 180 persons at a time, and the main meeting rooms are equipped for simultaneous translations for multi-language events. 67 rooms will accommodate about 180 guests. Mt. Pellegrino is about 10 km N of the city of Palermo. The hotel was scheduled to be open by the end of 1981.

Villa VILLORESI (C)
Via Delle Torri 63
50019 Sesto Fiorentino
(Florence) (055) 44 89 032

Authentic and lovely renaissance villa with terraces, gardens, galleries, reading rooms, bar, library and swimming pool. Modernized facilities in a 12th

Villa Villoresi

Castello Vorst

century villa, and a hotel since 1957. 27 rooms most with baths, central heat. 8 km from center of Florence, 3 km from exit "Prato Calenzano", Autostrado del Sole. (I)

Castello VORST **(NE)**
Foresta nr Merano
39022 Lagundo (Merano) **48 476**

Perhaps the most ancient among the castle hotels of Europe is Vorst Castle, encompassing a Roman fortress tower which itself was restored and enlarged in 1226 into a feudal castle of Prince Meinhard I of Tyrol, Austria. Later the castle was occupied by the Knights of Vorst (from which its present name derives) and several other noble families. Bought in 1956 by Hans Troyer of Meran (Merano), the castle was completely redecorated and its historical character preserved, and it became an enchanting hotel. Rooms are lavishly furnished with authentic antiques. There is a Tyrolean room with daily dinner music, a Tower Cafe in one of the Roman towers and a glassed-in sun deck atop a 2,000-year-old tower. Indoor pool and elevators. A dungeon now houses a bar. 22 rooms, 14 baths, central heat. Open Apr-Oct. In the Alps, on a river 4 km NW of Merano. (I)

Hotel Heintz

Hotel HEINTZ (NE)
55 Grand'rue
Vianden C-3 **Tel. 84155**

This old monastery is in the central part of the city, on the main street, and is furnished with many interesting antiques and works of art. The town has a medieval character and is dominated by Vianden Castle, Luxembourg's most famous castle ruin, which may be visited. Cable cars are nearby. Behind the hotel, which has balconies with many rooms, is a section of the old town wall and towers. Many celebrities have stayed in the hotel over the years. Notable cuisine, central heat, elevator, TV, gardens, children's playground. 30 rooms. Open Apr-Oct. 40 km N of Luxembourg city. (I-II)

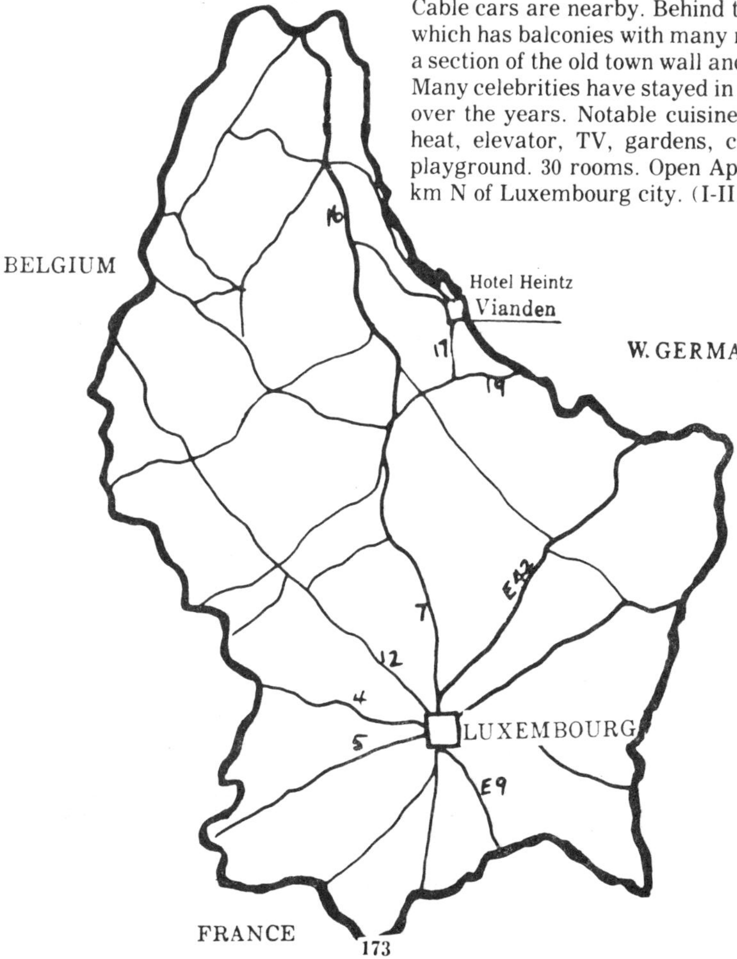

Norway

BARDSHAUG HERREGARD (NW]
N-7300 Orkanger (074) 81055

The country mansion, situated in spacious grounds, is a former private residence and is furnished in unusual elegance. There are dining rooms, library-lounge, bar, open-hearth lounge, cafeteria and banquet hall. Central and electric heat, baby-sitter service, trail riding, salmon fishing. 19 rooms in main building and annex. Open all year. Orkanger is on Rt. 65, 44 km S of Trondheim on the Trondheim Fjord. (II)

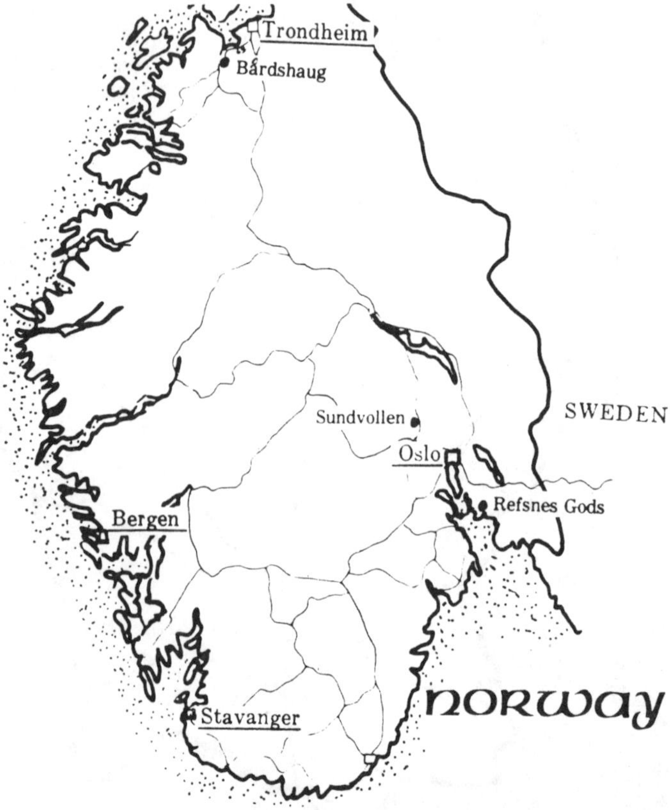

Bardshaug Herregard

Hotel Refsnes Gods

Hotel REFSNES GODS (SE)
Jeloy, 1500 Moss (Ostfold) 54 160

This old manor house stands in the midst of a large estate with ancient trees and its own beach along the Oslo Fjord. It has a fully licensed bar, pool, sauna, bicycling, boating, elevator, cruises and ferry service on the fjord. 62 rooms, all with baths or showers. (II)

SUNDVOLLEN Hotel (SE)
Sundvollen (Buskerud) (067) 39140

The old inn has provided accommodations for travelers for three centuries, and the present main building was built in the early 1700s. The older stone building is thought to date from the Middle Ages. The first guest of the place was the Bishop of Oslo in 1594, and since then there have been many notables including the Prince of Wales, Duke of Marlborough, Kaiser Wilhelm and several Kings of Sweden. It offers a recommended menu of wide variety and local specialties, and many drive up from Oslo for dining. Fully licensed bar, indoor pool, sauna, elevator, fishing, gym. 59 rooms. About 45 km NW of Oslo. (III)

Portugal

Pousada do Castelo
Guincho Hotel

Pousada do CASTELO (W)
Rua Direita,
Obidos 2510 (Leiria) Tel. (062) 95105

Obidos Castle dominates the ancient walled city of the same name, one of the best-preserved medieval towns of the Iberian Peninsula. The original castle was built at the time of the reconquest of Portugal from the Moors. Its walls, dating from the 12th century, now house one of the most attractive inns of the country. There are carefully restored antique furnishings, excellent cuisine, and wine cellars stocked with the delicate white wines appreciated by connoisseurs, reflecting the area noted for its vineyards. Central heat. This government-run pousada has only 6 rooms, early reservations recommended. 94 km N of Lisbon, and 22 km inland from the Atlantic; can be reached by train or car. (I)

GUINCHO Hotel (W)
Praia do Guincho
2750 Cascais (Lisboa) 285 0491
New York Tel. (212) 867-3123

This fine old medieval fortress, built in the 1200s, now offers deluxe hotel accommodations on a beautiful ocean coast. Situated on the westernmost point of land in Europe, it almost touches the Atlantic Ocean, commands an excellent beach, and enjoys a pleasant climate, with golf, fishing and water sports. Most bedrooms

Note: Reservations for the government pousadas in Portugal may be made in the U.S. through Marketing Ahead, Inc., 515 Madison Ave., New York, NY 10022, (212) 759-5170. This organization also handles reservations for the Spanish government paradores.

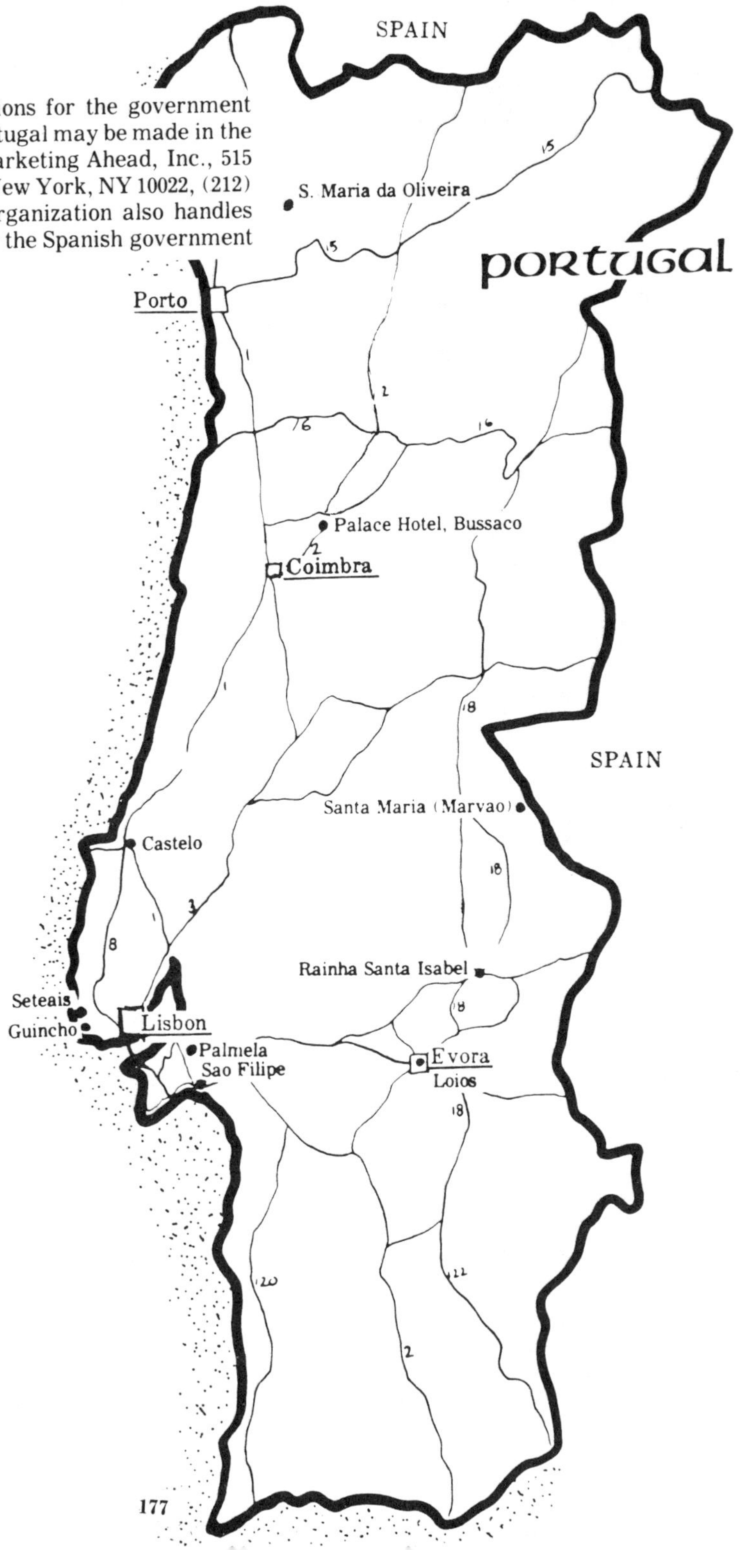

Pousada dos Loios

Roman Temple with Pousada Loios in background

face the ocean, and vaulted rooms and massive wood beams are characteristic. Air conditioned. 36 rooms and baths. 10 km N of Cascais, 35 km W of Lisbon. (II off-season; III high season)

Pousada dos LOIOS (S)
Evora 7000 24051

Evora is called the Museum City. Its ancient walls enclose one of the best preserved towns of the Middle Ages, with some structures still standing from Roman times. Tall columns and other remains of a Roman temple to Diana stand guard in the plaza outside the entrance to this government-run pousada. Loios is the original Convent of St. John Evangelist, and its first stone was laid in 1485. It was consecrated in 1491. There is a fine stone-columned and vaulted dining room, a grand marble staircase, and spacious guest rooms, furnished with antiques. Since 1965 it has served as a pousada (inn) with excellent food and accommodations. Besides the cloister, there is an interesting connected church. 28 rooms with baths. Evora is at the intersection of N18 and N114, about 140 km E of Lisbon. (II)

↓ Palace Hotel, Bussaco ⟶

PALACE Hotel (C)
Bussaco (Aveiro)
(Mail to: 3050 Mealhada) (0031) 93101

Built as a summer palace for the King of Portugal about a century ago, the Palace is an outstanding example of Manueline and Renaissance architecture. Exquisite stone carving dominates the exterior portico, facades and tower, as well as the interior public rooms, grand staircase and massive fireplace. The palace is also famed for its paintings and glazed tile work. The vast wine cellars hold some 200,000 bottles, vintages from local vineyards as well as from other areas. The building adjoins an old monastery built in the 1600s, and Cruz Alta, a cross at the summit of the highest hill in the surrounding great forest may be visited, by way of attractive footpaths. Bussaco Forest was the scene of a great battle in 1810 when Wellington's British and Portuguese forces defeated Napoleon's army. A military museum on the premises marks this event. Tennis, table tennis, billiards available. 70 rooms offer a wide range from moderate to expensive. Bussaco is 30 km NE of Coimbra, just off N234. (I-II)

Pousada de PALMELA (SW)
2950 Palmela 2351226

Although much of the structure of this government pousada is new, it also includes elements of a 14th century monastery. Just recently opened, its accommodations and furnishings have been carefully planned and selected to reflect the historical setting. The town is of historical interest, and stands atop a hill providing views all around. Palmela is about 8 km N of Setubal and 30 km SE of Lisbon. (I)

Pousada de Palmela

Pousada da (E)
RAINHA SANTA ISABEL
Estremoz 7100 (Evora) 22618

This government pousada is centered around a castle-keep dating from the 13th century, standing atop the highest hill in the picturesque village. Queen Isabel lived in the castle, and died there in the adjoining palace in 1336. Part of this palace also remains and is part of the restoration. Most of it was destroyed in an arsenal explosion in 1898 when the castle was used as a military installation. Reconstructed under government super-

← Pousada da Rainha Santa Isabel ↓

Pousada S. Maria da Oliveira

vision, the palace and castle were opened as one of Portugal's most luxurious hotels in 1971. Furnishings are 17th and 18th century Portuguese, and include not only furniture but also paintings, tapestries and ceramics of that period. Bedrooms feature exquisite four-poster canopied beds and matching furnishings, suitable for the president of Portugal who has stayed there. From the walkways near the top of the tower are fine views of the red tile-roofed village surrounding it below. Approach to the castle is made through narrow, winding streets with the flavor of the Middle Ages. Elevators, air conditioning, museum, an elegant dining room and cuisine are offered. 23 rooms and bath. About 60 km W of Badajoz, Spain. (II)

Santa Maria at Marvao

Pousada S. MARIA da OLIVEIRA (NW)
4800 Guimaraes **41893 (Braga)**

Set in the cradle of Portugal's founding kingdom, this government-owned pousada is a fortress-like palace built in the 1600s, and opened in 1980. The massive square stone corner towers are topped by crenellations. The town has medieval streets, handicrafts on sale, ancient churches, a museum, a nearby Marian Shrine at Penha, and neolithic remains at Briteiros. 16 rooms. Guimaraes is about 50 km NE of Porto. (II)

Pousada de SANTA MARIA (E)
7330 Marvao **93201**

In this ancient fortified town perched on top of a rocky prominence the government pousada is in a mansion built in the 1600s, crowded into one of the narrow village streets, just wide enough for one car. Parking is quite limited. Bar and dining room are in the new wing, and provide sweeping views of the surrounding countryside. Rooms are spacious and furnished in period antiques. Nearby there is a castle ruin which may be visited, parts of which are said to date from the Roman period. 8 rooms. Marvao is about 15 km N of Portalegre, just N of N246, about 5 km from the Spanish border. (II)

Pousada Sao Filipe

Palacio de Seteais

Pousada SAO FILIPE (SW)
2900 Setubal (065) 23844

This inn is part of an old fort, built in 1590, 600 feet above the busy fishing harbor of Setubal. It is approached by steep roads, through ancient walls, and the entrance is between massive walls and up ancient, dark, sweeping stone stairs. Porter boys will help with luggage up this slanting stair-tunnel. The fort is built in the shape of a star, with numerous corner sentry towers and massive battlements. Underground tunnels, gun embrasures and prison cells now serve as storage areas and wine cellars. An exquisite all-tiled chapel with its unusual ceiling is worth seeing. (Inquire at reception desk.) On Setubal's wharfs you can watch fishermen mending their nets, sailing and returning in their colorful dories. Fine cuisine and wines are featured in the attractive dining room. 16 rooms. Closed Nov. 40 km S of Lisbon. (II)

Palacio de SETEAIS (W)
8 Rua Barbosa du Bocage
Sintra (Lisboa) 293 3200

One of the great hotels of the country, this 18th century palace has been restored and furnished to duplicate its original state of the 1700s. Situated amid broad lawns and gardens, it is near the sea, and in an ancient, interesting old town. It overlooks a valley with lemon groves on the slopes. Public rooms are beautiful. 18 rooms. A half hour N of Estoril, and 20 km NW of Lisbon. (II-III)

Scotland

Airth Castle
Ardsheal House

ADAMTON HOUSE Hotel **(SW)**
Monkton, Nr. Prestwick,
Ayreshire **Tel. (0292) 70678**

The baronial country house, built in the 1700s, is a first class hotel with bar, restaurants and other amenities. Historic banquets are held in a "secret" room under the house. Nearby are sailing, fishing, golf at Troon, antique shops, and Robert Burns' birthplace. 30 rooms, all with baths or showers. Monkton is about 4 km N of Prestwick, and the house is about 2 km SE off B739. (II)

AIRTH Castle **(SC)**
Airth, by Falkirk,
Stirlingshire **(032) 483 411**

Airth Castle incorporates a tower or keep built in the late 1400's, and other sections from the 16th century. The original castle was burned in 1488 by James III, when it belonged to the Bruce family. Rebuilt, it was owned by several titled families and the present facade was added in 1803-1807. It became a hotel in 1971. Public and guest rooms are attractive, some of the latter with 4-poster beds, antique furnishings, and some tower rooms adapted as baths. Central heat, golf, fishing nearby, tennis, badminton, conference facilities. Cocktails and dancing on weekends in the old dungeons. Open all year. 23 rooms with baths. 32 km NW of Edinburgh airport. Hotel car will meet guests by arrangement. Location is off M9 toward

Kincardine Bridge, S side of Forth estuary. (II)

Atholl Palace

ARDOE HOUSE Hotel **(NE)**
Banchory Devenick,
Nr. Aberdeen, Grampian **(0224) 47 355**

A typical Scottish baronial mansion built with towers and battlements of solid granite, overlooking the River Dee and the countryside. Spacious rooms, fireplaces and the charm of a great country house greet the guests. The hotel has fishing rights along the River Dee for more than a mile, and nearby are golf and riding. Bar, restaurant, reception and conference facilities. Open all year. 20 rooms, most with baths or showers. Central heat. Banchory Devenick is about 9 km SW of Aberdeen. (II)

ARDSHEAL House **(W)**
Kentallin of Appin
Argyll PA38 4BX **(063) 174 227**

Towered and turreted, this old Stewart baronial mansion, built in 1545, stands on Loch Linnhe. Entrance to its 80 acres of grounds is at the head of Kentallen Bay. A game room is available, as are fishing, boating, climbing, tennis, riding, and golf at Oban. 12 rooms, most with baths. About 2 km W of the main Fort William-Oban road. About 24 km S of Fort William. (II)

ATHOLL PALACE Hotel **(C)**
Pitlochry, Perthshire

This imposing stone-towered mansion, more than a century old, stands on a hill with sweeping views down the Tummel Valley. Its 46 acres of parkland offer a swimming pool, various walking trails, and nearby tennis, fishing, sailing, riding and golf. The Pitlochry Festival Theatre is nearby, offering a variety of plays from April to October. Some 130 rooms are well furnished, and public and dining areas are spacious. About 48 km N of Perth. (I)

AUCHEN Castle **(S)**
Beattock, Dumfriesshire **(06833) 407**

This imposing baronial mansion with its two tall towers was built about 130 years ago as a private residence. It stands on a

Auchen Castle

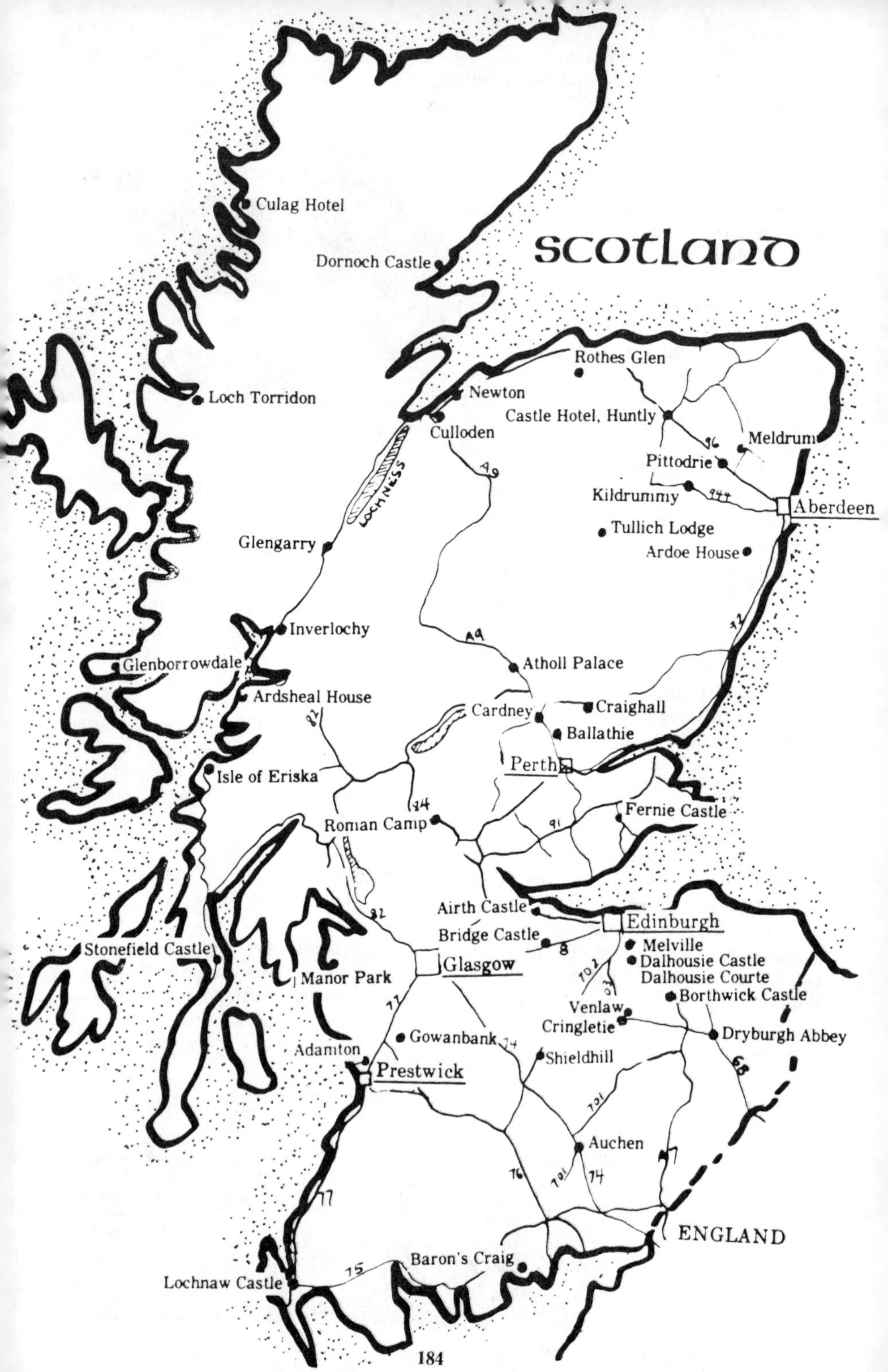
SCOTLAND
Culag Hotel
Dornoch Castle
Rothes Glen
Newton
Castle Hotel, Huntly
Meldrum
Culloden
Loch Torridon
LOCH NESS
Pittodrie
Kildrummy
Aberdeen
Tullich Lodge
Ardoe House
Glengarry
Inverlochy
Atholl Palace
Glenborrowdale
Ardsheal House
Cardney
Craighall
Ballathie
Perth
Isle of Eriska
Roman Camp
Fernie Castle
Airth Castle
Edinburgh
Bridge Castle
Melville
Dalhousie Castle
Dalhousie Courte
Stonefield Castle
Glasgow
Manor Park
Borthwick Castle
Venlaw
Cringletie
Dryburgh Abbey
Gowanbank
Adamton
Shieldhill
Prestwick
Auchen
ENGLAND
Baron's Craig
Lochnaw Castle

Ballathie House

Baron's Craig

hilltop, with a small lake, near the site of the orginal Auchen Castle of the 13th century. There is fishing in the stocked trout lake on the grounds, as well as tennis, golf, riding and sailing. Central heat. 37 rooms, all with baths. Open March-Oct. About 33 km N of Dumfries, 4 km S of Moffat. (II)

BALLATHIE HOUSE (E)
Kinclaven, by Stanley,
Perthshire (025083) 268

This mellowed stone towered baronial mansion built in 1850 stands in parklike grounds on the banks of the River Tay. Public and private rooms are tastefully furnished. There are 32 rooms with bath, in addition to three suites, all within the main hotel building. Also there are 14 bedrooms in a Chalet Block modern annex, designed mostly for fishing and grouse shooting parties, but suitable for families. Golf courses are nearby, and riding is available. The Perth Hunt Race is held twice a year and there is skiing at Glenshee and Aviemore. Deerstalking, handicap facilities. Central Heating. Open Jan.-Nov. Location is across the river from A93, N of Perth. (II)

BARON'S CRAIG Hotel (S)
Rockcliffe by Dal Beattie
Kirkcudbrightshire (055663) 225

A typical granite manor house built in the traditional Scottish castle style nearly a century ago. It stands on a rise in 12 acres of woods and gardens, with a view of Solway Firth and surrounding hills. Furnishings are largely antiques, and the 27 bedrooms have central heat as well as electric fires. Putting greens are on the grounds, a 9-hole golf course nearby, and a championship 18-hole course six miles away. Swimming, especially safe for children, and there is fishing in nearby lochs and rivers. Dining, bar, and other facilities. Open Easter-Oct. Rockcliffe is 11 km S of Dalbeattie and 35 km SW of Dumfries. Hotel cars will meet trains at Dumfries by arrangement. (II)

BORTHWICK Castle (SE)
Gorebridge,
Midlothian **Gorebridge 20514**

Built in 1430 by the first Lord Borthwick, the huge twin-towered castle was designed both for defense (walls up to 14 feet thick) and for elegance and comfort. Its 550 years have seen much history. A highlight was in 1567 when Mary Queen of

Borthwick Castle

Scots and her husband, the Earl of Bothwell, took refuge in the castle from their enemies. Bothwell, forewarned of a raid, escaped, followed by the Queen who, disguised as a page boy, departed through a small window in the Great Hall. Their apartment remains, and the chapel where she prayed is now part of the reception room. In 1650 the castle underwent a siege of Cromwell's cannon, and his letter of warning to the 10th Lord is still on display, and cannonball scars remain on the east wall. There are elegantly furnished public rooms such as the Great Hall and State Room, and private suites such as Lord Borthwick's bedchamber, a Mid-Dungeon Suite and others. Most have canopied beds and all have en suite bathrooms. Facilities are available for conferences. Cuisine features fresh salmon, Aberdeen Angus steaks and other specialties. Miss Helen Bailey, Keeper of the Castle, received the European Architectural Heritage Year Award from Queen Elizabeth, the Queen Mother, in 1975. Outside facilities include shooting, golf, sightseeing and walking. Location is 18 km S of Edinburgh. Guests can be met at Edinburgh Waverly Station, or the airport. (II)

BRIDGE Castle **(SE)**
Near Linlithgow,
West Lothian **Armadale 30228**

Erected in the 12th century to protect the road from the south to the royal palace of Linlithgow, 5 km away, the castle was later enlarged and extended, mostly in the 1500s. It came into the possession of Livingston, Earl of Linlithgow at that time. Dining specializes in Scottish and French cuisine. Riding, hunting available. Near A706, Armadale, S of Linlithgow, W of Edinburgh. (II)

CARDNEY House **(C)**
Dunkeld, Perthshire **Butterstone 222**

The laird and his wife (MacGregors) are hosts in this country mansion built in the 1700s. Rooms are comfortable. Extensive grounds. Fishing, golf, stalking, shoot-

Bridge Castle

Castle Hotel, Huntly

ing, tennis, riding and sailing. 23 rooms, 11 baths. About 5 km from the cathedral village of Dunkeld on Blairgowrie Rd A923. (II)

CASTLE Hotel (NE)
Huntly, Aberdeenshire (0466) 2696

Built by the Third Duke Gordon in 1752 as an adjunct to Huntly Castle, this ancestral home of the Gordon Clan now has become a modern hotel, though still maintaining its 18th century character. 4 poster beds, gardens. Much of the stone with which it was built came from nearby ancient Huntly Castle. Even in ruins, the medieval castle still is notable, and a major point of interest in this part of Scotland. The hotel has its own private stretch of the river Deveron for excellent fishing, and also offers golf, tennis, bowling and riding. Central heat. 26 rooms, 9 with baths. 64 km NW of Aberdeen. Open Mar-Dec. (II)

Craighall Estates

CRAIGHALL ESTATES (EC)
Blairgowrie, Perthshire

A castle, topped with chimney pots and spires, high on a bluff overlooking a river, Craighall offers a variety of self-catering guest apartments (flats). Some of the flats are furnished with antiques,. including four-poster beds. Bookings usually are made for the high

Cringletie House

season (July-Sept) or low season (Sept-Oct). Cottages are also available. Blairgowrie is at the southern edge of the Highlands on Rd 93, about 25 km N of Perth.

CRINGLETIE HOUSE Hotel **(SC)**
Peebles, Eddlestone
Peebleshire **(07213) 233**

This old Scottish baronial sandstone mansion thrusts its cone-roofed towers up to greet the visitor approaching the long drive from the main road from Peebles to Edinburgh. The castle-like building stands amid acres of woodlands. There is no reception desk; guests ring the bell for service; the atmosphere is country house rather than hotel. Bar, sitting rooms. Some of the rooms have fireplaces and turret windows. Putting, croquet, tennis are offered as well as golf and fishing nearby. Six of the 14 rooms have private baths. Central heat, electric blankets, elevator. Open mid-Mar-Oct 31, plus Christmas and New Year holidays On A703. (I-II)

CULAG Hotel **(NW)**
Lochinver, Sutherland **(05714) 209**

Located on the shore of Lochinver Bay with a pier at its feet, this towering old mansion was built prior to 1845 as the private residence of the Duke of Sutherland. Much of the food for its notable cuisine is taken from its own private gardens, and from the lochs and sea around. Lounge bar. Guests also can enjoy fishing for brown trout, sea trout and salmon in areas that are restocked continuously. Fishing boats ply to and from the pier daily. 45 rooms, central heat and elevator. Lochinver is about 75 km W of Lairg from which there are daily buses, and 160 km NW of Inverness. (II)

CULLODEN HOUSE **(N)**
Near A96, Inverness **(0463) 72461**

This estate was originally owned by the Chief of the Mackintosh clan and Bonnie Prince Charlie stayed in the original

Culag Hotel

castle the night before the great Battle of Culloden (1746). The present palace (the original was later burned), dates from about 1772. Some vaults and rooms of the original structure are incorporated in the present one. It is close to Loch Ness in the Highlands, and the Moray Firth. The guest rooms, including two luxurious Prince's rooms, are furnished in period style, and with baths en suite. Traditional Scottish food is served. Central heat. Reading room, salmon and trout fishing, golf at Inverness, deer stalking. 22 rooms. Culloden House is 3 km E of Inverness, S of the A96. Turn off at sign "Smithton, Culloden and Ballach"; 1½ km down this road. Hotel car service from Inverness Airport (8 km) by arrangement. (III)

Culloden House

DALHOUSIE Castle (SE)
Bonnyrigg (0875) 20 153

This 13th century castle offers highly rated hotel facilities. Standing amid open meadows and woodlands, the castle, still owned by the Earl of Dalhousie, is in a lovely setting. There is an attractive bridal suite in one of the towers, and a bar in the dungeon. 24 rooms with baths, color TV, nearby golf, fishing, shooting, riding. 8 km SE of Edinburgh, off A7. Watch for signs. (III)

DORNOCH Castle (N)
Dornoch, Sutherland (086281) 216

Ancient Dornoch Castle has dominated this seaside town since the mid-13th century. The tall massive stone building was mostly rebuilt in the mid-1500s, and today encloses 21 comfortable and well-furnished rooms. Views are of the mountains or across the Dornoch Firth and the North Sea. The grounds include gardens, and some of the castle's own foods are grown here. Central heat supplemented by electric fires, elevator, bar, lounges. Swimming and golf are nearby. A new wing was added recently. Open May-Sept. (II)

Dalhousie Castle

Dornoch Castle

Dryburgh Abbey

DRYBURGH ABBEY Hotel (SE)
St. Boswells,
Roxburghshire TD6 ORQ (083) 52 2261

Situated in the rolling hills of the Borders, this old towered mansion stands on the banks of the River Tweed. There is an ancient vaulted room of hewn stone where guests can relax by a fireplace, special menus feature fresh produce from the hotel's own gardens, and public and private rooms are well appointed, some with canopy beds. A scenic point, Scott's View is nearby, and there are interesting walking trails as well as points of interest for short car journeys. Fishing on the river, golf, shooting, riding, putting greens, and croquet are offered. Conference facilities. Open all year, 26 rooms. Location is N of St. Boswells, just E of B6356. (II)

Fernie Castle

FERNIE CASTLE Hotel (E)
Letham, Ladybank, Fife (033781) 209

Now a small luxury hotel, the castle was first documented in 1353 when it belonged to Duncan the 13th Earl of Fife. Although many alterations were made through the ensuing centuries, the 16th century fortalice (outer defenses), slit windows, and watchtower are still notable. The walls of the original structure are so thick that a modern bathroom was cut out of one wall. The lead bath in the East Wing, and the ice house in the rear, are examples of medieval items, few of which remain in this century. Some 4 poster beds. The castle now has central heating, air conditioning, and offers trout and salmon fishing, and golf. The Ladybank Golf Club is 2 miles away; St. Andrews is 25 min. away by car. 11 rooms and baths. Route A914, N of Ladybank, and about 1 km NE of Letham. (II)

Glenborrowdale Castle

GLENBORRODALE Castle (W)
Ardnamurchan (09724) 266

The towered and castellated structure, though built at the turn of the century, evokes the typical Scottish baronial stronghold, and indeed stands on the site of an earlier castle. Restaurant features specialties of the area including seafood and venison. The castle is beside Loch Sunart, in its own 120 acres of rugged countryside. In the western Highlands, there is hiking country, sailing, ferry service on various lakes and sounds. Picnic trips to the seal islands can be arranged. 35 rooms. Open Apr-Oct. A Trust House Forte hotel. Location is W of Fort William and Glencoe, near Rt. 8007, on the mainland just N of the island of Mull. (II)

Glengarry Castle

GLENGARRY CASTLE Hotel (N)
Invergarry,
Inverness-shire **Invergarry 254**

In the center of the Highlands, and 13 km south of Loch Ness with its legendary Monster, Glengarry Castle offers spacious and comfortable accommodations. On the broad grounds of the century-old baronial residence, are the imposing ruins of Invergarry Castle, seat of the MacDonnells of Glengarry. Trout fishing can be done in Loch Oich on the grounds where also canoeing and boating are offered. There are tennis courts, and walking trails, lounge with log-burning fireplace, spacious dining room and central heat. Open Apr-Oct. 30 rooms, also furnished cottages for let on the grounds. (II)

Gowanbank Hotel

GOWANBANK Hotel (SW)
Darvel, Ayrshire **Darvel 20533**

This castle-like, century-old mansion, has been converted to a hotel, with its owners, Mr. and Mrs. John Taylor, recreating the period style of the late 19th century. There is a Hunting Room restaurant for noontime snacks or three-course lunch, traditional Scottish High Tea is served between 5 and 7 p.m. and dinner is in the French style restaurant. Good salmon fishing and game hunting can be arranged. 7 rooms, all with baths, central heating. Location is high on the crest of the Irvine Valley in 7 acres of woodland. Just off A71, Ayr-Edinburgh road. (II)

INVERLOCHY CASTLE (N)
Fort William,
Inverness-shire **(0397) 2177**

Massive square stone towers with merlons and battlements characterize this Highland mansion, built more than a century ago. It commands long mountain views from its hilltop site. Elegantly furnished in both public and private rooms, it also has a notable great central

Inverlochy Castle

hall with frescoed ceiling. Built by the first Lord Abinger in 1863, it is close to the ruins of the 13th century Inverlochy Castle which is open to visitors. Not only is the hotel typically elegant Victorian, but in 1873 Queen Victoria with her daughter and retinue stayed a week as guests in the mansion. There are 50 acres of woodlands around it and salmon and trout fishing are available, as are also deer stalking and grouse shooting. Ben Nevis, one of Scotland's highest mountains, is close by. Inverlochy has won awards for its hotel and restaurant qualities. 11 rooms with baths. 4½ km N of Fort William on A82. (III)

ISLE OF ERISKA Hotel (W)
Ledaig, Connel,
Strathclyde (0631-72) 205

The castle-like towered and crenellated hotel is on an island about a mile long in the mouth of Loch Creran. There is some wildlife in the parklike setting, as well as gardens where produce is grown for the cuisine. An iron bridge and flower-lined driveway form the approach to the castle with its views of the Firth of Lorne and the mountains of Mull. Spacious rooms, period furniture, log fires, library, bar, riding, boating, fishing, tennis, croquet, nearby golf. 24 rooms with baths. Open Apr. to end of Nov. Location is about 19 km N of Oban. (III)

Isle of Eriska

KILDRUMMY CASTLE Hotel (NE)
Kildrummy, Mossat,
Aberdeenshire (03365) 288

The hotel, built on a beautiful site as a country mansion in 1900, takes its name from Kildrummy Castle which it faces on the opposite side of the River Don. The castle, built in 1245, was a leading stronghold through the centuries until it was finally abandoned in 1716. Since then it has become a historic monument and is open to visitors. (Glenbuchat Castle, built in 1590, also a historic site, is 7½ km from Kildrummy.) Kildrummy Castle Hotel offers fine accommodations and a varied menu, in an authentic Scottish country setting. Bar, 24 beds, many rooms with baths. Salmon and trout fishing. It is surrounded by beautiful grounds, and offers easy access to the Highlands. Open Easter-Dec. 56 km W of Aberdeen, near Alford; 4 km S of Mossat off A97. (I-III)

LOCHNAW CASTLE (SW)
Leswalt by Stranraer,
Wigtownshire 227

Dating from 1426, Lochnaw is one of the best preserved of the Scottish 15th century castles. It stands on a 160-acre estate on the edge of its private lake. Lovely antiques enhance the guests' rooms, reflecting the authentic historical setting. Squash, trout fishing, golf and beaches nearby. Ferries to Northern Ireland embark from Stranraer, and there is express train service from London. The area also has other interesting castles, including 16th century Galdenoch Castle. Location is 7½ km from the center of town. 6 rooms. Leswalt is about 3 km NW of Stranraer. (II)

Kildrummy Castle

LOCH TORRIDON Hotel (NW)
Torridon, Ross-shire Torridon 242

Many activities are offered by this old stone towered mansion located on the inlet from the sea called Loch Torridon. These include golf, trout and salmon fishing, sailing, croquet, tennis, mountaineering, hiking, deer stalking and others. The hotel is situated in the 33,000 acre Ben Damph Estate, one of the largest sporting areas in the western Highlands. Spacious public and private rooms, log fires, bar and other facilities. 28 rooms, most with private baths. About 32 km N of Stromeferry on the west coast. (II)

Loch Torridon

MANOR PARK Hotel (W)
Skelmorlie, Ayreshire (0475) 520832

The old mansion, of early Victorian vintage, is in a setting of lovely flower gardens and views of the nearby bay of Firth. The dining room has a popular menu and wine list, and serves the surrounding area as well as hotel guests. There is a bar, central heating, air conditioning. 14 rooms, most with baths,

Lochnaw Castle

Manor Park

Meldrum House

Melville Castle

and self-catering apts also available. Open Feb-Dec. On A78 just S of Wemyss Bay on the E side of the Firth of Clyde. (II)

MELDRUM HOUSE **(NE)**
Old Meldrum,
Aberdeenshire **(06512) 294**

A private castle, owned and operated by the Scottish Laird, Robin Duff, this 740-year-old towered and fortified residence has been a comfortable and personal hotel since the 1950s. The small, turreted castle has walls six feet thick, sections dating from 1236, and has been in the same family for nearly seven and one-half centuries. Its cuisine, supervised personally by the Laird, has won renown. Most of the produce is raised in the castle's own walled gardens. 9 rooms, central heat, open Apr-mid-Nov. Old Meldrum is about 32 km NW of Aberdeen on A947. (II)

MELVILLE CASTLE **(SE)**
Lasswade, Midlothian **(031) 663 6633**

A castle has stood on this site since medieval times and the present one, completed in 1788, stands on foundations of an earlier one. Today it is a mansion house set in beautiful woods along the North Esk River. The interior is notable for the spacious pillared entrance and an elegant "hanging" staircase surmounted by a lovely painted ceiling. The castle is referred to in Sir Walter Scott's writings, and it has long been the residence of nobility, also being visited by George IV. A bar and dining room have been built in the ancient wine cellars under the castle. Facilities include tennis, bowling and golf. 25 rooms. Located 16 km SE of Edinburgh. (II)

NEWTON Hotel **(N)**
Nairn **(0667) 53144**

The baronial style, towered stone edifice, with many gables and battlements, stands in 27 acres of grounds running

Newton Hotel

Pittodrie House

down to a golf course and the sea. More sun and less rain mark this area of the Highlands, and activities include golf on the Nairn championship course adjoining the grounds, plus another 18-hole course, putting greens, tennis, fishing, grouse shooting and skiing. Visits can be made to nearby tweed mills and distilleries, as well as to Cawder Castle. Central heat, handicap facilities, elevator, lounges with open fireplaces, notable cuisine. 44 rooms with baths. 24 km NE of Inverness on the Moray Firth. (II)

PITTODRIE HOUSE Hotel (NE)
Pitcaple, Aberdeenshire (04676) 202

Dating back to 1480 and going through many changes, this private castle-like residence was converted to a hotel in 1977 by the owner, G.R.T. Smith. It maintains the character of a private house and family furnishings and antiques have been left. Bedrooms are individually furnished, most have private baths and some have four-poster beds. The estate is secluded and quiet, near Bennachie Mountain, in an area steeped in history. The castle garden is over 200 years old and is divided by 20-foot-high holly hedges. Vegetables for the varied menu are grown here. Fishing, rough shooting, deer stalking on advance notice. 33 km NW of Aberdeen, 3 km W of the A96. (II)

ROMAN CAMP Hotel (C)
Callander, Perthshire
FK17 8BG (0877) 30003

Built in 1625 as a hunting lodge for the Dukes of Perth, the lodge resembles a small French chateau, mainly because of its towers with conical roofs. The name derives from military construction on the site in 142 AD by Roman legionaries of

Roman Camp

Antonius Pius. Defense embankments from that period are still visible. The present estate was acquired in 1908 by the 2nd Viscount Esher, advisor to Queen Victoria. Later owned by Lady Wilson, who restored the 20 acres of grounds and gardens. It is now owned and run by the Wood family. Public areas include dining room, bar, drawing room, glass-enclosed patio, oak paneled library with sculptured plaster ceiling, and a chapel. It offers: fishing in private run of River Teith on the grounds, 18 hole golf 1 km, Gleneagles course is 40 km, walks to waterfalls, mountain crags and forests. 11 rooms, most with baths. Callander is 88 km NW of Edinburgh; 12 and 25 km respectively from Doune and Stirling Castles that are open to visitors. Transport arranged from Stirling station or Glasgow or Edinburgh airports. (II)

ROTHES GLEN Hotel (NE)
Rothes, Morayshire (03403) 254

Located at the head of the Glen of Rothes, this country seat has a lovely character with its numerous conical towers, a massive square castellated tower and its many chimneys. The building was designed by the architect who built Balmoral Castle, one of the residences of the English monarchs. Completely refurbished recently, the hotel still retains its ancient character with many period pieces of furniture and art. There are 40 acres of land in the hotel's domain, and within 20 miles there are seven golf courses, and a nine-hole putting course on the grounds. Deer stalking, and private salmon fishing can be arranged on the Spey River, and quiet fishing villages of Moray and Banffshire are just north on the Firth of Forth. Dining rooms, bar, central heat and other facilities complete the amenities. 20 rooms, some with bath. Open Mar-Nov. About 9 km S of Elgin and 5 km N of Rothes on A941. (I-II)

SHIELDHILL HOUSE Hotel (S)
Quothquan, Biggar,
Lanarkshire (0899) 20035

The Shieldhill property has been owned by the Chancellor family since about 1185 and the present castle-manor house has evolved over a period of 750 years. It stands in 10 acres of parkland with views of the River Clyde and the Lanarkshire Hills. Lounges, bars, log fires in season, restaurants featuring local produce, central heat. Trout fishing and golf available. 20 rooms. Biggar is on Rt. 702 and 701. (II)

Rothes Glen

Stonefield Castle

STONEFIELD CASTLE Hotel (W)
Tarbert, Loch Fyne, Argyll (08802) 207

Overlooking Loch Fyne in a setting of 100 acres of private parkland ablaze with rare Chinese rhododendrons, rare shrubs and ancient trees, Stonefield Castle offers accommodations in the Scottish country tradition. The present castle was built in 1837, replacing an earlier ancestral home of the McAlisters and later the Campbells. It remained a private residence until 1949 when it was adapted as a hotel. It now has an elevator, central heating, fine public rooms including a library, and offers tennis, putting clock golf, sailing, shooting, heated pool, sea bathing, and deer stalking. Sauna, conference rooms, beauty shop, handicap facilities. Open Easter-Oct. 34 rooms most with baths. Reached by road, or daily mail boat from Gourock; 3 km from Tarbert; 80 km S of Oban. (I-II)

Tullich Lodge

TULLICH LODGE Hotel (NE)
Ballater, Aberdeenshire (03382) 406

At the top of a steep, winding drive stands turreted Tullich Lodge, dominated by its square tower and battlements. Its setting is in five acres of woodland garden with good views of surrounding Royal Deeside scenery. Beautifully furnished rooms are a feature of this country house. Good food is served in the walnut paneled dining hall, and there is a large variety of whiskies in the bar. Rooms for 20 guests all have private showers or baths, with central heating. Location is above the Aberdeen-Braemar Road (A93), 64 km W of Aberdeen and 2 km E of Ballater. The Queen's royal castle, Balmoral, is about 16 km away. (II)

Venlaw Castle

VENLAW CASTLE (S)
Edinburgh Rd.
Peebles, Peebleshire **Peebles 20384**

A typical towered mansion, Venlaw Castle, built 1782, is just north of Peebles in the heart of Scotland's lowlands, and

Dalhousie Courte

from the top of its wooded hill dominates the surrounding countryside. It stands on the site of a much older castle, destroyed during the upheavals of Medieval Scotland. A few miles from Venlaw, Neidpath Castle still stands as a reminder of those times. Excellent accommodations at a moderate price, central heat and wonderful scenery are offered at Venlaw, but its great charm is the spacious guest rooms, most of them with fine views of gardens and woods. On clear days great portions of the lowlands may be seen, while at night the illuminated castle shows its impressive mass to travelers miles away. Open Mar-Oct. 16 rooms. 40 km S of Edinburgh. (I-II)

MEDIEVAL BANQUETS

DALHOUSIE COURTE, Cockpen, Bonnyrigg, 5-6 km SE of Edinburgh. Jacobean banquet. This is about 1½ km from Dalhousie Castle. (031) 663 5155.

Spain

Parador de los Condes (NW)
ALBA y ALISTE
Plaza de Canovas,
Zamora **Tel. (988) 51 44 97**

Much of the ancient splendor of the old monastery, built in 1459, has been preserved. There is a monumental staircase with Lombard carvings, and a Renaissance cloister. Weapons and banners on display, and armored knights astride horses add to the fantasy of the Middle Ages in this government parador. Air conditioning, swimming pool and other amenities remind the guest of the 20th century. Zamora is about 250 km NW of Madrid. (I-II)

Parador ALCAZAR del (S)
REY DON PEDRO
Carmona (Sevilla) **(954) 25 32 60**

This massive feudal castle was the seat of Pedro I, King of Spain (1350-69), who was also known as Peter the Cruel. The whole town is a national monument, and part of it is still enclosed by walls with Roman gates. The parador was opened by the government in 1976 and is 4-star rated. 55 rooms, many with balconies. (I-II)

Alba y Aliste

Par. Alcazar del Rey Don Pedro

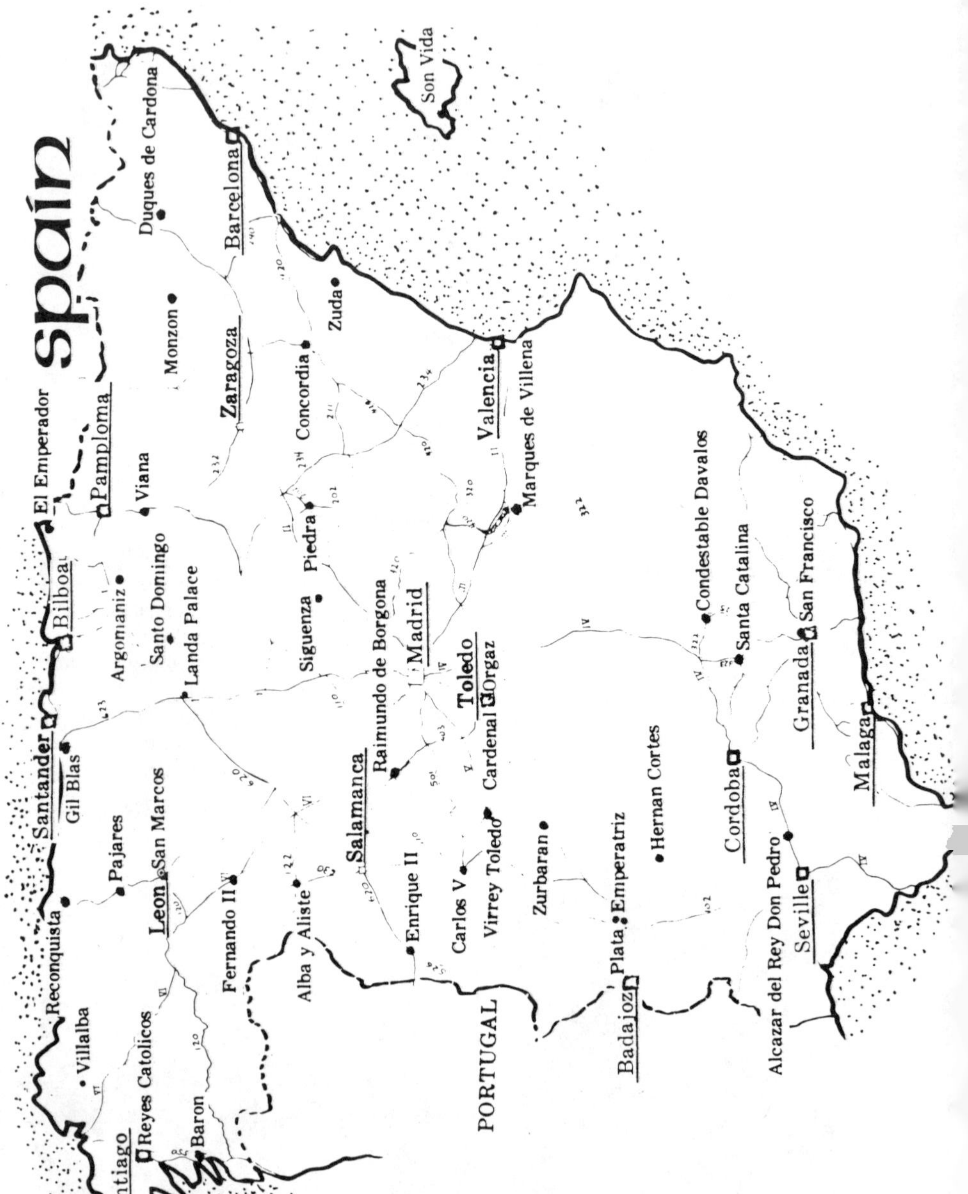
Spain
El Emperador
Pamploma
Bilboa
Santander
Gil Blas
Reconquista
Villalba
Santiago
Reyes Catolicos
Baron
Pajares
Leon
San Marcos
Fernando II
Alba y Aliste
Argomaniz
Santo Domingo
Landa Palace
Viana
Zaragoza
Monzon
Concordia
Zuda
Piedra
Siguenza
Salamanca
Raimundo de Borgona
Madrid
Toledo
Cardenal Orgaz
Enrique II
Carlos V
Virrey Toledo
PORTUGAL
Zurbaran
Plata
Emperatriz
Badajoz
Hernan Cortes
Cordoba
Alcazar del Rey Don Pedro
Seville
Granada
Malaga
San Francisco
Santa Catalina
Condestable Davalos
Valencia
Marques de Villena
Barcelona
Duques de Cardona
Son Vida

Parador de ARGOMANIZ **(N)**
Argomaniz (Alava) **(945) 24 22 00**

This parador is in an old converted palace in this small town in the northern part of Spain near the French border. It is a picturesque location, about 2,000 ft. above sea level, and some 60 km S of San Sebastian. 3 star hotel. Central heat, garden. 54 rooms. (I)

Parador Casa del BARON **(NW)**
21 Maceda, Pontevedra **(986) 85 58 00**

Former castle-palace of the Counts of Maceda, this 17th century mansion is located in the old quarter of a picturesque town of ruined walls, street arcades and ancient houses. Central heating, bar. 47 rooms. 34 km N of Vigo toward Santiago. (I)

Par. Casa del Baron

Hostal del CARDENAL **(C)**
Paseo de Recaredo, 24
Toledo **(925) 22 08 62**

This former palace of Cardinal Lorenzana, Archbishop of Toledo in the 1700s, now offers elegant accommodations, just inside the city walls about 100 yards from the main city gate. The beautiful courtyard, and patios, with trees, shrubs, flowers, fountains and walkways make a quiet place for alfresco refreshments. Lovely dining and public rooms, and a highly rated restaurant add to the enjoyment. Suckling pig and lamb, roasted in the big oven in the old Castillian manner, and other specialties of the region, including special marzepan desserts, are served. From its location adjacent to the old town walls a guest can traverse the catwalks of the defenses of the ancient Spanish capital. 27 rooms, all with baths. (I)

Parador CARLOS V **(WC)**
Jarandilla de la Vera
(Caceres) **(927) 56 01 17**

Dating from the 1300s, this state-operated restored castle was built by Alvarez

Hostal del Cardenal

Parador Carlos V

Parador La Concordia

de Toledo, and was the residence of Carlos V (Charles V of the Holy Roman Empire, and Charles I of Spain). Medieval furnishings, four-poster beds, armor, and other traditional objects add to the charm of the massive walls, turrets and battlements. There is an open patio, a fountain, and surround gardens and woods. Facilities include a lounge, bar, library, swimming pool and central heat. 23 rooms with baths. Located at the foot of the Gredos Mountains, about 216 km W of Madrid; about 60 km NW of Oropesa. (I)

Parador la CONCORDIA (NE)
Alcaniz (Teruel) (974) 13 04 00

Situated in a historic medieval 13th century style "Castle of the Calatravos", this four-star hotel offers air conditioned comfort as well as central heat, restaurant, bar and interesting surroundings. High ceilings mark the dining room, lounges and guest rooms. The castle, part of which is still in ruins, dominates the town's hilltop. 12 rooms. Alcaniz is 100 km SE of Zaragoza. (I-II)

Par. Condestable Davalos

Parador (S)
CONDESTABLE DAVALOS
Plaza Vasquez de Molina
Ubeda (Jaen) (953) 75 03 45

Like many of the old Spanish palaces, this parador has a somewhat plain exterior which conceals a beautiful interior court with carved stonework, a veritable greenhouse of plants, a monumental staircase, and other typical Spanish accoutrements. Built in the 1500s as the palace of Dean Ortega, it was adapted as a hotel in 1930 and now has central heat, bar, and other amenities. Sr. Ortega also built the adjacent Church of the Savior, which you may visit if you can locate the family living in its confines at the rear which has the keys. Surrounding mountain country offers fine scenery and hunting and fishing. 25 rooms and baths. 3-star rating. About 50 km NE of Jaen. (I)

Parador HERNAN CORTES (SW)
Plaza de Maria Cristina
Zafra (Badajoz) (924) 55 02 00

A massive castle-fortress whose construction began in 1437 as the feudal seat of the Dukes of Feria. Cortes lived in the castle before setting out for the New World to become the conqueror of Mexico. Notable is the octagonal gothic chapel with flamboyant 15th century decor, and the Golden Room of the same period. The castle is square with a round tower at each corner, two towers flanking the entrance, and a massive round keep in the rear. A typical open court occupies the center area. Narrow winding shopping streets of the town are within a block or two of the castle. Lounges, bar, garden, swimming pool, central heating and air conditioning, are included in this four-star hotel. 28 rooms with bath. Zafra is about 66 km SE of Badajoz and about 130 km N of Seville. (I)

Parador Hernan Cortes

Parador DUQUES de CARDONA (NE)
Cardona (Barcelona) (938) 69 12 75

The original fortress church was begun in 789 A.D. by King Ludovico Pio, and rebuilt in 981. The present massive castle-like complex was erected in its place in 1020-1040 by Bremundo, Viscount of Cardona. Many battles have raged around it, but the castle has never been conquered. It was once owned by Ramon Folch, nephew of Charlemagne, whose descendants are entombed here. This is said to be a perfect example of Romanesque architecture in Spain, and since 1931 it has been protected as a national monument. A gothic court and chapel, part of the original structure have been converted into a museum. It was only in 1976 that it was opened as a government-run parador, quartering guests in 65 rooms, all with private bath. Good food and accommodations are typical of the paradores. Cardona is 96 km N of Barcelona city via Monserrat and Manresa. (I-II)

Par. Duques de Cardona

Parador El Emperador

Parador el EMPERADOR (N)
Plaza de Armas
Fuenterrabia (Guipuzcoa) (943) 64 21 40

A government-operated parador, that was opened in 1968, in the old castle-fortress of Charles V, Holy Roman Emperor and King of Spain (1519-1556). The castle was also called "Palace of the Captains". Central heat, bar, reading room and other facilities. 16 rooms. It is in the extreme northern corner of Spain, near the French border, about 65 km N of Pamplona. (I)

Hotel Emperatriz

Hotel EMPERATRIZ (SW)
Plaza de Espana 19
Merida (Badajoz) (924) 30 26 40

Located on the main square in this historic Roman city, the 15th century palace offers a quiet central court, beautiful stone arcades, staircases and vaulted rooms -- a notable example of architecture of the period. The town's stone arch bridge, Puento Sobre el Rio Guadiana, dating from Roman times, is still in use. Other Roman remains include an Arch of Trajan, a theatre and an amphitheatre. Central heat. 44 rooms with bath. Main road between Madrid and Seville, 55 km E of Badajoz. (I)

Parador Enrique II

Parador ENRIQUE II (W)
1 Castillo
Ciudad Rodrigo
(Salamanca) (923) 46 01 50

The great square keep of this 15th century castle dominates the old walled town as you approach across the plains. The old fortress is built into the town wall, and you can walk completely around the town on top of the wall in a little over an hour. Below the castle flows a river, crossed by stone bridges, where black-clad local women do the family wash along the banks. The walls are partly Roman but mostly 12th century, and the whole town is a National Historic Monument, but nevertheless a bustling busy community. Air conditioning, central heating, bar. 28 rooms. Rt. 620, 90 km SW of Salamanca. (I)

Parador Enrique II

Par. Rey Fernando II de Leon ↑
↓

Parador Rey (NW)
FERNANDO II de LEON
Benevente (Zamora) (988) 63 03 00

The historic building has a most impressive, spacious, stone reception area and bar, with massive beams and vaulted alcoves, decorated with wall medallions and tapestries. Facilities include air conditioning, central heat, restaurant, garden, hunting and fishing. 30 rooms. Benavente is 65 km N of Zamora. (I-II)

Parador de GIL BLAS (N)
Plaza Ramon Pelayo 11
Santillana del Mar
(Santander) (942) 81 80 00

A government-operated hotel with good accommodations and meals, located in a 16th century palace in a medieval village on the sea. The village has grown up around the 6th century monastery of Santa Illana. Designated a National Monument, it is one of the most picturesque villages in Spain. Nearby are the Caves of Altamira, famed for their prehistoric color paintings dating back possibly 20,000 years. Central heat, bar. 24 rooms. 30 km W of Santander. (I)

Parador de Gil Blas

LANDA PALACE **(NC)**
Burgos **(947) 20 63 43**

This massive square keep, adjoined by an old palace, offers comfort with a 5-star rating. There is a good restaurant, indoor and outdoor pools, air conditioning, central heat, tennis, fishing, and an elevator. 39 rooms, all with baths. (II)

Landa Palace

Parador Castillo de MONZON **(NE)**
Monzon de Campos
(Palencia) **(988) 80 80 75**

Monzón is a massive, virtually windowless 12th century castle atop a mountain. Its guest rooms look inward to a Spanish enclosed court, but the dining room grudgingly provides a panoramic view. 3-star, 10 rooms, garage, restaurant, central heat, open all year. About 30 km N of town of Palencia. (I-II)

Par. Castillo de Monzón

Parador Conde de ORGAZ **(C)**
Paseo de los Cigarrales,
Toledo **(925) 22 18 50**

This four-star parador, recently built, is included here because of its convenient location at Toledo, and for its spectacular site overlooking that old walled city. The town is nestled within the big U-shaped bend of the river, and the parador is across the river at the base of the U, south of the town. It is on a high hill overlooking the whole scene. Many of the 22 rooms have private balconies. Restaurant, bar, central heat, air conditioned. (I-II)

Par. Conde de Orgaz

Parador Puerto de PAJARES **(NW)**
Pajares (Oviedo) **(985) 47 36 25**

This parador, with a high tower typical of the architecture of the region, is situated high in the mountains of northwestern Spain, providing sweeping views of peaks and valleys. Fishing and mountaineering, hunting available. 30 rooms. Central heat. Pajares is about 49 km S of town of Oviedo, and 58 km N of Leon. (I)

Monasterio de PIEDRA (EC)
2 Nuevalos
Piedra (Zaragoza) (976) 84 90 11

A well-preserved monastery founded in the 12th century by Cistercian monks, this hostelry now offers an unforgettable experience for the 20th century traveler. The 800-year-old Torre del Homenaje (Tower of Homage) especially is a Romanesque-Byzantine landmark. There is a great staircase, the monastery kitchen, gothic cloisters and other sections of architectural and historic interest. The first class hotel offers rooms which were once monks' cells, with sunny private galleries. Tennis courts, swimming pool, waterfalls, lakes, grottoes, air conditioning, central heat and bar. 61 rooms. Open April-Oct. Between Madrid and Zaragoza; 22 km SE of Alhama de Aragon. (I)

Par. Puerto de Pajares

Monasterio de Piedra

Parador Via de la PLATA (SW)
Plaza Queipo de Liano 3
Merida (Badajoz) (924) 30 15 40

An old convent with elements going back to ancient times forms this government parador. You will see storks nesting on the chimneys of this four-star hotel, but otherwise a rather plain exterior hides charming interior courts, arcades and archways, decorated with antiquities including many Roman artifacts. Some of the columns are Visigothic with Arabic inscriptions. The town dates from Roman times with a stone bridge, aqueduct and other remains. Air conditioning, central heat and bar. 45 rooms with bath. 60 km E of Badajoz. (I-II)

Par. Via de la Plata

Parador RAIMUNDO de BORGONA (C)
Marques de Canales y Chozas 16
Avila (918) 21 13 40

This ancient town, surrounded by a spectacular wall with 88 towers and keeps (and 2500 merlons, if you care to count them), is a landmark of the plains of Castile. It is one of the finest examples

Par. Raimundo de Borgona

Los Reyes Catolicos

of military construction surviving from the Middle Ages. The city was recaptured from the Moors some five centuries ago by Raymond of Burgundy, whose name was given to this government parador located in the northern section of the walls. It was originally the Palacio de Piedras Albas (White Stone Palace), but much of it was rebuilt about 70 years ago. It surrounds a court and includes a square tower in which some of the guest rooms are located. Lounges and rooms are furnished in the rustic style. Elevator, central heat, bar and shops. 27 rooms and baths. 100 km NW of Madrid. (1)

Hotel de la RECONQUISTA (NW)
Gil de Jaz, 16, Oviedo (985) 24 11 00

A modern 5-star hotel has been created within the elegant royal palace constructed in the mid-1700s. Superbly furnished rooms, public and private are accented by grand staircases, carved wood ceilings, collonaded courts and arcades. There is a restaurant and grill with private salons, snack bar, American bar, gym, sauna, air conditioning, shopping arcades within the palace complex. Convention facilities. Nearby are golf, riding, tennis, game hunting such as wild boar, lake excursions and river fishing. It is located in the center area of Ovieta, which is not far from picturesque coastal towns. (II-III)

Los REYES CATOLICOS (NW)
Plaza de Espana, 1
Santiago de Compostela
(Coruna) (981) 58 22 00

A monumental gothic-renaissance complex built in 1499 by Ferdinand and Isabella as a shelter for pilgrims. Its elegant carved stone portals, facades, cloisters, sculptures, some 600 canvases, coffered ceilings, canopied beds and authentic antique furnishings still make it a favorite stopping place for 20th century travelers. Restaurants, and a wide range of accommodations for dorm-

Hotel de la Reconquista

Parador de San Francisco

San Marcos

itories to royal suites are available in this five-star hotel, including air conditioning central heat, shops, beauty parlor and bar. 157 rooms. The town is 65 km S of La Coruna on Rt 550. (II-III)

Parador de SAN FRANCISCO (S)
Bosques de la Alhambra
Granada (958) 22 14 62

Though a first class hotel, this ancient palace and monastery also is a first rate sightseeing spot among Spain's many historic monuments. One of the oldest buildings in the Alhambra, it was rebuilt in the 14th century by Yusuf I, and in 15th century it became a Franciscan monastery. Since 1945 it has been a popular hotel, providing an authentic historic Spanish setting of elegant interior, cloisters, arches, towers and exquisite gardens. Air conditioning, central heat, bar, 26 rooms. Make reservations as early as possible. 110 km NE of Malaga. (I-II)

SAN MARCOS (NW)
Plaza de San Marcos, 7
Leon (987) 23 73 00

Built in the 1500s, this old palace of the Knights of St. James is now one of Europe's fine five-star hotels. Beautifully furnished rooms have different styles and periods, with many antiques and art objects. Setting is in spacious gardens and terraces, and food includes regional specialties. Air conditioning, central heat, swimming pool, elevator, beauty parlor and bar. Over 250 rooms with bath. 100 km S of Oviedo. (II)

Castillo de SANTA CATALINA (S)
Jaen (953) 23 22 87

Spectacularly situated on a mountain top, this parador has been built into the complex of a 10th century castle of the Moorish Kings. If you make an inquiry, you can explore the old castle areas with a caretaker-guide, walk along the walls, climb the towers, and enjoy some spectacular views of the old city below, the olive groves and mountains. In the great keep you will discover that the high arching brick and stone vaulting has been repeated in a larger scale in the main lounge of the more recently built parador. Styled to blend with the medieval castle, the furnishings are done with taste, and the dining room looks like a knights' hall. A four-star hotel, its food and wines are a blend of typical Andulus-

Castillo de Santa Catalina ↑ ↓

ian specialties as well as of La Mancha. Greatly enlarged recently, it now has more than 60 rooms, many with balconies. Air conditioning, central heat, bar. 95 km N of Granada. (I-II)

Parador SANTO DOMINGO de la CALZADA (N)
Santo Domingo (Logrono) (941) 34 03 00

The parador has derived from a 12th

Par. Santo Domingo de la Calzada

century monastery and stopping place for pilgrims. The patron saint who built it also erected a causeway or bridge (calzada) from which the town took its name and which still stands. Central heat, bar, 27 rooms. 69 km E of Burgos and 42 km W of Logrono. (I)

Parador Castillo de SIGUENZA (C)
Siguenza (Guadalajara) (911) 39 01 00

The whole town of Siguenza is a Spanish National Monument, and the parador is built within the great 12th century castle-fortress. The towers and battlements rise above the town providing guests with a broad view. 4-star, restaurant, bar, air conditioning, central heat, 66 rooms. About 130 km NE of Madrid. (I-II)

Hotel SON VIDA (E)
Palma de Mallorca (971) 23 23 40

Except for a turreted tower and some battlement-topped walls, this five-star hotel has a modern look about it belying its history. Standing for several centuries, it was recognized as one of the most important houses on the island of Mallor-

Par. Castillo de Siguenza

Hotel Son Vida

Par. Principe de Viana

Condes de Villalba

ca (Majorca) by 1701. A century later it was so badly damaged in a storm that its upper story was removed. Enjoying the hospitality of Son Vida have been such personages as Edward VII, Isabel of Bourbon, and more recently, Gen. Franco. It was transformed into the present deluxe five-star hotel with air-conditioning, central heating, totally fitted with private baths, and completely modernized in 1961 when Prince Rainier and Princess Grace of Monaco officially opened it. Tennis, riding, golf, swimming pool and 1400 acres of private sub-tropical park. 175 rooms. 9 km from Palma. (III)

Parador Principe de VIANA **(N)**
Plaza de San Francisco
Olite (Navarra) **(948) 74 00 00**

Built within a medieval royal castle's walls and towers, the entrance is through an imposing stone facade topped by battlements. Furnishings include antiquities in harmony with the surroundings, and the dining room has the castle ambience. 39 rooms and baths. Air conditioned. 40 km S of Pamplona. (I)

Par. del Marques de Villena

Parador Condes de VILLALBA (NW)
Valeriano Valdesuso
Villalba (Lugo) (982) 51 00 11

The parador incorporates an unusual octagonal fortress keep 125 feet tall, thought to date from the 1200s. It is the ancient seat of the Counts of Andrade. Entered over a drawbridge, the tower has five main floors. Reception area and a fine medieval restaurant occupy the first floor, and upper floors house guest rooms with fireplaces. Summer dining is on a terrace. Elevator, central heat, bar. 6 double rooms. Located in the far NW corner of Spain. 35 km N of Lugo. (I)

Parador del Marques de VILLENA (E)
Av. Amigos Castillo
Alarcon (Cuenca) (966) 33 13 50

Accommodations are in a reconstructed 8th century castle, with several rooms in the 75 foot high tower and around a court. Site is on a hilltop with walls and towers below, remaining from fortifications of the Middle Ages. The Jucar River's deep gorge forms a natural moat. Great halls fly medieval heraldic banners, and there are displays of armor and weapons. Superb views, rustic antique furnishings, elevator and central heat. 11 rooms. Just off N3 and E101, main road from Madrid to Valencia, 75 km S of Cuenca. (I-II)

Parador VIRREY TOLEDO (WC)
Plaza del Palacio
Oropesa (Toledo) (925) 43 00 00

This royal medieval castle stands atop a hill dominating the whitewashed village and is approached through extremely narrow, winding streets. Olive groves climb the slopes, and the snow-capped Gredos Mountains are in the distance. A massive keep and walled enclosures are open for exploring. Most guest rooms are in the attached mansion of the Counts of

Parador Virrey Toledo

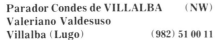

Par. Castillo de la Zuda

Oropesa. The castle, which survived many wars and two orders for its demolition, and the attached town walls are thought to date from 1366. It was badly damaged during Napoleonic invasions, but has been restored into a four-star hotel with elevator, central heat, air conditioning, bar, lounges and chapel. Food features regional specialties. 47 rooms with bath. 150 km SW of Madrid. (I-II)

Parador Castillo de la ZUDA (NE)
Tortosa (Tarragona) (977) 44 44 50

This converted castle on the Mediterranean coast between Valencia and Barcelona, is in a picturesque setting. Guest facilities are modern, built into the remains of an ancient Moorish castle. A few elements of the original castle remain in parts of the parador. 4 star

hotel, central heat, bar, garden. 82 rooms. (I-II)

Parador Nac. de ZURBARAN (WC)
Marcues de la Romana, 10
Guadalupe (Caceres) (927) 36 70 75

This palace was built in the 1500s and faces the basilica in this small town. It features an open court center patio, public and private rooms which are decorated in rustic antique style, with the white walls, arches and wood beam ceilings so typical of Spain. Elevator, bar, swimming pool and central heat. All 20 rooms with baths are on the first floor. 175 km SW of Toledo on a mountain road about 4 km N of N401. (I)

Parador De Zurbaran

Sweden

BÄCKASKOG Castle (S)
529034 Fjalkinge (Skåne) (044) 532 50

Built about 1250 as a monastery, Bäckaskog was fortified as a castle in 1537, and the church tower was added nearly a century later. The Crown housed high-ranking military leaders in it for a time, and later it was the residence of the Crown Prince (Oskar I), whose son Karl XV later used the castle as a summer residence. By 1900 it was used for farming. In 1956 it was restored and adapted as a hotel. Today it offers a historic setting on Lake Ivo for modern facilities, a restaurant, boating, tennis, and other activities. Other historic sights nearby include a church dating from 1280. Bungalows and an annex have been added making a total of 50 rooms, 27 with baths. Handicap facilities. On Rt. 15, about 15 km E of Kristianstad. (II)

LANSMANSGARDEN Manor (SW)
S68600 Sunne (Värmland) (0565) 103 01

The old manor house, located on Lake Fryken, is in a beautiful area frequently visited by tourists. The manor is featured in the famous novel "Gosta Berling's Saga" by the late Swedish Nobel Prize winner, Selma Lagerlof. There is a huge lounge with fireplace, decorated with antiquities and objects of art. Swimming, boating, hiking, fishing available, with golf nearby. 30 rooms. Location is approximately midway between Stockholm and Oslo and makes a good place to stop overnight or for a longer stay. 380 km W of Stockholm, 237 km E of Oslo. (II)

← Backaskog Castle ↓

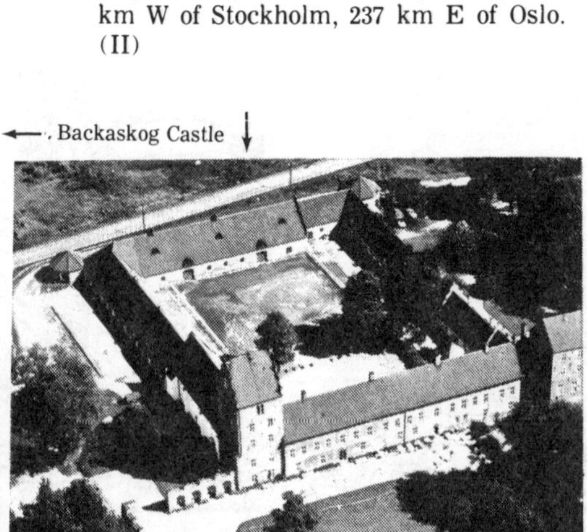

SWEDEN

(Northern part of Sweden is not shown)

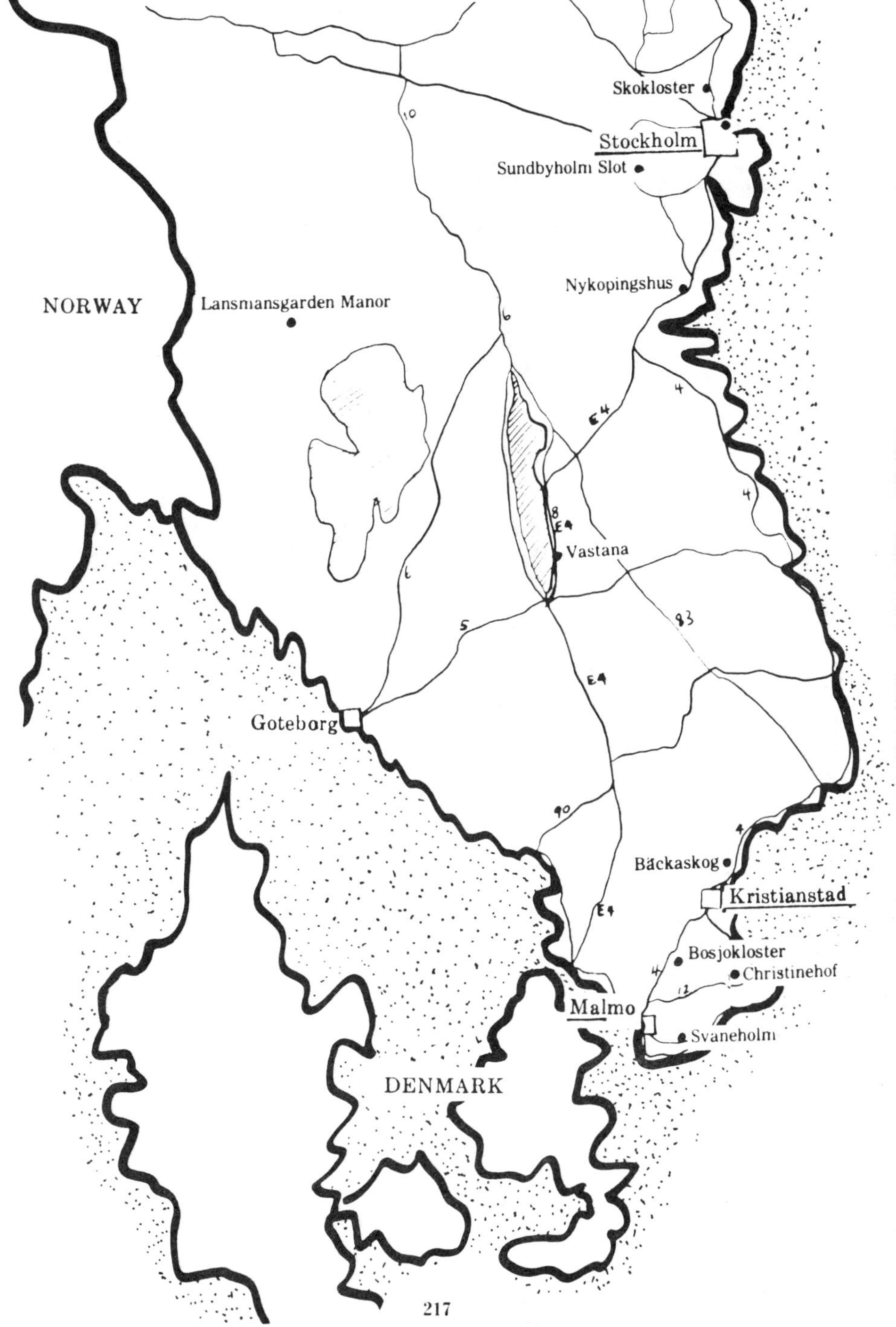

Skokloster Castle ↑ ↓

SKOKLOSTER Castle **(SE)**
Skokloster (Uppland)
S-19800 Balsta **(018) 38 61 00**

The towered white castle, in a setting of green trees and vegetation, is owned by the state. It is authentically restored, has an interesting interior, and a notable collection of arms and art. The old stable has been converted into an attractive restaurant featuring home cooking. Hotel accommodations are not in the castle itself but in an adjacent inn with 72 rooms. Activities include sailing, swimming, fishing, and a gymnasium. An exhibition of antique autos is nearby. Skokloster is 37 km S of the city of Uppsala, W of Rt 4. Open May-Sept. (II)

SUNDBYHOLM SLOT **(SE)**
S-63590 Eskilstuna
(Sodermanland) **(016) 962 90**

Built in 1640 by the Lord High Admiral Gyllenheim, an illegitimate son of King Karl IX, the castle was restored and served as a popular restaurant for a number of years. More recently guest rooms were fitted out and excellent accommodations are now available in addition to dining and other public facilities. A conference center has been added with 62 rooms, and there are in addition, 30 rooms for regular guests. The castle is about 13 km NE of Eskilstuna, and about 100 km W of Stockholm. (II)

VASTANA **(S)**
Granna, Smaland **(0390) 107 00**

The old manor house is situated near the south end of Lake Vattern with a lovely view and setting. It has spacious grounds and tree-shaded areas. In the Middle Ages it was owned by Count Per Brahe who ruled that part of Sweden virtually as a king. Since 1796 it has been owned by the Count Gyllensvaan family. Luxury accommodations and breakfast. Meals available in nearby Golden Otter Inn. 10 rooms. Open June-Aug. On Rt 1, E side of Vattern Lake. (I-II)

Castle Restaurants

There are several interesting restaurants in old castles, manor houses, and similar historical settings in Sweden. Following are a few, and you can inquire about others at the various Swedish government tourist offices in major Swedish cities.

Bosjökloster Castle

BOSJÖKLOSTER CASTLE, in the town of the same name, near Hoor, is a former Benedictine convent founded in 1080, with a vaulted refectory from those times still standing. The Convent Wall restaurant-cafeteria serves up to 300 people. There is a park area with animals, a children's zoo, boat rentals, fishing and swimming. The castle is owned by Count Thord Bonde, who might show you around the castle if you happen to be there at the right time. About 50 km NE of Malmo. Address: 24300 Hoor (Skåne) (0413) 250 48.

CHRISTINEHOF CASTLE, Lovestad, built 1737-40 by Countess Christina Piper, was opened as a museum and restaurant in 1963. It is a few km NW of Eljarod, close to the Ystad-Kristianstad road. Southern end of Sweden. Address: S-27030 Lovestad (Skåne) (0417) 261 04.

NYKOPINGSHUS CASTLE, Nykoping, was built in the Middle Ages, and a 17th century room now serves as a restaurant. 105 km SW of Stockholm. Address: Tovastugans Vardhus, Box 11, S-61101 Nykoping (Sodermanland) (0155) 171 90.

SVANEHOLM CASTLE was built in 1530 as a fortress, and a century later was converted into the style of a Venetian palazzo. A fine restaurant is located in the cellars and ground floor, and there is also a museum. Boating and fishing are available on Lake Svaneholmssjon. 40 km E of Malmo. Address: S-27400 Skurup (Skåne) (0411) 409 82.

Switzerland

Hotel Les AMURES (SW)
1, Puits St. Pierre
CH-1204 Geneva **Tel. (022) 28 91 72**

Located in the Old Town section of this international city near the Cathedral of St. Peter and the Hotel de Ville (City Hall), this elegant hotel was once the residence of bishops and counts of the 13th and 14th centuries. Every modern amenity has been included in a recent renovation before it was opened as a hotel late in 1980. Some wall frescoes and other works of art from past centuries are part of the decor. (III)

Hotel-Restaurant BAEREN (N)
Hauensteinstr. 16
BL 4438 Langenbruck **(062) 60 14 14**

This historic country inn, dating from 1577, has hosted many famous people through the ages, notably Emperor Franz Josef II in 1777, and Napoleon Bonaparte in 1797. Cafe-restaurant, terrace and a bar with dancing, conference rooms, and a casino are among the attractions. 46 beds. Open all year. The town is about 35 km S of Basle on Rt 12. (I)

Hotel-Restaurant Baeren

Schlossli Bottighofen

Weiherschloss Bottmingen

Schlossli BOTTIGHOFEN (NE)
8598 Bottighofen TG (072) 75 12 75

A former summer residence of the Bishops of Constance, the hotel was built in 1674-76. It later belonged to several cloisters. It was adapted as a hotel some 40 years ago and has taken advantage of its beautiful location on the shores of Lake Constance (Bodensee) with gardens and a park area on the lake. It is away from the traffic and offers fine views, lake swimming, water sports, boat excursions, shore walks, and a new marina nearby. Cuisine features fish specialties. 12 rooms. 4 km E of Kreuslingen. (I)

Weiherschloss BOTTMINGEN (NW)
Bottmingen (Basle) (061) 47 15 15

Restaurant Only

This moated castle, built soon after 1409, has been kept virtually in its original form, except for a later remodeling to a more baroque style. It fell into neglect some 50 years ago, until Dr. Carl Roth and the Swiss Castle Association rescued it with popular funds and aid from the city and Canton of Basle. Today it is owned by the association and government and is beautifully restored, complete with drawbridge, Patrons of the fine restaurant include many foreign business people. The dining room serves 30, and 100 can be accommodated on a terrace. There are rooms for private luncheons, dinners, weddings, etc., for 5 to 150 persons. Closed Mondays and for 10 days at Christmas-New Year, and 2 weeks during the Basle Carnival in late Feb-March.

Schloss BRESTENBERG (N)
Am Hallwilersee
AG5707 Brestenberg/
Seengen (064) 54 22 12

Count Rudolf von Hallwil built this spacious castle in 1625 and surrounded it with beautiful gardens on the north end of Hallwilersee (Lake). Modernized for

Schloss Brestenberg

SWITZERLAND

W GERMANY
Basel
Bottmingen
Baeren
Brestenberg
Roter Turm
Solothurn
Biel
Neuchatel
Bern
Hirschen
FRANCE
Thun
Interlaken
Couronne
St. Georges
Lausanne
Martheray
d'Ouchy
Montreux
Siecle
Le Chateau
Geneva
Amures
Sion

Schaffhausen
Worth Rheinfall
Drachenburg
Bottighofen
Hagenwil
Baden
Zurich
AUSTRIA
Vaduz, Liechtenstein
Luzern
Gutsch
Engel
Vitznau
Sargans
Ragaz
Chur
Zuoz
St. Moritz
Locarno
Seeschloss
Castello
ITALY
Lugano

Le Château

guests, the castle now offers an elevator, dancing, private beach, fishing, tennis and riding. There is a garden restaurant. 40 beds. Closed Jan. 40 km N of Luzern. (I-II)

Albergo del CASTELLO (S)
TI6600 Locarno (093) 31 23 61

Renaissance building on the site of the medieval Visconti Palace adjacent to the Castello di Locarno and the Mayor's Palace. Furnished with priceless antiquities such as medieval altars, paintings, objects of art and a 15th century "locanda" (tavern). Swimming pool, garden, central heat and elevator. 60 beds. Open Mar-Oct. Locarno is on Lake Maggiore in the Italian section of Switzerland. (I-II)

Hotel Drachenburg

Le CHATEAU (W)
1844 Villeneuve
VD1820 Montreux (021) 60 13 57

A lovely, towered building from the 1600s, in a spectacular mountain setting, the castle-like baronial mansion is the former residence of the Bouvier family, related to the house of Savoy. Wood beamed ceilings, rotiserie restaurant, dining on the terrace. Accommodations on the second and third floors for 20 guests. Villeneuve is on the eastern end of Lake Geneva, SE of Montreux and not far from the famed Castle of Chillon, which is open to visitors. (I)

Gasthaus Engel

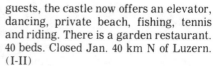

Auberge de la COURONNE (W)
VD1522 Lucens (021) 95 82 31

This old relay station for stage coaches was opened in 1451, giving it time to have seen a lot of coaches. During the centuries it has hosted many famous personages, and maintained a good reputation for hospitality for five hundred years. It was recently enlarged and modernized and is an international meeting place, with French cuisine, diet food and dancing. 38 beds. May be closed some winter periods. On Rt 1, about 35 km NE of Lausanne. (I)

Hotel DRACHENBURG (NE)
8274 Gottlieben (Lake Constance)
(Turgau) (072) 69 14 14

This beautifully furnished inn was built in the 13th century as a Bishop's castle. It is now said to be one of the finest historic buildings on Lake Constance. Elegant rooms are furnished in different styles: Renaissance, Empire, Louis XV, etc. 53 rooms. 4 km W of Konstanz. (I)

Gasthaus ENGEL (C)
SZ6403 Kussnacht am Rigi
(Lake Luzern) (041) 81 10 57

Built as a municipal palace in the 1400s in the cradle of Switzerland, this hostelry is under the management of the Ulrich family which has run it for over 400 years. Beautifully ornamented facade and typical carved wood interior. 20 beds. NE corner of Lake Luzern, 9 km E of city of Luzern. (I)

Château Gutsch

Chateau GUTSCH (C)
Kanonenstrasse
LU6000 Luzern (041) 22 02 72

One of the city's most magnificent views is from this chateau as it stands on 13th century foundations and ramparts overlooking the old walled city and the Lake of Luzern. Private cog-railway (funicular) runs from the street, bus stop and railway station just below. The main towered building was built at the turn of the century but the adjoining building is much older. Rooms range all the way from genuine antique with canopied beds, to modern with mezzanine bedrooms. In the original castle on the site, the Corpus Christi Brotherhood was founded in 1467, and it was a fortress during wars of the 1600s. Guests have included Queen Victoria, Prince George of Prussia and other royalty. Attractive decor and furnishings, medieval armor, objects of art, chests and paintings. Several dining rooms with spectacular views, and a restaurant in a dungeon-like vaulted room features open fireplaces and live music. Elevators, swimming pool, diet menus. 75 beds. Open all year, 4 star. (II)

Schloss HAGENWIL (NE)
Hagenwil b. Amriswil

Various parts of this moated castle were built from 1220-1403, with a drawbridge, and a strong keep in the half-timber style of architecture. It was the seat of Abbot governors as well as barons of the region. Hagenwil has been privately owned for about 180 years. In an ancient engraving

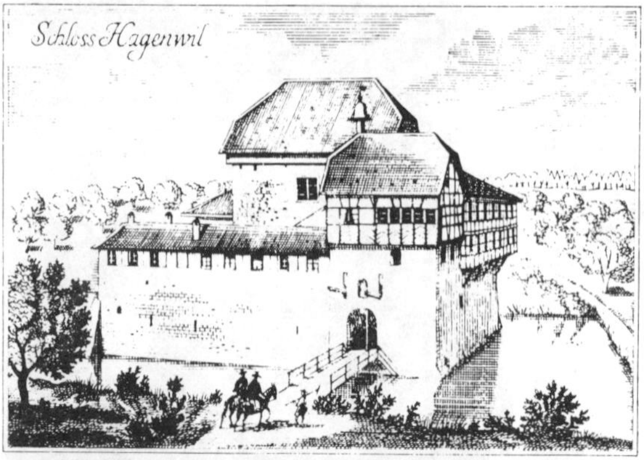

Schloss Hagenwil
(Today, and in a centuries-old print)

it appears exactly as it looks today, complete with moat and drawbridge. It is a good base for excursions into the mountains and around Lake Constance. Rooms for only 6 guests. The village is about 5 km S of Amriswil, Rt 34 N of St. Gallen. (I)

Hotel Hirschen

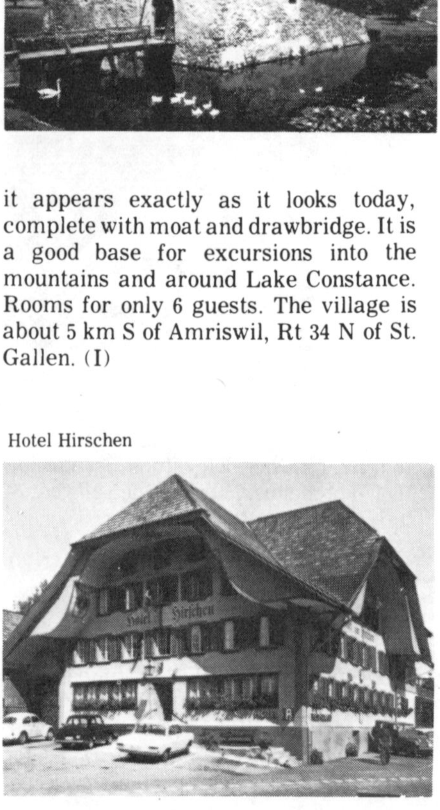

Hotel HIRSCHEN (C)
BE3550 Langnau in Emmental (035) 2 15 17

A typical Swiss Chalet and inn which deceives you as to its age. As early as 1467 it was mentioned in the town's chronicles as a wine tavern and meeting place and the present building dates from that time and from 1626. The Hirschen has had a wine license for 300 years. Offers a sauna and nearby are facilities for swimming and tennis, and hiking is popular in the region. 32 beds. Langnau is on Rts 10 and 94, about 30 km E of Bern toward Lucerne. (I)

Chateau du MARTHERAY (W)
VD1268 Begnins (022) 66 14 09

The single-towered castle was constructed in 1180 by the Noblemen of Begnins. It was remodled, mostly to its present form, in 1661, and has been owned by the Mennet family since 1863. It has been a hotel and restaurant for more than a century. Not a first class rating. 28 beds. Begnins is about 8 km N of Nyon near Lake Geneva. (I)

Le Chateau d'OUCHY (SW)
Place du Port
VD1006 Lausanne (021) 26 74 51

A 12th century stronghold of the Bishops of Lausanne on Lake Geneva. Site of the Louis de Savoie treaty in 1300, the castle became a government custom house in the 1700s. A hotel was built around the castle in 1884, and the Lausanne Peace Treaty was signed there in 1923. The castle's 800-year old Salle des Chevaliers (Hall of Knights) is especially interesting. Elevator, dancing, tennis, excursions. 70 beds. On shore of Lake Geneva. Open all year, 4 star. (II)

Schloss RAGAZ (NE)
SG7310 Bad Ragaz (085) 9 23 55

Stone towers and walls give this baronial mansion of the early 1900s the aspect of an old castle. Now a resort hotel, it offers extensive grounds, a spa, golf, swimming, carriage rides and other pleasures. Dining rooms and suites were enlarged and redecorated in 1968, and rooms are also offered in cottages on the grounds. Well-appointed lounges and fine cuisine, also diet menus. Impressive views of the snow-capped Alps. 120 beds. Central heat, air conditioning, open all year. Bad Regaz is near the borders of Austria and Liechtenstein. (II)

Hotel-Restaurant ROTER TURM (NW)
Hauptgasse 42
CH4500 Solothurn (065) 22 96 21

This ancient stone tower was first mentioned in history in 1485 and was

Roter Turm (Red Tower)

Château Martheray

Château d'Ouchy

Schloss Ragaz

Schloss Sargans

rebuilt about 1570. It was associated with a tavern through the centuries, and after a renovation in 1960 and adaption as a small hotel, it still serves that function. Solothurn is said to be the oldest town in Switzerland, deriving from a Celtic settlement which pre-dated the coming of the Roman legions. Rooms in the old building are modern. There are two restaurants, a roof garden, hairdresser, elevator, air conditioning. A 3-star hotel in the old section of the famed watchmaking town. (I)

Seeschloss Castello

Schloss SARGANS **(NE)**
7320 Sargans **(085) 2 14 88**

Restaurant Only

This spectacular old castle has a high tower that can be seen for miles around, and has become somewhat of a landmark, having stood since 1282. In 1396 it became the property of the Duke of Austria. In 1415 the castle's 8-foot-thick walls were stormed unsuccessfully by the people of Appenzell, and again unsuccessfully by Swiss Confederates in 1445. It later was sold to the Confederates and was the seat of the Bailiffs whose coats of arms are painted on the balcony ceiling. Earthquakes and other damage caused the restoration of some parts through the centuries. It has been owned by the government in more recent times. Today Sargans Castle is a restaurant and also holds banquets and other events. Check ahead for opening times, etc.

Hostellerie ST. GEORGES **(W)**
FR1663 Gruyeres **(029) 6 22 46**

This palace-like hotel dates from the 1600s and has the mountain country atmosphere of the charming little town in which it is located. The village is credited with the origin of Gruyere cheese, and sits astride a mountain ridge with an old castle. Restaurant, rotisserie, terrace, dancing. 25 beds. Open all year. About 35 km S of Fribourg, and E of Rt 77. (I)

Hotel SEESCHLOSS CASTELLO (S)
TI6612 Ascona (093) 35 18 03

Built about 1250 by the ruling family of Milan as a four-towered castle, surrounded by water. The park of the castle borders on the beautiful mountain-studded northern end of Lake Maggiore. Nearly 700 years after it was built, the castle was adapted as a guest-house in 1910 and completely redecorated in 1960. Swimming pool, garden, central heat. 65 beds. Open Mar-Oct. (II)

XVIeme Siècle

Hostellerie du XVIeme SIÈCLE (W)
Place du Marche,
Angle rue Delafiechere
1260 Nyon (022) 61 24 41

As the name states, this hotel is of the 16th century, and has a mellowed exterior and interior. The dining room has ancient exposed stone walls and wood rafters. Restaurant closed Sundays. 20 rooms, elevator. Open all year. Nyon is on the northeastern shore of Lake Geneva, between Lausanne and Geneva. (I)

Park Hotel VITZNAU (C)
6354 Vitznau (041) 83 13 22

Located in the beautiful Luzern lake and mountain region, Park Hotel Vitznau is a spacious, towered, Victorian-style building offering first class accommodations,

Park Hotel Vitznau

Schlossli Wőrth Rheinfall

restaurant, and swimming, sauna, tennis, mini-golf, water skiing, fishing. Golf within 20 km. 80 rooms, elevator. Location is E of Luzern, near Rigi Mt., which has a cogwheel railway. (II)

Schlossli WORTH RHEINFALL **(N)**
8212 Neuhausen am Rheinfall **(053) 2 24 21**

Restaurant Only

Built on a prominence of land jutting out into the Rhine River, this 900-year-old fortress faces "Europe's Niagara", the Rhine Falls. Through the years, Worth Castle has played an important part in Swiss history because of its strategic location on the great river. Conference and banquet rooms, snack and grill, terrace dining with a spectacular view of the falls. Varied menu. Point of departure for boat trips to the falls rocks. Open Mar-Nov. 4 km S of Schaffhausen.

Castell ZUOZ **(E)**
GR7524 Zuoz **(082) 7 12 21**

The castle-style hostelry is in an outstanding location west of this attractive, scenic village in the Engadine. Offers elevator, swimming pool, tennis, dancing, bar, garden, park, ice skating, outdoor curling, child care. Closed April, May, Oct., Nov. 126 beds. 20 km NE of St. Moritz. (II)

Glossary

OF CASTLE TERMS

Barbican—defense house or tower above a gateway or entry bridge

Bastion—a projection or outward extension of a wall or tower designed to give a wider firing range

Battlements—low wall usually atop a tower or wall with open spaces for shooting, or an architectural design in this style.

Bower—a boudoir, or lady's apartment in a castle.

Burg—in Germany: a fortified castle, as contrasted with "schloss", a more elegant version. (Often used interchangeably.)

Castellan—the head or keeper of the castle. Also chatelain in French.

Catapult—ancient device for hurling stones or large objects over castle walls. Usually a container on a long arm is pulled down under tension and suddenly released.

Coffered—decorative sunken panels, usually in a ceiling or vault

Chatelaine—the lady of the castle

Crenellations—the battlements on top of a wall or tower

Curtain wall—the wall enclosing other elements of a castle

Drawbridge—a bridge which can be raised or lowered, usually over a ditch or moat at the entrance to the castle. (Today, most of them have been replaced with permanent stone bridges.)

Embrasures—opening in a wall or battlement, usually tapering from a wide one inside to a window or narrow slit on the outside

Enceinte—wall enclosure, like a curtain wall

Fortalice—a tower or other defensive outwork

Fosse—same as moat—ditch or trench around a castle, often filled with water

Gargoyle—a grotesque carved figure protruding from a roof eve, usually functioning as a waterspout with water draining through the open mouth

Keep—central or strongest tower of a castle.

Loophole—a hole or narrow slit in a wall or tower for looking or shooting

Machicolations—open spaces over a castle entrance through which stones or hot liquids could be thrown on intruders

Mangonel—a device for throwing stones or objects (see Catapult)

Merlons—the upright sections of battlements

Meurtriere—from the French "murderer" —an opening at an entrance from which an intruder could be attacked

Moat—a protective ditch around a castle, usually filled with water

Oilette—a round enlargement at top or bottom of a loophole

Portcullis—heavy wood or iron grating gate which can be dropped in grooves to shut a castle entrance or town gate.

Postern—a back or side entrance to a castle, sometimes underground or hidden

Schloss—a German castle or baronial mansion of more elegance, or a later period, than a feudal castle (which, in German, is a "burg"). The terms nowadays are often interchanged.

Photo Credits

Frontispiece and pages 6 and 7, color photos by the author (except Trigance, Fr.).

AUSTRIA--By the author: Itter, Klosterbrau, Munichau. Austrian National Tourist Office: Feyregg, Igls, Picklarn, Rabenstein, St. Martin.

BELGIUM--Jeannie and Tony Taylor: Vert Gazon. Belgian Consulate General: Amigo, Brasschaat.

BRITAIN--Author: Caldicot, Great Fosters, Langdon Court, Manor (Castle Combe), Manor (Moretonhampstead), Moonfleet, Old Court (exterior), Old House, Pennsylvania, Tregenna, Welcombe, Weston Manor (exterior and interior). British Tourist Authority: Ballygally, Brecon, Cardiff, Culloden, Knock-na-moe, Seaton Delavel, Slieve Donard, Thornbury.

DENMARK--Danish National Tourist Office: Bygholm, Dragsholm.

FINLAND--Finnish National Tourist Office: Haikon, Valtion.

FRANCE--Author: Celle, Chaumontel, Trigance. French Government Tourist Office: Caze, Cheronnac, Coudree, Creissels, l'Escaladieu, Levezou, Montesquiou, Poste, Retival, Vallee Bleu.

GERMANY--Author: Blomberg, Burghaus, Engelsburg, Furstenhof, Hirschhorn, Hornberg, Lembeck, Ronneburg, Sababurg, Spangenberg, Tremsbuttel, Wilkenhege. German National Tourist Office: Lauenstein, Schonburg.

HOLLAND--Author: Neubourg, Wittem.

IRELAND--Author: Ashford. Irish Tourist Board: Black Rock, Bunratty, Dunguaire, Knappogue.

ITALY--James Eversole: Cappuccini Convento, Labers.

PORTUGAL--Author: Castelo, Rainha Santa Isabel (interior).

SCOTLAND--Author: Dalhousie Castle, Melville. British Tourist Authority: Auchen, Inverlochy, Tullich.

SPAIN--Author: Carlos V, Emperatriz, Orgaz, Virrey Toledo. Spanish National Tourist Office: Alba y Alista, Baron, Concordia, Emperador, Enrique II, Fernando, Gil Blas, Pajares, Piedra, Plata, Raimundo, San Francisco, San Marcos, Santa Catalina, Santo Domingo, Viana, Villalba, Villena, Zuda, Zurbaron. Jeannie and Tony Taylor: Alcazar del Rey Don Pedro.

SWEDEN--Swedish National Tourist Office: Backaskog, Bosjokloster, Skokloster. Other photographs were supplied by managements of the various hotels.

SPECIAL ACKNOWLEDGMENT is due to several "Castle Romantics" who send us valuable reports on their extensive travels: Carol Blodgett, Connecticut; Sylvia Eversole, New York; Dr. Leonore Levit, Illinois; Wallace Sokolsky, New York; Jeannie Taylor, Hawaii.